Christmas House

Rosemary Hamer

In loving memory of my mother Dora Hamer (nee Roberts/ nee Catherine Jane Goules) who died Nov 28th 2007.
This is her story, which I am privileged to tell, and this is what she would have said:

'Sometimes when I have a moment, and I've many moments these days, I gaze through the window and think back – and wonder what I can tell my daughter about my life. How did I know I would ever have a daughter? That was the one thing I was always sure about – the rest was never so clear.

I have told Rosemary so many stories over the years about my childhood and growing up. Sometimes she was bored and would say 'Oh I've heard all that before, Mum,' and sometimes she was so busy that she'd rush off before I had a chance to finish the story. I do wonder, once I've gone, what she'll make of it all.

It's difficult to piece together now. That's what it's become – just pieces in a puzzle. Pieces that should have fitted together now my time's nearly over and yet like every true story never did. I will leave it to my beloved daughter to try and make sense of it all if she so chooses.'

(Dora Hamer – Gloucester, 2005).

PROLOGUE

1925 – Aberystwyth, Christmas

'Dora – Dora Roberts,' the voice boomed – cutting through the silence in the room. There was no response.

'Dora, Dora Roberts – come here at once,' the voice persisted.

Dora never even glanced up, far away, lost in thought, replaying the events of the previous week. Memories of last Friday afternoon had left her feeling stunned and shocked. Where had it all gone wrong?

∞

It had started so well. Going home from school that foggy afternoon, Aberystwyth decked out in its Christmas finery had never looked so inviting. Even before the lamps were lit, the town seemed to sparkle with a feeling of suppressed excitement that was hard to resist.

Dora loved this time of year, staring longingly into tinselled shop windows, gawking at ducks and turkeys hanging outside butchers' naked without their feathers. Red, green, silver and gold trimmings, making her gasp, and the sweetmeats, pink fluffy marshmallows, sugared almonds and gingerbread men with scary button eyes hanging from miniature Christmas trees enticing her. Mouth watering and tummy rumbling loudly, if only she could, ----but it was no use. There was only the halfpenny that one of the summer visitors had given her. Dora fingered it carefully in her pocket?

What if you were rich enough to go in and buy anything you wanted? Dressed in silks and ermine she would march in demand to see the manager, and make him parade all his goods before her as if she was Queen Mary herself.

Anyway it was no good pretending as Dora knew she should be getting home. She was dying to tell Gran that she'd got a gold star for her English composition.

Idly she wondered what she might get for Christmas. It was no use asking for anything as that would be the last thing she'd get. She'd learnt her lesson there. No doubt her mother would give her something practical, but perhaps Dada and Gran would try to give her just what she wanted. There were so many things she'd like, she thought wistfully.

But wasn't that music coming from somewhere?

Dora spun round fast, catching sight of the Salvation Army on the opposite corner. Smartly uniformed with instruments gleaming, they were just beginning to play her favourite 'Come all ye Faithful', so maybe she should stay a little longer after all music always made her feel happy.

Dora crossed over to join the crowd and started singing as loudly as she could. A girl about her age in a bonnet beat time on a tambourine. After the carols, she came round collecting proffering the tambourine like a collection plate. When the girl reached her, Dora hung her head. Then on second thoughts and with great reluctance carefully drew out her last precious shining halfpenny, and placed it precisely in the centre of the tambourine willing her finger and thumb to let go. The girl looked at it with disdain but thinking better of it smiled, thanked her and moved on.

Sometimes it was hard to do the right thing, despite Gran quoting regularly from the Bible, that "God loves a cheerful giver". Dora wasn't at all sure she felt virtuous or cheerful about losing her treasured halfpenny, but never mind it was nearly Christmas with lots to look forward to.

With a sudden spurt of energy Dora kicked up her heels and ran, skidding and slipping her way across the icy pavement.

She shot up Chalybeate Street making for Baker Street and home but glancing down towards Tivvys' the Bakers, she saw a big crowd of people clustering round their window.

What were they doing? It would just take a minute to see what all the fuss was about. Dora ran full pelt into the throng, wriggling her way to the front. Right in the middle of the window was an enormous frosted house covered in snow and icicles. What a sight! Dora's mouth fell open - eyes on stalks. There were so much to look at it was hard to take it all in.

The house, its red tiled roof sprinkled with snow, and with tiny puffs of smoke emerging from the two chimneys, was as big as an oversized doll's house. Through the garden gate a frosty path with a plump snowman led to the open front door, where a 'Welcome' mat decorated with holly had been placed. Each of the rooms was lit and tiny people sat on exquisite miniature furniture.

It was mesmerising. Dora gazed and gazed, finding herself dreaming of sitting in those little iced seats or moving from room to room, absorbed with the colours, the lights and the decorations.
If only this was her house! She imagined being 'lady of the house' greeting her family at the end of a day, pouring out tea from a fancy silver teapot into delicate china cups, wearing a blue velvet gown, and offering tiny cucumber sandwiches with slender white hands. Her husband and children would be sitting round a roaring fire, whilst their little dog lay on a satin cushion, stretching itself. Everyone would be wishing her 'Merry Christmas'. There would be flowers and presents, oh and of course, crackers and a tree with ornaments. Even a piano, where she would play gentle melodies and everyone would sing and dance together. What a wonderful life!

A sharp thwack on the head brought Dora back to earth with a bang, and the dream was broken. There were stars, chaos and mayhem.

'Where've you been all this time? What have you been doing?'

Each question was punctuated with yet another box to her ears.

'I've been up to the school twice ----- round and round the town. Don't tell me missy, you've been standing here all this time?'

Clutching her sore and now throbbing head, Dora turned to see her mother stretched to her full four foot ten, hand raised to give another slap, boiling mad, practically frothing at the mouth.

'What've you been doing? Why didn't you come straight home?' Even the questions were like darts stabbing her poor head. 'Two hours! Two hours- would you believe -----I've got a stack of ironing and all the teas to get yet, and I've wasted all this time looking for you.'

Dora cowered under the onslaught of rage, folding her arms round her body to protect herself. Had she really stood there that long? When had it got so dark? Even the lamps were lit now.

With no time for explanations, Sarah grabbed hold of her coat and frogmarched her straight up North Parade to 8 Baker St., pushing her along at a relentless pace.

Gran was in the hall when they arrived. Taking one look at her daughter's tight lips and furious expression she resisted saying anything, and stood back whilst Sarah prodded Dora towards the front stairs.

'Up to bed my girl, no tea for you when you behave like this. Now up you go – and I don't want to hear a murmur from you tonight.'

Behind the slammed bedroom door, in the dark with no lamp or even a candle, Dora cried and cried until she couldn't cry anymore. What had she done that was so wrong, maybe she'd been a long time getting back from school but why was that so bad? Usually her mother was so busy she hardly bothered when Dora came in. It was always Gran who made her tea. Where was Gran? Why wasn't she coming to comfort her? She felt so alone and miserable. It wasn't fair; it had been such a lovely time. Now it was ruined. How could she ever feel about the Christmas House in the same way?

Much later, after Dora had cried herself to sleep, there was a gentle knock on the door. Gran and her father still in his work clothes stood there with a tray and a lamp looking concerned. Jack's lined face frowning more than usual.

He sat down on the bed putting his arm around her, 'You gave your mother a bad fright today, Dora. She thought she'd lost you. That's why she was cross. She was frightened. You know fear makes people angry, and sometimes they react without thinking, but she's calmed down now.' He wiped his daughter's tear stained face tenderly, 'Don't cry anymore.'

Giving her his hanky he said, 'Give that red nose of yours a good blow, and tell me what you were doing all that time?'

Dora gulped, and shakily told them about the cake house.

'Did anyone come up and speak to you?'

Dora shook her head, 'No, no I was on my own.'

'Are you sure no one spoke to you?'

Dora again shook her head. Her father breathed a sigh of relief.
Dora wondered why it mattered if someone had come up and spoken to her?

Gran added, 'Dora, didn't you realise how long you'd been standing there? Your mother and I were so worried we---' Her voice seemed to peter out suddenly and Dora could barely hear the last few words 'may have lost you forever.'
She looked across at her son-in-law and he gave a barely perceptible shake of the head. They seemed to visibly pull themselves together, and turned back to Dora.

'Tell us about the cake,' they said in unison.

'The Christmas House,' Dora insisted, going into a long description. They agreed it must have been a sight to take up her attention for so long, and promised to take her for another viewing.

Dora felt better with their reassurances, but wondered why her mother hadn't come upstairs too. There seemed to be something that both of them were unwilling to tell her.

∞

Reluctantly dragging herself back from her daydreams about that afternoon, Dora vaguely thought she heard her name being called.

'Dora Roberts, you've got your head in the clouds again. Where are you this time? I've called your name I don't know how many times.'

A heavy hand landed on Dora's shoulder. 'Come up to my desk immediately, I want to talk to you.'

Dora reluctantly and with leaden feet moved towards Miss Lloyd's desk.
'Do stand up straight Dora don't hunch your shoulders like that. Be proud of your height.' (Dora hated being the tallest girl in the school).

'Dora,' the teacher said in an unusually quiet almost confidential tone, 'you'll have to stay in at playtime today. See me in my room when the bell goes. I'll find you something to read. Now go back to your seat.'

Dora wondered what she'd done, but couldn't think of anything. She looked across at her best friend. But Eluned head down, mouth open and tongue out was painfully copying neat loops above and below the line with a scratchy pen trying to avoid blots.

Hoping she'd done nothing bad or there would be trouble at home Dora looked across the sparse brown and cream room, and fastened on the only picture in the room. 'Christ at the door of the world'. The picture always warmed her – it was so golden and welcoming with Jesus holding the lamp high, and opening the door to another world. She often wondered what was on the other side of the door, maybe something soft, comforting and friendly. She must ask Gran. Gran would know.

When the bell rang, Dora made her way to Miss Lloyd's room. Although small it was neat and tidy, with carefully cross stitched samplers on the walls reminding pupils to 'Respect your parents', or 'Home Sweet Home'.

Dora tapped on the door. Miss Lloyd sat her down in the far corner away from the window, and gave her the Mabinogian to read. It was a gift, as Dora knowing it so well, would regularly escape into a world of heroes, giants, beautiful ladies and white horses. Miss Lloyd said forcibly, 'Dora, don't on any account leave this room till I come back.' There was something in her tone that discouraged disobedience but Dora didn't mind. Though she loved to skip or run round the yard this was infinitely better, even if it was some sort of punishment.
As the afternoon classes moved on, Dora began to feel worried. Had she done something that would have repercussions at home?

7

When the final bell went and she saw her mother outside the door her fears seemed justified. What was her mother doing there? She rarely came near the school. Not only that but she had on her second best suit, and on a Monday. What did it all mean?

All the class lined up to leave, until there was just her, her mother and Miss Lloyd. They said to her, 'Wait here whilst we have a chat,' and moved out into the corridor.

Dora edged quietly towards the doorway straining to hear, and catching the odd word or phrase. 'It's no good----- worried-----this woman --------- regularly------ tempting Dora with sweets.'

Miss Lloyd seemed to be pacifying her mother '—Mrs Roberts, Dora is fine, she has no idea--- I'll keep her in for a few days---- ----- perhaps the woman will give up.'

Dora wondered who the woman could be, wrinkling her brow and trying to think who they were talking about. There was that strange woman from last week of course. In fact the woman had been there several times in the last few weeks waving to Dora. This particular time however she had brandished a bag of sweets smiling and beckoning to Dora.
Seeing no harm in it Dora had run over to talk to her through the playground bars, but then the woman had bombarded her with lots and lots of questions that confused her. What did it matter if she was happy and well cared for, and if her parents were kind to her, it was surely nothing to do with this person? Dora had taken the sweet politely but then shaking her head, had backed away to join the skipping, sucking the outside of the sweet till she tasted the bitter centre and out of sight spitting the thing out.

By now her mother and Miss Lloyd had finished their business but neither showed any inclination to take Dora into their confidence.

Over the next weeks her mother delivered and collected Dora from school, maintaining a deadly silence, with Dora biting her lip and allowing her hand to be held tightly. There was no more running up Baker St with her friends just the rigid formality of walking properly with her mother. Dora hoped this wouldn't go on forever. She was much too old for this. It was almost as if her mother was frightened of losing her. Surely the incident with the Christmas House hadn't upset her that much!

As Christmas approached, her mother seemed to relax, becoming kinder and more patient and running up matching blue velvet dresses for Dora and her doll to wear on Christmas Day. Dora wondered about the choice. It was almost as if she knew about the lady in the Christmas House, or perhaps it was just a coincidence. Anyway what did it any of it matter anymore, as long as there was a new dress to wear!

HOME LIFE

1

1917 - Beginnings at No '8'

Life at No 8 Baker Street, Aberystwyth was never predictable. Sarah Roberts always called Sis by her family, her baby daughter Dora and her mother Zipporah Reynolds made an unlikely trio. Prior to no 8, the three of them had lived in a flat in Terrace Road with Sarah working at a tobacconist all day and Sarah's husband Jack away at War. Never on the best of terms the confined space had forced mother and daughter into an uneasy truce. Later, taking on the Convalescent Home at no. 8 in 1917, put even more pressure on them.

When things reached boiling point, Zipporah would succumb to cutting comments, 'I always thought with your cold nature Sarah, you would never marry. I'm surprised you and Jack waited so long. You don't know when you'll see him next if ever.'

Dora, though still barely a toddler, was always a bone of contention. Neither could agree on what was best for her.

'You forget I brought up you four children well enough,' Zipporah would exclaim passionately.

But Sarah wouldn't rise to the bait, instead she would freeze her mother out for days at a time until they moved back to their usual conciliatory positions, and then it would all begin again. It was no good them falling out completely as Zipporah penniless at sixty two had nowhere else to go, and though Sarah wouldn't admit it she needed her mother's help.

Dora herself was too young to clearly remember the Convalescent Home. It had all started the day Sarah had come home from the tobacconists hardly able to contain herself with excitement.

This was so unlike her usual cool demeanour and so contagious that even Dora at eighteen months started jumping up and down in her high chair.

'Goodness Sis, what on earth has happened to you?' Zipporah exclaimed, far from happy about any upset to her routine, 'and why are you home so early?'

Sarah calmly announced, 'I've been offered a new job, well a business really. One of my regulars, Ernie Simms, came in as usual for his pipe tobacco, and started talking about his job. He acts as an agent for the Red Cross, and they're looking to open a type of convalescent home by the sea for soldiers and sailors recovering from their wounds.'

'What's that to do with you?' her mother asked curtly, 'Are you thinking about going back into some sort of service for them – and what about Dora and I?'

'No of course not Ma,' Sarah replied angrily. 'He's asked me to find a suitable house to lease in Aberystwyth. The Red Cross would pay and provide the furniture, and I'd run it.'

'I don't see how, Sarah,' her mother always called her formally by her first name when they quarrelled – 'after all you've no nursing experience or even run a business before.'

'Don't worry Ma, there'll be Red Cross volunteers to help, and these men are recovering so don't require proper hands on nursing. Anyway it's going to happen whatever you think. There'll be plenty of room for Dora and of course you if you deign to come,' Sarah said in a voice edged with sarcasm.

'What choice do I have?' Zipporah retorted bitterly, 'None of your brothers want me. I've no money to set up on my own as you well know. I suppose (looking fondly across at Dora) we'll have to make the best of it.'

11

Sarah true to her word full of entrepreneurial spirit, found the perfect house in the centre of town with twelve rooms on three floors. She immediately began the work of furnishing and refurbishing it. The house was called 'Dolegwyn', 8 Baker St., but Sarah never keen on Welsh names she didn't understand always referred to it thereafter as 'No 8'.

It was as if Sarah had finally come into her own gaining a new lease of life, seeming to be everywhere at once; negotiating with the estate agent, visiting sale rooms and taking on volunteers.

Dora loved the freedom of it all, after having been cooped up in the tiny flat. She tottered round after Sarah as the floors were scrubbed and polished. Ma had finally decided to enter into the proceedings though still complaining and murmuring 'it'll never work', as she washed down windows and doors, sorted through laundry and seamed curtains.

The first groups of invalid soldiers came early in 1917 before Dora had reached her second birthday. Horse ambulances brought them in stretcher upon stretcher until the three storeys of the house were bulging, 'Where do you want these, missus? Point us in the right direction and we'll unload them and there's two more ambulances behind us.' Aides were positioned on each of the landings, pointing out the rows of truckle beds laid out in readiness. Sarah efficient as ever had it all planned like a campaign. Her stern looks and command kept everyone calm and collected.

Most of the patients seemed to be suffering from 'shell shock', and Sarah despite all her years of housekeeping experience had never envisaged dealing with anything like this. It seemed as if the Red Cross having dealt with their physical wounds, had no idea what to do with this type of mental or emotional suffering, and dispatched many of the worst cases to Aberystwyth to convalesce.

Night times at no. 8 were the most traumatic; men would wake screaming with nightmares about being buried alive. Fear would send them into paroxysms of crying and shouting, with the other men doing their best to quieten them down.

Loud knocking on Sarah's bedroom door would be followed by the cry, 'Mrs Roberts, Mrs Roberts, come quick, 'It's Frank. He's real bad again. You'll have to come we can't do anything with him.'

Sarah would gather up brandy and laudanum, and on her knees try and persuade a frightened boy out from under the bedstead, 'Frank, there's nothing to be afraid of, let me help you now.' She would soothe his hair from his eyes and murmur quietly to him. Sometimes he came out like a lamb. Other times he would fight her all the way kicking and screaming and start tearing up his bedclothes, believing he was still buried under the dirt and soil of the Somme.

On many a day Sarah would end up with a black eye and bruises, elbows and knees having been launched full pelt at her. Zipporah, now called Gran by everyone, would tut tut under her breath remarking, 'Sis – this is no job for a woman, tell the Red Cross to take them back to the hospital. They should never have been let out in this state.'

But Sarah was never daunted, 'Ma you don't understand- these men are just as sick as if they had physical wounds. I must do my best by them. Jack would want me to.'

Gran helped by taking care of Dora. Together they would sit in the gloomy back kitchen, Dora propped on cushions handing potatoes and vegetables one at a time to Gran who would patiently peel bucket upon bucket. Gran would regale her with stories about Birmingham and hers and Sarah's childhoods. Dora would sit quietly, big eyes taking it all in, 'Tell, tell more Gran,' she would plead, anything to avoid bedtime.

The fitter men able to move about helped with the fires, and doing the lighter jobs. They all loved Dora and would spoil and cosset her as a pet. Sarah was never in favour of this, saying brusquely, 'They'll ruin that child. She'll be good for nothing as she grows up.'

Often at night an exhausted Dora would sit on an available knee whilst one of the men sang softly to her until she slept. This seemed to give the men some much needed peace, bringing out their long forgotten gentleness. Dora liked it best when the wives and sweethearts started arriving. They'd stay at the Railway Hotel, bringing her embroidered handkerchiefs and little gifts they could barely afford. Once they arrived, she was banished from the kitchen, whilst they sat at the table hour after hour with Gran or Sarah, weeping and berating the War, and how things would never be the same, asking over and over– 'Mrs Roberts, will my John ever get back to normal like the man I married?'

Truthfully, no one knew. The ones pronounced fit and well, were soon shunted straight back to the Front. The damaged ones were left to be rehabilitated as best they could, so they could be returned to their families whenever the War ended.

When that day finally came - November 11th 1918, the Armistice, the day the Great War ended, Dora was too young to realise how her life was to change again. All she ever remembered afterwards was the excitement, the noise, the laughter and the dancing.

Jonno had come racing into the kitchen shouting hysterically – 'Mrs Roberts, Gran I mean Mrs Reynolds – have you heard the news? – have you heard the news?' He was gasping so much that he almost fainted. Almost out of breath he got out, 'It's over –I can't believe it – it's all over---- at last-- at last,' he mumbled, and then fell into a chair in some sort of swoon.

'Ma,' Sarah shouted, 'don't just stand there gaping, quick get me the smelling salts,' and she deftly put the stopper under Jonno's nose, and shoved his head between his knees.

Before she could think what on earth had come over him-there was a dull roar from the castle's maroon gun. Then all hell let loose with bells pealing, cheering, and men running in and out of the kitchen.

Dora was completely bemused by it all but joined in, running in mad circles, until Danny picked her up and launching her onto his shoulders, started singing at the top of his voice, 'Pack up your troubles in your old kitbag----'

Sid Briggs lifted Sarah off her feet, and swung her round and round. 'Put me down, Sid,' she puffed 'put me down immediately.' But there was no holding him back, he placed her gently on a chair and then started dancing with Gran.

'Stop, stop', Sarah ordered 'you'll give us both heart attacks, and Dora will be sick in a minute, she's only just had her breakfast – give her to me.'

'But it's over—Mrs Roberts, 'the War I mean – it's finally over and we've won.'

'I gathered that,' Sarah said dryly, 'Now let's all calm down and have a cup of tea.'

'Tea's the last thing we want, missus – what about a snifter?'

'Absolutely not Private Briggs, settle down, help your friend Jonno here. He's suffering from shock.'

However eventually and against her better judgment Sarah carefully unlocked one of the cupboards taking out a prized bottle of brandy.

She poured each of them a tiny tot - giving a slightly larger one to Jonno, and a half wine glass of milk to Dora.

The War had lasted four years, fourteen weeks, and two days.

Sid echoed all their thinking in his toast, 'Here's to the returning soldiers especially your Jack, Missus, - to the ones who will never come back and the ones who will never recover, to peace, and getting back to our families.' They all looked at one another for a long time and clinked glasses.

Once the Armistice was declared, everything was a blur – all the men packed up and left. At first, Dora had been glad. The house was so empty; she had the freedom to run about from room to room, her footsteps echoing against the bare boards. It was strange to be just the three of them again. But maybe now her mother might pay her more attention.

2

1918 - Jack's Return

It was the arrival of the Marconigram that heralded the change that was to come. It read:

Cariad Stop Coming home Stop Arriving Aber Thursday midday train Stop Love Jack Stop

In truth Dora had forgotten about Jack. She knew he was her father, and was serving in the Sudan. Her mother would show her postcard pictures of him sitting on camels or standing to attention in full uniform amongst the Arabs. A framed photograph of him and her mother at their wedding in 1912 stood on top of the piano. But he never seemed real, just a picture book character whom she kissed goodnight. Dora was used to men in the house but most of them had been sick and very young. What would her father be like and what if he didn't like her?

But there was no time for anxiety for once Sarah was thrown out of her usual ordered routine, hurriedly running up dresses for herself and Dora ready to meet him at the station. She seemed unexpectedly nervous, and more abrupt than usual.

Eventually Gran chided her saying 'Do relax Sis – you're making us all edgy –I'm sure Jack will be fine, and pleased to see you after so long.'

Arriving at the station the three of them were confronted with the town band, and coloured banners welcoming the returning troops, as they struggled through the hordes.

Gran held tightly to Dora's hand, 'Don't let go, child, or we'll lose you. Stay close.'

When the train finally steamed in, there was pandemonium.

Everyone surged forward. Sarah left them and fought her way to the front, rapidly scanning the carriages. She was completely distracted hurrying this way and that, and then to Dora's utter astonishment, she saw her mother take to her heels and run up to a man disembarking at the far end of the train, throwing her arms round him. They caught up with her, Gran puffing and wheezing, and Dora amazed at her mother's show of emotion.

Regimental Sergeant Major John Herbert Roberts (or Jack) was a sight to behold as he shouted orders to his men, 'Careful, Dai with that trunk. There's valuable stuff in there. I want to get it home in one piece.' Bronzed to the colour of mahogany by the desert sun, his black hair now bleached and streaked, he stood solidly in his breeches, puttees and boots, toupee under his arm. It was as if he had brought the flavours and scents of North Africa back with him. Dora took one look and loved him on sight.

'So this is Dora.' He was delighted with her – rubbing his handlebar moustache against her face, and bouncing her high in his arms until she squealed with fright.

'Jack, you need to be gentler with her. She's only used to very sick men who would just pat and play with her.'

But there was no holding him back.

'Sis, I've bought you, Dora and Ma – all sorts from Egypt,' he said excitedly, 'slippers, material, ornaments, jewellery.'

'Never mind that now Jack, let's get you home to Baker Street.'

Sarah chivvied him along in her usual pragmatic way, cutting through the crowds and purposefully striding out towards home. Her mother and Dora lagged behind, finding it hard to keep up the pace, but there was no stopping Sarah when she had the 'bit between her teeth'.

18

Jack was full of vigour and energy. He kept saying 'It's so good to come home after so long.' Having left behind a bride of mature years in 1914 in rented rooms, he'd returned to a very different household; an elderly mother-in-law, a young daughter and a twelve roomed house. But he was not in the least perturbed. He was soon calling his mother-in-law 'Ma', and teasing her mercilessly. She took it all with a just a faint quirk of the lips, as having three sons herself she enjoyed the banter. Dora hung on his every word and would sit on his knee for hours playing with his watch chain.

True to his word he paraded out all his souvenirs, and would hang jewellery and necklaces round Dora's neck , turning her into an Arab maiden, and putting slippers on her feet telling tall tales of the Arabs, Egypt and the desert but little or nothing of the actual War itself.

'Now Jack, you are not to give all this to Dora. She has already been fussed over enough by the invalids we had. I don't want her growing up a spoiled child.' It was clear from the start that Sarah's word was going to be law in the house and the family, even ex-Regimental Sergeant Major Roberts used to giving orders and who adored the ground Sarah walked on, was never going to stand up against his wife.

In the following weeks and months, with the lease on Baker St extended under a new landlord, Sarah and Jack rolled up their sleeves and painted and papered all the rooms. Much of the furniture was left by the Red Cross and once they had sorted out the rest, the house was ready for business as a boarding house. There was still the question of what Jack would do but for the moment he contentedly worked in the house.

He had also started helping out at a market garden on North Road with an old army mate and his father, though Sarah was not at all sure about this arrangement. In her hard headed way she said to her husband, '– do you think he's alright?'

'Of course, – he's a real old mucker and got me out of many a scrape in the Sudan. I'm sure we'll work well together.'

'I don't know Jack, wartime is one thing, peacetime another. You really are too trusting, always looking for the good in everyone. I hope he proves you right.'

Months went by and Sarah was pleased to see Jack full of enthusiasm and working so hard. He did however, seem to be coming home later and later, but always had time to sit and chat with Ma, or dandle Dora on his knee, and play 'pat-a-cake' with her.

Sarah would often say, 'Late again tonight, Jack, you look so tired, get off to bed and I'll boil you some milk and bring it up.'

Finally it came to a head. Jack came home during a busy dinnertime. He plonked himself on one of the kitchen benches dejectedly, 'You were right Sis it's not going to work. Davy is busy drinking away all our profits at the Coopers hotel every day. I've had to pull out. I've absolutely no idea now what I can do.' Sarah had never seen him so down and dejected, as whatever happened he was always 'gung-ho', full of life, energy and purpose.

'Don't worry Jack. Something will come up. Perhaps it's come at the right time I badly need your help in the house now. Ma isn't getting any younger and more of her time is spent taking care of Dora rather than helping me.'

A few days went by and then out of blue, when they were all sitting down for the evening, Ma and Sarah crocheting and Dora playing by the fire, Sarah said, 'I think I've got the answer Jack '

Jack didn't need to ask 'the answer to what?'

All he ever thought about these days was their future and how he could earn a living.

'Why not work for yourself just as I'm doing.'

'But Sis, we've got no money for me to start a business. Anyway what could I do? I only know about soldiering.'

'That's not all you know Jack – What about gardening? D'you remember when you first came down from North Wales, you did lots of odd jobs around the garden when you were driving old Dr. Evans. You've learnt a lot about planting with Davy and seem to really take to the outdoors. There's lots of spare land about now the War's over. With all this tuberculosis, people will want fresh fruit and vegetables again.'

Ma said encouragingly, 'It sounds a good idea, Jack. You could build greenhouses and sheds. All you need is some land to rent.'

'I don't know – it would need money, and it would be a lot of work starting from scratch.'

Ma scoffed, 'and when have you been frightened of a bit of hard work, me lad.'

Sarah added, 'and I've got a bit put by to give you a start.'

Jack laughed 'I think you're both ganging up on me. There's only Dora who's got nothing to say.'

He said jokingly, 'Now Dora, bach, what do you think to your Dada running a market garden?'

'Will there be flowers?'Dora piped up.

'Definitely.'

'And can I pick the flowers?'

'I don't think so Dora my girl –we'll be selling them or making bouquets or wreaths with them, but perhaps you can have your own little garden.'

None of them knew where to go from here, but Sarah ever patient and persistent would tap her nose wisely and say, 'Just you wait and see – if it's meant to be, it'll happen.'

Jack always believing in her, waited, and applied himself to the work at No 8. For once, fate seemed to be on their side. Sarah, out and about shopping, made enquiries about land and eventually heard of an acre and a half big enough for a market garden about a mile away.

The following Sunday afternoon, Sarah pulled on her cloche and coat, 'Jack- leave the washing up, Ma will finish, and Dora's down for her rest. Why don't you and I go for a walk, I could do with a breath of fresh air.'

Jack only too keen, having been housebound all week, bounded out the door before she could say another thing. When Sarah purposefully turned down towards Plascrug and the Avenue, he said 'Where are we going then? I thought you'd want to go down the Prom to see the sea.'

'No, Jack, I feel like a walk in the country. We never go out of Aber. It'll be a change to see some trees.' They cut through the cemetery grounds, until they turned right past a few large houses. There in front of them was a waste piece of ground with a sign on it 'For Rent or Lease' and a great banner with the words, 'In Negotiation' slapped across it.

'Stop a minute, Jack. I can't walk at your pace. Let me get my breath.'

They both stood and looked at the land.

22

Eventually Jack remarked, 'This would be ideal Sis, for a market garden, the right place and the right acreage. It's a pity it's gone. 'As they went to move on, a man standing on the ground with his back to them, turned and hailed Jack: 'Well I'm blowed is that you Sgt Major?'

Jack turned like a shot, practically standing to attention, 'Brigadier,' he stammered- fancy seeing you round here.'

'I live just over there', the Brigadier gestured to an enormous detached house opposite—'this is my land, what d'ya think of it?'

'We were just saying it would make a lovely market garden. Pity it's not available.'

'Well to be honest, I haven't made up my mind what to with it, and I don't want to sell it as a building plot as it would ruin my view. Take a turn with me, and tell me what you would do with the land?'

Heads together they wandered off across the field, with the Brigadier saying, 'I hear you're heavily involved in the British Legion these days, Jack.'

'That's right Sir. I felt it ought to do as much I can for the soldiers who need help. I had some narrow escapes myself and was grateful to come back in one piece.'

Sarah took a few steps back, watching them whilst they paraded up and down the block, heads together, talking ten to the dozen. She enjoyed a quiet grin to herself, hoping the Brigadier wouldn't give her away. Being ex-military men together they would soon think any plans they hatched would be their own brainwave. After all women had no part to play in the world of men's affairs.

Jack was so excited on their way home he could hardly contain himself, thinking what an amazing coincidence it had been. Fancy them finding the right land for a market garden just like that, with a landlord he knew and for a rent he thought he could afford. Whilst he was telling Ma and Dora, Sarah caught Ma's eye and for once they both burst out laughing at his evident enthusiasm and his innocence.

Now they all had something to work for. It was never going to be easy but they were a family at last, and would have to pull together.

3

1921 - Summer

Summer was the time that Dora loved best. At the turn of the century Aberystwyth rather pompously advertised itself as:

ABERYSTWYTH - The Biarritz of Wales
HEALTH, SUNSHINE, SCENERY
ABERYSTWYTH affords all the advantages of Foreign Travel
without its expenses and inconvenience.
A Powerful Restorative of Convalescents and Invalids. The
town faces the Atlantic and receives the full force of its life-
giving breezes
Exceptionally pure supply of Drinking Water
313 Days of Sunshine last year

Dora knew this was why her mother had come to Aberystwyth originally, suffering weak lungs from the pollutions of Birmingham. Her mother used to say sardonically when she stepped off the train that first time it had felt like travelling to the ends of the earth. There was nowhere to go after Aberystwyth, it was the end of the line – you just fell off into the Irish Sea. Sarah made her views very plain saying it was a foreign land where the natives spoke a different language and weren't at all friendly, in spite of the fact that she'd married one of them.

But Dora was in her element this time of the year. There were hordes of summer visitors. A silver band played on the band stand. There was ice cream; donkeys; carts full of oysters; whelks and cockles; pleasure boats; rowing boats; charabancs bringing in day visitors; Pierrots and singers on the Pier.
Dora could never get enough of the colour, the noise, the music and the laughter.

No 8 was full to the rafters with summer visitors, Dora had been deposited on a trundle bed in Gran's room and Sarah and Jack on mattresses in the back kitchen.

The Rogers' family from Birmingham had written earlier in the season:

'Dear Mrs Roberts,
As you know we'll all be coming again for Wakes Week,
Frank and I can only stay the week but Mildred and her family
have a few extra days. As usual we'll want full board and be
bringing a sack of potatoes, Frank's runner beans, and some
bottled blackberries. We're all looking forward to seeing how
much Dora has grown, and be on the eight o'clock charabanc
on Friday night. Can Mr Roberts meet us at the Station with
the pushcart?'

And so the summer would start. Sarah had to be well prepared. Cooking full board for so many people with so many different meals took some doing. She would set Gran up, like the old days, in the yard with all the potatoes and veg to peel. This took forever even with Dora helping, and doing her best to keep out of her mother's way. After a while she would get restless, jump up and down impatiently whispering, 'Gran are we nearly finished yet?'

'Hold your horses young lady, 'a watched pot never boils'. Gran loved to come out with these little sayings. Dora was never sure of their meaning, but there was always a proverb or a Biblical saying for every occasion. Once the chores were done, they were both free to do what they liked.

Sarah would say roughly, 'Get out from under my feet you two.' Dora and Gran chortling like children would put on their Sunday best and make good their escape.

Gran would put on her very r--ef—ined voice and say, 'Well, I say Dora, where shall we go today? A brief sojourn on the Promenade I think. Would that suit your ladyship?'

26

Dora giggling her head off would curtsey and offer her arm to Gran and they would meander slowly up the street, at a pace that suited them both. They always took the same route.

Gran liked to look in all the shops in Eastgate, and remark on the quality and price of the goods. The Jewish couple, who kept the bakers on the corner, always waved and called out 'How are you Mrs Reynolds? Going for your usual constitutional?'

But Gran never answered, turning her face purposefully towards the street. Dora would pull at her arm, 'Gran, Gran, didn't you hear Mr Blumberg?'

Gran would toss her head, 'A lady doesn't respond if she hasn't been introduced - foreigners have a different way with them.'

Dora said, 'But Gran, they've lived here most of their lives – '

'Dora, you've not experienced war. At the end of the Great War, all sorts of riff raff came here even Germans. We may have to live with them, but that doesn't mean we have to acknowledge them.'

Dora wondered if people ever forgave and forgot. War was quite beyond her comprehension. All she remembered were bells pealing when the Armistice was declared, and dancing with all the soldiers celebrating. There was no more to be said. They made their way past Thomas the Outfitters, and Miss Jones, the Wool, but didn't loiter. Today they had a special appointment.

Before the summer had started, Gran and Sarah, working together, had made a special white broiderie anglaise dress for Dora, tied with a pink satin sash, Gran pinning and tucking and Sarah treadling away on her beloved Singer. Dora noticed when they were working together they seemed more of a mind. She just wished they could be like that all the time.

Fitting it on Dora, Gran said 'She looks a picture, Sis. Between us we've done a good job.'

'I think you're right, Ma. Perhaps we'll have a photograph done at Pickford's. There's just her hair to sort out now.'

∞

Dora's hair was the bane of her life. Her mother relished Dora's thick hair, now long enough to sit on. There was no use in asking to cut it. Gran had told her that when her mother was young and courting, her hair had been her pride and joy. Now it was so much finer and thinner it seemed that Sarah was going to make the most of Dora's locks instead.

Every Friday night, the torture began – the washing of the hair. Sarah was definitely of the opinion that 'cleanliness was next to godliness'. There was no question as who would be the victor in the battle.

Gran, seeing Dora's appealing face, would say, 'Sis let me do Dora's hair – you've got such a lot to do. You can get on with the supper if I do this.'

'No Ma, it's a difficult job and needs a firm hand. It would be too strenuous for you and takes up so much time. I need to get it done before Jack comes home for supper.'

Dora, ears full of soapsuds and up to her neck in boiling water, thought resentfully of it being called 'a difficult job'. It's as if she didn't exist as a person just a vast amount of hair. She would visualise a great silver chopper coming down, and slicing it all off in one clean stroke. Wouldn't it be wonderful to be free of the wretched stuff? Buried in her mother's pristine apron, she could barely move her legs, so tightly were they pressed up against Sarah's bombazine skirt.

Feeling imprisoned and suffocated, her poor head was thoroughly mashed and mangled by those delicate but tough little hands – nails scoring her scalp. Once that was over, it had to be wrung out thoroughly like the bed sheets. Winter was the worst time for this, as in summer Dora was allowed to let her hair dry naturally in the sun. But in the winter, she was marched to the sitting room and sat on a chair in front of the fire to dry. This was never as bad as what was to come.

Gran would pat her hand and say reassuringly, 'The worst is over now, Dora. Think how pretty you will look tomorrow.' But that was never any consolation. The combing out was bearable enough except for the occasional knot – but the brush. The hard coarse bristles of the brush banged and grazed her scalp. The brushing would become more and more forceful as if her mother was beating out rugs on the line. If she didn't sit still there was the odd box to the ears and bang on the head as Dora tried to duck and dive. It had to be a hundred strokes at least.

Even then it wasn't finished Sarah believed to be beautiful you must have some sort of ringlet curls, that could be tied back with a bow. This was always a challenge with Dora's poker straight hair. Out would come the rags, each strand rolled up so tightly that Dora thought her head would burst. After this there was some peace. Dora would have her supper, and then go off to bed trying to reconcile herself to her enormous rag rolled head and find a comfortable position to sleep.

∞

Despite the dreaded ringlets, Dora's pleasure in her new dress on this special day couldn't be suppressed. All the way up Eastgate and down Pier Street, she spun and pivoted, catching brief sights of herself in the shop windows.

'Dora you are such a vain child.' Gran reproved laughingly, her tone tinged with love and pride.

At the photographers' a chair was produced for Gran. Dora was cajoled into posing next to a flowered trellis, first with a parasol and then with a handbag. Dora didn't mind any of this but smiled and curtseyed when told. It seemed a fiddly business.

Why the photographer had to disappear under that black cloth was a mystery- and what was that huge flash, and why was everything upside down? No one explained anything to her, and she was never expected to utter a word of complaint. It took so long Dora began to think of what they would do next.

Knowing better than to ask, she counted off the possibilities in her head; Straight home – surely not with her in a new dress, what a waste; perhaps a walk and a sit on the Promenade; maybe, even an ice cream on the Pier, perhaps both of the last two. The anticipation was almost too much to bear.

Gran settled business with the photographer, and then it came. 'You've been such a good girl I think we'll go for a little walk down to the Promenade. Your mother won't mind. She's so busy and won't miss us for a while. Perhaps we'll take a dish of ice cream on the Pier.'

This is exactly what Dora had been waiting to hear. She could hardly contain her excitement and kept forgetting herself, and dancing along the pavement while tugging on Gran's hand.

'We won't get there any quicker Dora, if you keep tugging away at me. I can't walk any faster. Please remember you're a young lady.'

There wasn't a cloud in the sky. Gentlemen politely doffed their hats. Gran never dressed in anything but full black mourning after the death of her young husband. People would often remark on a likeness to Queen Victoria in her widow years, but Dora liked it best when they noticed and mentioned what very blue eyes they both had and the close family resemblance.

Heading on to the Pier, Dora felt the familiar apprehension. She carefully placed her small feet on the middle of each of the wooden slats which had wide gaps, where you could see the sea rising and falling below. One day she was sure she would fall straight through and be lost forever in that boiling sea.

Once on the Pier it was like a dream. They sat at a carefully pressed linen clothed table by one of the windows overlooking the Promenade and Constitution Hill. Silver dishes of ice cream were brought to them. Dora thought it was like being out with Royalty, the way Gran acknowledged every small detail with only the slightest nod of the head.

After the ice cream, Gran consulting her precious fob watch decided there was enough time for them to walk a little further down the promenade to the bandstand. Gran always liked to sit in the shade accordingly elderly gentlemen would hasten out of their seats to accommodate them in the front row. Gran took this as her due, and settled down to listen to the latest Sousa marches.

Once the band had finished, they slowly made their way home. Gran would point out landmarks – 'Look Dora, there's the Queens' Hotel, where your mother came to work as a maid all those years ago. Can you believe it has eighty three bedrooms – your poor mother had to work so hard and only had one evening and one day off a week?'

Further on, they ambled up Terrace Road, 'There's the Coliseum Theatre where your mother first met your father. Do you know he hardly spoke any English at all?' And she chortled rather vulgarly, 'I expect he learned quickly enough.'

Dora would relish these bits of information about her mother, clutching them tightly to her chest like tiny nuggets of gold.

After such a lovely day together, their slower and slower pace showed their reluctance to go home.

Gran would say, 'These poor old lungs won't let me go up Portland Street, we'll go the long way round, shall we, the slope from the Westminster Bank isn't so steep.' Dora never disagreed. Not knowing what mood Sarah would be in, made them both thoughtful – but neither gave voice to their thoughts. Dora was much too young to say anything, and Gran knew better.

4

A 1920s Childhood

Everyday Gran told Dora that she was 'special'. Dora would pester and pester Gran and say 'How'm I special, Gran?'

But Gran would just laugh and tap her nose, as if there was some great secret between them, '<u>You</u> are special to me, Dora.'

At the end of a day working in the house if it was sunny Gran would sit with Dora in the backyard, Dora on the wide back wall on a cushion, and Gran in the old somewhat disreputable Lloyd Loom chair, her knees covered by a rug. There were young children often playing out in Baker Street, but Sarah didn't approve. Gran would sometimes plead, 'Sis, let the child make a few friends in the street. She needs some company.'

But Sarah was obdurate, 'Playing in the street is common, only for guttersnipes.'

One afternoon when Gran and Dora sat soaking up the sun, all of a sudden Gran said, 'Your mother's gone for her rest, why don't you bring Girlie down for an outing? You know your mother's made her a new dress.' Dora was surprised. Girlie was a family heirloom and never meant to be played with. Girlie, a life size child doll, with a beautiful porcelain face and cherubic lips, had long human hair, but was rather let down by her disjointed body and splayed limbs attached by springs, though Dora never minded or even saw her imperfections. When she was younger Dora had blotted her copybook by hugging and kissing Girlie too much, even when the giant doll was nearly suffocating her. Finally the doll was wrested from her grasp and put in a trunk for safekeeping.

However her mother seemed to have gone to a lot of trouble recently.

Girlie was now proud and smart in a new taffeta dress cut down from one of Dora's dresses, with a crocheted shawl, a bonnet and even small boots for her rather ugly plaster feet.

'Oh Gran isn't she beautiful. What an elegant little lady!'

Gran watched indulgently as Dora fussed over plaiting and braiding the doll's hair, and rearranging her bonnet coquettishly whilst whispering in the doll's ear, 'If only you could speak, you could be my sister – what fun we'd have.'

After a while one of the Hughes' little girls from next door popped her head over the wall, 'Ooh Dora is that your doll?'

'Yes,' Dora said proudly, 'this is Girlie. Isn't she fine?' and then in a rush, 'my mother made the new dress and bonnet and shawl and boots. Do you want to come over and see her?' The little girl carefully climbed on a chair to sit on the wall beside her.

Seeing them so absorbed, Gran said, 'I'm just going to close my eyes for a moment Dora. Mind and make sure you take Girlie back upstairs before your mother gets up. Are you listening child?' This seemed to be some sort of coded message. Dora tried to work out why her mother had gone to all the trouble of redressing Girlie if she didn't want Dora to play with her.

'Yes Gran, Mair and I will just be a few more minutes.' They put their heads together examining the doll and moving her arms and legs about, with Dora making sure that Girlie had disappeared back into the trunk before Sarah got up.

But now Girlie was so resplendent Dora could never resist taking her out on the quiet and playing with her.

She never told Gran but kept it her own deep dark secret. It was always exciting to do something just a little bit risky, something only she knew about.

∞

It was Gran who helped Dora get a real live breathing companion. She often thought how lonely the little girl was with no brothers or sisters, no friends allowed to the house and surrounded by adults. Being the wise woman she was, she decided to start with her son-in-law. Pointing to an advertisement one day in the local paper, she said, 'Look Jack, here's the very dog for Dora. Isn't that the type of breed you had as a boy?' Jack always fond of his mother- in- law studied the advert carefully.

Dora who was sitting at the end of the table listened with interest. A dog, wouldn't that be grand! She could imagine playing with him, taking him for walks. She could train him to catch balls He could sleep on her bed, the possibilities were endless.

'I don't know Ma. We've got enough to do without looking after a dog. It's really up to Sis.'
That sounded ominous, Dora thought well that's that then, her mother would never agree.

Sarah responded as predicted, 'I'm not sure Dora is old enough to look after a dog.'

Dora was biting her lip with the effort of trying not to say, 'Yes I am old enough- and I can take care of a dog.' But she daren't, no one would expect her to have an opinion.'

Days went by and then surprisingly Sarah said to Gran, 'Jack seems set on this idea of having a pup for Dora. I don't know, I've no time to train a dog. There's bound to be accidents, and what will the visitors think?'

Gran kept her counsel. There were times in life, when it was best to take a back seat.

Jack, deciding on a course of action, was never one to delay. He sent off for the dog in the advert, paying out a considerable sum, and putting the case to his wife by saying, 'We'll get a good pedigree if we're going to have one.'

When the dog came, it turned out to be a runt and Jack was furious, 'Ma, we can't keep this pup. There's too much wrong with him. He's going to have to go.'

Dora was in tears but there was nothing for it. However the owner refused to take the dog back or return Jack's money.
Holding the little pup close to her chest, Dora pleaded and pleaded with her father, 'He's so sweet Dada can't we keep him anyway?'

But Jack was adamant, 'No Dora, he's not perfect and there are always problems with runts. I'll take him to work with me.'
He didn't elaborate – and Dora kept wondering, 'what will he do with him?'

Jack mouthed quietly to his wife, 'I'll drown him in one of the water butts tomorrow,' and attempting to reassure his daughter said, 'I'll find you a better animal – don't worry.'

Dora knew she'd have been happy with little Johnnie as she'd named him. It didn't matter that he wasn't perfect she would love him, but of course it was never her decision.

True to his word, Jack heard of a terrier puppy from a good home and within a week, he and Dora were off to collect it. Dora was beside herself with the new pup, insisting on calling her Judy.

'Now Dora,' her mother said emphatically, 'Judy is your responsibility. You'll have to train her and keep her from under my feet. She'll sleep in the backyard lavatory till your father makes a kennel. I'm not having you sneak her in to your bed.'

Dora didn't care about the instructions. She had a companion at long last and someone to pour all her love into. Gran of course was the one to thank. Neither of her parents seemed that interested in the animal, only complaining when Judy got in their way, but Dora never tired of teaching Judy new tricks, 'Look Gran. Judy's so clever now – see how she pretends to lie dead. Shall we take her to church on Sunday now she's so well behaved?'

Gran didn't approve of mixing animals and religion especially with St Michael's being High Church, 'Dora, I think the vicar would be apoplectic.' Dora had no idea what that meant but it sounded frightening. However not giving up easily, she raised pleading eyes to Gran who could never resist her.

'Well just this once Dora, and she'd better be good or we'll both be thrown out. I can't think what God would say about taking dumb animals into his house!'

The following Sunday they got ready for church. Dora put on her best coat – cleverly making a little pocket between the top buttons. She sneaked out of the house whilst Gran kept her mother talking in the hall. Judy was quite content in her hiding place – her little nose snuffling in the air.

The vicar was at the main door to meet and greet his congregation. Despite her strong faith Gran could never abide the Reverend Elwyn Davies, thinking him rather oily and unctuous, but this time she hailed him pleasantly: 'Reverend, how are you this fine day? I hope you're giving us a good sermon today. Dora, go in and find a seat near the back- my old bones can't take a long walk.'

'Mrs Reynolds – what a pleasure,' the reverend said silkily, 'Perhaps I could offer you my arm and help you to your usual pew.'

'I'm quite capable, Reverend, of making my own way,' responded Gran frostily leaning heavily on her stick, 'and I'll sit where I please thanking you.'

He huffed and puffed off down the aisle full of good intentions, leaving Gran to broadly wink at Dora. They carefully left just before the end of the service, Dora hugging Judy close to her chest.

'Dora, you know we've committed a mortal sin, hoodwinking that poor man. Still it was worth it. Put Judy on her lead now and give her some freedom. I haven't had so much enjoyment in a long time. You're a wicked child tempting me off the straight and narrow!'

They laughed all the way home, Dora sliding herself and Judy into the house behind Gran's skirts. At Sunday dinner Sarah remarked drily, 'I didn't realise how much fun there was to be had in going to church on Sunday. You two seemed to have had a fine old time today.'

'You'd be surprised, Sis – you should try it yourself sometime,' Gran winked naughtily at Dora, who giggled behind her hand carefully masking her grin from her mother.

5

1923 - Sisterhood

Dora was never sure later how it had all come about. Without warning her mother had ordered her to, 'Run upstairs Dora, and put on your Sunday best- we're going out- and don't dawdle.'

Dora was always pleased to dress up. Her mother had just run up a new outfit in the sailor style with a dropped waist. She pranced about in front of the mirror to see the complete effect.

Downstairs her mother was already calling, 'Dora do come on I'm ready and waiting.' Hurriedly doing up the last button on her boots, Dora shot down the staircase as if her life depended on it, jumping the last few stairs.

'What've I told you about jumping and running – try to act like a young lady not a hooligan.'

This wasn't a good start Dora was dying to know where they were going. Silently she fell in behind her mother and they walked through the town, straight down North Parade lined with trees in full leaf and beyond Northgate to open country, making Dora concerned about where they could be going. It seemed a long way and a long time before her mother said anything, 'Do come along Dora, we've a way to go yet.'
She seemed to mumble to herself, and sigh loudly '---- so far– I don't know if it's practical-----' Dora knew she wasn't expected say anything and kept silent.

They came to some big gates and a driveway. Her mother stopped abruptly.
 Taking Dora by the shoulders she spat on a hanky and rubbed her face hard, tidying her plaits and smoothing down her dress, 'Now Dora – stand up straight, shoulders back, and only speak if spoken to.'

They marched through a garden scented with perfumed flowers. Dora wondered if she was perhaps going to work here – wasn't she too young at eight? Perhaps she was going into service as a Tweeny, or maybe a beautiful lady wanted her as her companion. Currently reading 'Jane Eyre' with Gran, Dora hoped there wasn't a Mr Rochester in there. It was intriguing though. She was definitely curious.

The grounds were beautiful and mysterious leading to an old house. Standing in front of the stout oak door, Sarah pulled hard on the bell and a small grid slid open. A smaller door set in the main door opened, and they stepped inside. It was cool and quiet in the main hall, and very silent. A tiny lady in some sort of black and white dress scuttled off to say they had arrived.

Sarah eventually seemed constrained to say something, 'Dora this is a convent. We have an appointment with the Mother Superior, the head of the convent. Behave yourself-----and don't on any account let me down.'

The only time Dora had ever heard about convents and nuns was in books. What was a Mother Superior? Perhaps her mother was going to leave her here. Perhaps she'd become a nun, though she wasn't entirely sure that she wanted to be one–weren't they always on their knees praying a lot?

Time elapsed and finally they were shown into a vast book lined room, overlooking the gardens. The lady that greeted them had a kind wrinkled face. She gestured Sarah to sit, and found a little stool for Dora to perch near the window.

Dora could hardly take her eyes off the books. Oh what a treat to spend your life reading in a room like this. There was so much to take in. She could barely concentrate on what her mother was saying.

Sarah as usual took the initiative, 'Madam, I'm not sure how I should address you?' and then quite brusquely stated, 'We're not Catholics you know. I'm not at all used to nuns.'

'You can address me as 'Mother' Mrs Roberts, that'll do fine. How can I help you?'

'It's my daughter,' Sarah continued, gesturing towards Dora, 'my mother and I are tired of hearing her banging away at our piano constantly. She's been doing this from a very young age, and we wondered if she has any real talent for music. Then my husband heard that you sometimes offer private music lessons, so we thought this was the place to come.'

Mother Superior considered thoughtfully for a few minutes, 'I don't know, Mrs Roberts. She's about the right age to start. But the sisters are very busy with the school and the other tuition we provide.'

Dora's ears pricked up surely she wasn't going to have piano lessons and what's more did she really want them? It was true she loved to bang away at the piano pretending she was a famous pianist, so learning to play properly might be fun. Anyway no doubt her mother would make any final decisions.'

Sarah– never one to be deterred from her goal, said proudly, 'We may not be Catholics – but we can certainly pay.'

Mother Superior obviously cut from the same cloth, responded in a firm commanding manner, 'You don't have to be Catholics, Mrs Roberts. We could give Dora a trial if you like, to see if it's worth her having further lessons. That way you won't be wasting your money.'

Sarah begrudgingly admitted this was fair. So they agreed on a day and a time for Dora to start.

On the way back her mother said, 'Do your best at the trial next week Dora. If it's meant to be, we'll find the money for lessons. You're a very lucky little girl, and don't you forget it.'
Not at any time did she take into account Dora's wishes or ask her what she thought. Sarah had made her mind up and that was that.

Back home Gran was delighted, 'You know Dora, I could play quite well as a girl. Of course my poor fingers are crippled now. But it will be a joy to listen to some music. Why your mother ever bought that beautiful piano I don't know. She can't play a single note.'

Dora was not so enthralled. And neither was Jack. When they all sat round the tea table he said 'I don't know Sis. Why do you want Dora to learn? It's going to be money we can ill afford.'

'Jack, I never had the chance myself. Pa promised me a piano – he was so musical – we used to sing little songs together.
He wanted me to have lessons. Once he died of course, there was no time or money –and I had to look after the boys, and then there was a living to earn to keep us all,' Sarah looked pointedly at her mother, 'I'm determined to give Dora the opportunity I never had. Whether she'll make anything of it we'll have to see.'

There was a distinct frostiness in the room. Gran got up abruptly, obviously riled, tossed her head and left.

Jack took his paper and made a swift departure to the outside lavatory, leaving his wife and Dora to clear the table. Sarah pursed her lips, as she banged plates together, gesturing to Dora, 'Come along child, we've not got all night, do hurry up. I've not seen such a slow coach.'

∞

Once the trial week at the Convent was over and proved to be a success, Dora started attending once a week, considering it her special time. Of course, she loved the music but more than that she loved going to the Convent. Though it was a good three quarters of a mile away, surprisingly enough Sarah thought her old enough to go on her own with just Judy for company.

Out of Sarah's sight, Dora and Judy would race through the town at breakneck speed to get there early. Once they entered the gates Dora would let the little dog off the lead and they would scamper up and down the paths, the very air scented by the flowers in the walled garden. Exhausted at last they would collapse on the steps, and wait to be called in.

Passing nuns would ask, 'Can we help you, who are you waiting for?'

'My sister,' Dora would reply.

'What's her name? Is she having a lesson too?'

'Of course not,' Dora would say indignantly 'it's my lesson with my sister.'

Eventually, whilst they tried to untangle it all, a smiling Sister Marie-Amelie would float into sight in her black habit, gliding along as if she was on castors. Dora would look at her adoringly. Her pure white wimple framed her Madonna like face, which was always wreathed in smiles.

'I think you'll find she means me- she's waiting for her lesson with me. Do-va always calls me her sister. I think she counts me as one of her family, don't you Do-va?'

Coming from France, Sister could never quite get the pronunciation of the 'r' in Dora.

Dora thought it made her name sound exotic and interesting far better than plain old 'Dora'.

People used to joke about her name being the initials for the 'Defence of the Realm Act.' How she hated that name. Why couldn't she have been called Zipporah like Gran or Sarah like her mother?

They were soon immersed in the lesson whilst Judy sat patiently outside.

'You are doing so well Do-va, but---,' and then Sister would tap Dora's fingers, '------- more practice I think. You are such a clever girl Do-va, but you must work harder at your lessons and then you'll be able to go to the County School.'

'But Sister I'm not good enough, my arithmetic is so bad.'

'I don't know Do-va how can that be? You count notes and work out the music here.'

But it was no use, Dora always thought of music as one thing, and school as quite something else. She knew she was far too stupid to go to the County.

On their way home Dora would think how lucky she was to have Judy, her Sister and Gran in her life. They were always so kind to her and understanding, never telling her off but loving her as she was. Of course her father was very loving too, but he would never show her any form of affection in front of her mother.

Idly she wondered what it would be like to be Catholic. They all seemed so kind, patient and serene. Never shouting, being angry, or hitting even when she played a wrong note. Of course Catholics had to attend confession regularly, and Dora wasn't at all sure that she could tell a priest the things she got up to. Her sins were probably far too wicked.

Occasionally Sister would let her sit in the chapel if there was no service. The chapel was painted in such vibrant colours with pictures and statues of the Virgin everywhere. Dora felt she could soak up all the gold and blue into her very being. So much more attractive than plain St Michael's or the cream washed walls of the local chapels. 'Perhaps when I grow up I'll think about becoming a nun, and then I'll be surrounded by music, books and paintings,' she would muse to herself.

It always seemed she had a heavy heart when it was time to go home. Still Tuesday was always her favourite tea – fried fish and baked tart with gooseberries fresh from her father's Market Garden. There were always consolations.

6

Childhood Interrupted

'Dora---- come here a moment.' Her mother was in the back kitchen clattering pans. Dora hastily covered Girlie with a rug, and raced into the kitchen.

'Stop running everywhere, stir this custard. Don't let it get lumpy.'

It was the start of yet another summer, the sun burning strongly through the scullery window casting shadows on the newly scrubbed flagstones and glancing across gleaming copper pans hung over the range.

Dora sincerely hoped the stirring would not have to go on for too long as she was halfway through giving Girlie a new hairstyle, and she had to get her back to the trunk before her mother noticed. After that she had her new 'Alice in Wonderland' to read. Alice was just about to drink from the bottle, and Dora was dying to know what happened next.

Concentrating hard on stirring, she vaguely heard her mother say in the distance, 'It's the start of the summer holidays.'

Well of course it is, thought Dora indignantly- does she think I'm stupid or something?

Having just reached her tenth birthday, she was relishing the thought of the long summer holidays stretching into the far distance, no school till September. She would take Judy for long walks on the beach, or perhaps go with Gran for a saunter on the Promenade. On Saturdays now she was older her father would say, 'Sis why don't I take Dora off your hands today. She can give me a hand in the Garden.' They always called his Market Garden 'the Garden.'

Her mother hands on hips would hum and har, whilst Dora looked beseechingly at her father, 'Look Jack, I just washed her hair last night – I don't want her or her hair getting dirty.'

'Don't worry Sis, I've just got a bit of watering to do, and then we'll be home for dinner.'

Sarah could never resist her husband, and eventually gave in brushing out Dora's semblance of ringlets and tying them firmly back with ribbons. 'Make sure she wears her pinafore if she's planting anything Jack and don't be late home.'

Sunday mornings when she didn't go to church with Gran, were precious to Dora, as in the summer she would often go with her father to the Pier, where he looked after all the hanging flower baskets. He would lower the baskets, and together they would carefully water each of them. Once they were back in place, he would say, 'Well Dora, that's a job well done – what about some payment- a Knickerbocker Glory perhaps?'

When the dessert was placed in front of her, Dora would sit and gaze for so long at the tall glass adorned with cherry and a fan shaped wafer that her father would tease, 'I don't know Dora if you don't eat that soon it'll melt. Perhaps I should give it to another little girl?'

Eventually digging deep with the long silver spoon, Dora would uncover and anticipate layer after layer of the jelly, the ice cream and the meringue, each more mouth watering than the last.
Back home her mother knowing exactly what they'd been up to, would protest loudly, 'You're too bad Jack. I bet you've been giving that child one of those big ice cream things again. She'll never eat her dinner.'

∞

Dora suddenly noticed her mother was still talking to her whilst she'd been mechanically stirring, and dreaming.

'From now on,' her mother said, 'you won't be going to Birmingham for the summer.'

In past summers since the age of six, Dora had been labelled and bundled off on the train to Birmingham, under the guard's beady eye, to stay with her mother's relatives. Dora liked some of them, but some were Gran's age. This meant she was expected to be quiet and amuse herself.

At other times her mother would say, 'You know Uncle Ron and Auntie Mary, who come every year for their holiday. They've written and asked if you'd like to go and stay with them for a few weeks in Edgbaston.'

Dora knew that her mother, father and Gran were busy in the summer, but sometimes it did make her feel like an unwanted parcel being handed round. The people she went to were always kind and tried to make her feel welcome, but she was always glad when it was time to come home.

'Dora, are you listening? Do stop dreaming. You'll dream your life away.' And then it came --. 'After you've done your piano practice, you're quite old enough to start helping me in the house and I'm going to teach you to cook.'

Dora felt sick even faint. Her head was swimming. What? No more freedom and on top of that, spending more time with her mother. In one fell stroke, it felt like her childhood was over.

Sarah prodded her hard in the back, 'Keep stirring. After that you can do the same with the gravy.'

Dora peered into the enormous vat of custard. Her arm ached from all the stirring. It would never do to let it burn.

Moving on to the gravy, it was more of the same, a battle against lumpiness. Dora wondered if this was all she was ever destined for. Surely there was something besides custard and gravy – why did people need so much of them. Gran came in at just the right moment, 'Sis, this child really needs some fresh air I'll take over here.'

Later on, stroking Girlie's locks for perhaps the last time, Dora was stricken by her fate and plaintively asked Gran, 'Why can't I go to Birmingham for the summer anymore?' Going away would be better than this.

'Well, child, your mother is so busy; anything you or I can do to help is what matters. Your mother started work very young even younger than you are now. When my lovely William died so quickly---,' Gran's eyes filled with tears.

'Oh Gran please don't cry, I never meant to upset you,' Dora said contritely, lovingly stroking her face.

'No, you need to know, child. After his death, I fell apart, you see. Your mother who was barely 12, had to look after Walter, young William and Tom the baby singlehandedly,' she gulped – choking back the emotion, 'I was no use to anyone. I thought I'd die of grief. We'd been young sweethearts, and then he was gone.'

'Please Gran it's too painful for you.'

'I must, Dora - so that you can begin to understand about your mother.'Gran continued, 'There was no more school for Sis. We needed money badly and she had to go to work travelling everyday into Birmingham, and still looking after the boys. I couldn't cope for a long time. It's been a hard life for her and still is now, but she thinks you're old enough to help her. '

Dora wasn't at all sure about that, but she knew she must try.

As long as Gran was around to confide in and support her probably life wouldn't be all that bad. Sometimes Gran would tell her little odd and ends about her mother's life in Birmingham, but Dora could never ask outright or the shutters would come down.

One of the stories she liked best was the one about the tin teapot factory. Sarah had been just fifteen when she joined Hart and Sons of Birmingham. Sharp and bright and being one of the few who could read and write, she was soon promoted to supervising the production line and checking on rejects.

The manager Mr Frobisher, an unpleasant portly man in his fifties, never left his office or visited the line or even the shop floor. Late on Friday afternoons at the sound of the klaxon Sarah was expected to report to his office with the week's figures-whether she missed her tram home or not. This particular afternoon he wanted to know the names of people not pulling their weight and those producing most rejects so he could sack them.
'Come on girl, give me their names. Who produced these useless specimens (pointing to a rejected tray of teapots)? What's the point of promoting you if you don't do what you're told?'

But Frobisher hadn't bargained on Sarah's temper finally erupting after suffering weeks of his appalling rudeness and laziness. Standing ramrod straight she fired back at him, 'I'm not your personal spy or stool pigeon, and I'm not doing your dirty work for you. If you want to get rid of anyone, come down to the line and do it yourself, instead of just sitting on your fat, idle backside.'

Frobisher was furious at this chit of a girl speaking up to him like this, 'Sarah Reynolds, who do you think you are, speaking to me like that. You're sacked. Get out of my office and my factory this minute.'

Sarah always one to have the last word said, 'Don't worry I'm going,' then in a terrible fit of rage picked up the last tray of teapots and threw them straight through his glass door, 'Here have your teapots – may they bring you much good,' she yelled, leaving him practically frothing at the mouth.

Dora had experienced her mother's bad temper on many an occasion, but to think her mother had actually walked out of a paid job, and stood up to a man more than three times her age. It was heroic, and did give her some pause for thought.

∞

That year though, the summer felt longer than ever. So much washing up, cleaning and cooking – would it never end? The only escape was the trips to the Convent as even her daily piano practice had become a chore. Usually Dora was reluctant to return to school in September after the long holiday, but this time it was a relief. At last all the summer visitors had departed. There were only a handful of lodgers for the winter, Jack's Garden was much quieter, and Dora could get back to her friends and the routine of school with no more household jobs to do, and time to spend with Gran.

7

1928 - Leaving School

Dora blinked. Was that a ray of sun? Surely she could draw the curtains now – it was bound to be a lovely day out there. Tentatively she pushed the window up, trying to catch a glimpse of Judy in the yard. Who on earth got measles at thirteen? Surely it was a childish ailment; she certainly wasn't a child anymore. Lying in bed for the last three weeks in freshly laundered sheets had been lovely, but the castor oil and the dark had been torture.

When there was no one around Dora would read with a torch under the bedclothes. After all how could being covered in spots affect your eyes? Even missing the daily piano practice was a relief, it was just so lovely to lie in bed and be waited on. True it was a bit boring now but better to make the most of it, it wasn't going to last much longer.

At least there was Gran for company. After doing jobs downstairs, she would come and sit and read to Dora, 'Now Dora what shall I read you today? We've not had 'The Little Match Girl' for a while, have we? What do you think?'

'Please Gran not that book again – it's so sad and she dies every time. What about 'The Scarlet Pimpernel?'

Gran would nod, 'Perhaps a bit of excitement and adventure will do you good now you're on the mend, but don't let on to your mother or she'll think you're getting too agitated, and it could make you feverish again.'

This morning Gran was still busy in the downstairs back kitchen and Dora tired of her books, skittered to the top of the front stairs and her usual vantage point to find out what was going on down below.

She peered over the banister and down the front passage, thinking she could hear a familiar voice – in fact raised voices. Very quietly she crept down to the bottom stair, near enough to listen in to the visitor in the front room.

Wasn't that Mr Thomas's voice? She shuddered. What was the headmaster of her school doing here at this time? Dora hoped she hadn't done something wrong. Being head of Alexandra Road Board School, Dora hardly ever saw him. He led assemblies and doled out punishments, but that was all. It was said that Mr Thomas was a learned man busy studying and doing research, and far too erudite to talk to pupils or teachers. Praying he hadn't brought her homework, Dora instinctively crossed her fingers. It was the last thing she wanted. Maybe a composition wouldn't be too bad but please not sums.

Dora had to crouch nearer the door to hear his quiet but authoritative voice. 'Now Mrs Roberts, I think you don't understand, the law says that Dora cannot leave school yet,' Despite no immediate response, Mr Thomas persevered. He was not a man to be crossed. Though learned and academic, he was very much in charge, punctilious in interpreting procedures.

Sarah never one to be put down by either the law or an errant headmaster replied, 'There's no point. Dora isn't that good at her lessons. She'd be leaving anyway. There's only the summer term. I've plenty of work for her to do here rather than wasting time at school.'

Mr Thomas tried a new tack, and a more pleading tone, 'But Mrs Roberts, Dora is not 14 until June, surely a little more time with her school friends and more learning will help her mature. Dora is very good at English. If she'd studied harder at her arithmetic she'd be going on to the County School.'

'Mr Thomas, I really don't think there's anything more to be said on the subject. Dora's still in bed with the measles. She'll not be returning to school when she's better. That's an end to it. I started work at 10, with little education, so I don't see what the problem is.'

Mr Thomas became officious, not used to being spoken to like that by a woman, 'I must warn you Mrs Roberts, that I will have to report this. There may be serious repercussions.'

Dora could imagine her mother bristling. Even though she was tiny, few people were brave enough to stand up against her.

∞

On the one hand Dora would love to leave school behind, especially arithmetic which she hated with a passion. On the other, what about all those times with her friends, Eluned, Beryl and Phyllis. All four of them would sit in class, their shoulders often shaking with ill contained laughter and nearly wetting themselves. Playtime they'd double skip in the yard reciting rude verses, throwing balls, shooting ink pellets over the boys' wall, with Beryl balancing on the shoulders of a bigger girl, gurning and laughing. Eluned would be leaning up against the outside wall, too shy and reserved to join in whilst Beryl organised everyone into gangs, not worrying about ripping or dirtying her clothes.

Beryl came from a big family at the top of Baker St, –rough, tough and often dirty with threadbare clothes, and no shoes on their feet– they ran wild but there was lots of love and fun in their house. Dora always felt envious, and when she went to call, she had to do it on the quiet. Her mother called them 'layabouts and scoundrels'. Her opinion was that they were 'no better than they should be', which was a term she used to describe at least half the population in the street, and even the town.

Of course school hadn't all been plain sailing, particularly when Dora was younger and she'd encountered Miss Lloyd. She'd certainly been a force to be reckoned with, a spinster in her last years of teaching. Weariness and pain had woven deep carved patterns into her cheeks culminating in thin narrow lips. The rumour was that she'd lost her young man in the Great War. Dora thought that unlikely. In Dora's view there were only beautiful heroines who deserved Prince Charmings. Surely Miss Lloyd with her body crippled by polio, and her bad temper had never had a beau!

But then there'd been her favourite teacher Miss Davies. She always asked Dora to be ink monitor and clean the blackboard. She was such a pretty and kind woman, that Dora never minded doing anything for her. Last Christmas she'd wanted to give the young teacher a present.
Broaching the subject with her mother, Sarah had just snorted, 'What's it coming to when we give presents to people just doing their job? Anyway no doubt she'll marry soon and leave.'

Gran however had been listening in and had come up trumps. She'd found a tiny little butterfly brooch in her belongings and given it to Dora, who'd packed it carefully in soft tissue paper. Her teacher was delighted with it, pinning it straight on to her blouse, with Dora basking in the pleasure of giving.

∞

But in her wandering thoughts Dora had missed some of the conversation downstairs. It seemed to be coming to an end. She couldn't be caught listening.

Sarah's voice had gone up a pitch or two, 'Mr Thomas, thank you for coming and for your concern. I have said my last word. I think you can find your own way out.'

And that was it. Dora knew her fate was sealed.

Very much like the loss of her beloved summer holidays – now her whole life would be bound up in the house. She scuttled back to bed. What sort of future would she have? No doubt some of her friends would go to the County School, others would go as maids in the local hotels, or into service and yet others would probably go to work in shops, hairdressers, banks. Just not her! She'd be in the house fulltime, working hard trying to keep her mother happy, in captivity for life!

Dora lay back in bed, wondering what the next weeks would bring. She consoled herself by imagining herself imprisoned in a turret, with a prince on a white charger or even a flying unicorn coming to rescue her and steal her away to a land of freedom and happiness. Anything but this, it was unbearable.

8

The Daily Grind

'Dora, I've called you twice already.' The sharp rap on the door and the peremptory tone shook Dora.

This was harsh reality. To think it was nearly two years now since she'd left school. What had her life become? It was no use dwelling on it. Being an eternal optimist, she said to herself, 'Perhaps something good will happen today.'

For a fleeting moment she wondered what sort of mood her mother would be in. But there was no time for that. Quickly splashing cold water on her face from the bowl on the dresser, and tiptoeing from the rag rugs onto the freezing lino, she pulled on her chemise and thick lisle stockings. An all over sponge wash in the winter months was usually perfunctory, and sometimes she skipped it, longing for the warmth of the kitchen range.

Sarah wouldn't knock again and the icy coldness of the water would be nothing compared with her mother's iciness if she was late. Her woollen dress was cold and damp sticking to her skin and her petticoats. With just time to pull the rags out of her hair, brush and plait it, Dora was ready for another day's work.

No '8' had never looked more gloomy, with its dark brown paint and polished mahogany wood. Dora stole a look in the hallstand mirror to check her hair, spitting on her fingers to wet down the odd wayward lock. The mounted animal heads in the hall looked back menacingly at her reflection as she put her tongue out at them and raced through the glass conservatory to the back kitchen.

Her mother was already clanging the big pots of porridge and gave her only a cursory glance, 'About time too, stop running like a herd of elephants. Take this tray in for the Gladstones.

We've a lot to do today. Beds need changing and rooms will have to be bottomed out. Come back and take this tray up to Gran.'

Gran was spending more and more time in bed these days. Dora missed her companionship and mischievousness as doing routine jobs together was so much more fun than working on your own.

Taking in the breakfasts was always a bit of a treat though. The lodgers made such a fuss of her, 'Dora come and tell us what you're doing today,' or 'Dora you look so pretty in that dress – the blue matches your eyes.' But she daren't linger.

Once everyone was out of the house, she and her mother would make all the beds. Sarah was like a tornado and Dora could barely keep up with her. There was a lot of, 'Dora, you've got to learn to make hospital corners or we'll be here all day,' 'Dora, you're not folding that linen neatly enough,' or 'Dora, get the brasso – the bedroom knobs need polishing.'

Then there was the range to black lead and what about the front door step? The one thing Sarah could not abide was a dirty front step and letterbox. She would say to Dora, 'People will judge you by your step and your windows. The outside reflects the inside. You don't want to look like you're running a slovenly house.' So it was out with the chair, and up with the vinegar and newspaper to shine the windows.
As well as the door step, Dora was even expected to brush the pavement in front. This was a job she didn't mind as people would stop to chat to her, although this was regarded by Sarah as a terrible breach of etiquette as one must not be seen to be cleaning, and should be done first thing in the morning before too many people were about.

It was also Dora's daily job to wash and polish all the bedroom floors. Doing the floors was a heavy job, but it had its compensations.

Once the boards were washed and the polish laid down, Dora would tie dusters to her feet, walk up and down reading the book she'd hidden earlier, rubbing as she went. It would never do to be found out so often she would tip toe quietly to the landing listening hard in case her mother was coming up the stairs.

Mondays were wash days and out would come the boiler. Dora was put in charge of the dolly, pushing and prodding the wash as it boiled and bubbled away, whilst her mother worked on her father's stained overalls on the washboard. Then it was mangling. This was heavy and hot work. Dora often felt that her arms would drop off folding and pushing the heavy cotton sheets through the roller. She thought longingly of those lovely days at school when she could play in the yard or just sit and feel the sun on your face. But Sarah was a hard task master – there was no time to sit or even take a break.

'Come on Dora, you can put this first lot on the line.' Dora would climb up onto the wide outside wall, bring down the line pulley and carefully spread the sheets out. There didn't have to be a sign of creases, as it made ironing all the harder.

Usually twice a day Dora would escape Baker Street for a quick trip to the Dairy, 'Dora, take a jug and get the milk, perhaps some cream for Gran's porridge.' Dora would be halfway out the door before a harsh voice would haul her back, 'Just a minute young lady – off with that pinafore. Tidy your hair before you go. I don't know what the neighbours would think? Never never be seen in your work clothes, always remember you must at least look like a lady. A lady never gets her hands dirty.'
Dora could never fathom this. How could you be a lady and clean the house if you weren't to get your hands dirty? It was a real poser.

Dora would take her time getting to Terrace Road. She loved going there. The staff would tease and pull on her plaits playfully, 'Well, little Miss Roberts s'mae – have you come to milk the cow again?' They would take her jug and pour her a long glass of cold frothy milk to drink whilst she waited. Covering the filled jug Dora would walk carefully back – trying her hardest not to spill a drop. This was never an easy task, but worth every effort to stop her mother complaining.

However today her mother was in a good mood, 'Dora, you can have the night off. Go and see your friends.'

This was always at the last minute, and not as simple as it sounded. Leaving school so young and always working in the house, Dora never had any time to see friends during the week, let alone make arrangements with them. Baker St had a telephone but it was reserved for business, and not many people she knew had telephones.

Though Dora was often too exhausted to go out it was better to do something, or her mother might think twice about giving her evenings off, but who could she could call on? Eluned was her best friend at school but Eluned's mother being deeply Welsh never approved of their friendship, so going round to her house was definitely not a good idea. When they used to walk to school together, Dora would skulk about waiting for Eluned to wave goodbye to her mother and catch her up. Dora never knew whether it was because she wasn't a Welsh speaker, or was there perhaps some other reason?

There was Mary of course, but she was older and an apprentice to a dressmaker and usually worked late. Finally there was Beryl, a bit of a flibbertigibbet but fun to be with, and always game for anything.

Dora tried them all – but with no luck, 'Dora if only I'd known earlier, I could have come – but I've promised to help my sister cut out a pattern.'

Everyone was busy at home or not wanting to go out on such a freezing night. After running round the streets for an hour, the intense cold made Dora dig her mittens deeper into her pockets. Well she might as well go home –but on the other hand, it was so lovely to have time to herself there must be something she could do.

Fingering her pocket money, Dora had a sudden brainwave– what about the pictures? She had enough pocket money. Loving the silent films because of the music, she would often go home and reproduce the same music on the piano to her father's delight. But once the talkies arrived it was far more realistic and exciting to hear what people said rather than just reading words on a screen.

The last time Dora had been to the pictures was with her father. Jack enjoyed taking her when he wasn't busy as they both loved Errol Flynn's swashbuckling and piracy on the high seas, but Dora had never been on her own. Did she dare? The thought of it was frightening but exhilarating at the same time.

Putting aside her apprehension, Dora raced down to the Coliseum Cinema. Paying her money she sped up the stairs to the balcony, not even checking to see what was on. With the luxury of the red plush walls, the gold paint and décor, it was like stepping into a palace. For a moment Dora could pretend she was royalty. The pictures always thrilled her with glimpses into other lives and other worlds.

As she entered the darkened balcony, old Mrs Gale, the owner, stepped out of the shadows, dressed from head to toe in black mourning veils since the death of Queen Victoria, and nearly frightened Dora half to death. 'Just the one?' she hissed menacingly.

Dora straightened her shoulders and held her head up, 'Just the one,' she said proudly.

The old lady huffed and puffed, making a great business of cutting the ticket in half and a poor show of helping Dora to her seat but Dora didn't care. Beaming with pride in herself, Dora delved around in her pocket for her last Walnut Whip of the week, and sat back to enjoy the picture.

Returning home she was brimming with enthusiasm but her mother didn't ask anything about her evening or 'Have you had a good time?' showing absolutely no concern or interest.

Dora thought resentfully, 'I could have been robbing a bank for all she knows or cares.'

But there was always one person to tell of course, Gran her partner in crime, even when she hadn't physically been there. The next day she and Gran went through every detail with Gran chortling at the thought of Mrs Gale in all her veils stepping out of the gloom.

Gran said, 'You're so brave Dora, d'ya know I've never done anything on my own. I wish I'd had your sense of courage and independence when I was your age. Perhaps life would've been different.'

But Gran you were brave when you ran off with your husband. Didn't you tell me you eloped down a ladder and ran off together and your family wouldn't have any more to do with you?'

Gran nodded knowingly, 'But then you see it was my William who was the strong one. He took good care of me 'til he died-and then it was your mother I looked to.'
Dora treasured these times with Gran. She didn't want to think about the fact that Gran was already nearly eighty, much older than anyone else in the street and one day wouldn't be around to be her confidante.

9

1930s - The Garden

Dora decided this was going to be a good day. Her father as usual was working late and had a long day ahead of him, so her mother said, 'Run down to the Garden, Dora. Take these sandwiches and flask to your father, or he'll suffer with his stomach. Perhaps you could stay and give him a hand.'

There was no holding Dora back. This was a job she loved, anything to get away from Baker Street for a few hours. She would run the mile and a half as fast as she could, wind in her hair, long legs pumping away. Racing down the Avenue and through the Cemetery she could reach the Garden in less than fifteen minutes, always trying to break her past record. Freedom beckoned, and time spent with her beloved father was a bonus.

As soon as she got there, her father was always welcoming, 'I'm glad to see you Dora. Just the person I need. Soak some of those frames for me. There's a funeral tomorrow and I've a lot to finish yet.'

Sitting in the back shed opposite him, Dora could smell the familiar scents of foliage, damp earth and pine mixed with the recently creosoted timbers and the pungent smell of Jack's pipe. Dora would say, 'Who's died Dada? Doesn't it upset you making wreaths?'

He'd laugh indulgently, 'No Dora cariad, I don't know the person who's died. It's not upsetting unless it's someone young. We all have to die sometime, you know.'

'Will you go to the funeral?'

'No. All I do is deliver the wreaths. You see it's a business. I can't sit and cry over everyone who dies, all I can do is a good job.'

They sat there in silence wiring each flower, feeling comfortable in one another's company.

Jack over the last years had developed a love and passion for plants and flowers, nurturing them like his children. He was never more at home than in the Garden. He appreciated living things growing and greenness after his time in the desert.

Having spent most of the Great War in Africa there were tales to tell and Dora would be agog and dying for him to reminisce. It always felt like the Arabian Nights when he started:
'You see Dora, everything we needed in the camp, had to be brought in by camel. It was quite a sight to see them coming loaded in the middle of the night. If the moon was full we could see quite a distance – four or five miles at least. The sky in the desert was filled with thousands of stars. Of course in the day we could see further, maybe one hundred or two hundred miles. The air was so different. Distance would play tricks on your eyes. It could seem as if there were vast flat lakes of water sitting on the surface. Sometimes I would think I could even see the mountains of my home in North Wales. But it was an illusion. Your eyes were deceived, there was nothing there. The natives called it a mirage.'

Dora could envisage him as Lawrence of Arabia standing on the top of dunes, pith helmet on straight, khaki shoulders always at attention, shading his eyes to look into the far horizon.

He added, 'It would have been a splendid place to grow tomatoes, Dora. Of course, they'd have had to grow without water or earth and be wired off from camels and jackals.'

Dora thought surely not many soldiers would have thought about gardening in the middle of the desert and in the middle of a war.

Her father was a definite one off, telling her all sorts of tales about befriending many of the Arabs he served with, visiting their encampments, sampling their food, and bargaining with them,

Dora realised what an unusual man he was. A true man of nature with something of the desert remaining, as over the years he had continued to wear the breeches and long socks he'd worn then complaining that ordinary trousers made his legs cold.

'Tell me some more Dada about the Sudan.' But Jack never liked to be pressed too often. His experiences of war had been mixed and he never dwelt on its savagery.

'Not just now Dora –we need to take more care as we wire the flowers into the frame. It's a delicate job. We don't want to bruise the blooms.' He would take her small hand in his and together they would insert the wired flowers, until the whole frame was covered. The scent of the blossoms was heady. 'They just need watering now Dora, and then we can go on to the next one.'

Being a man of variable tempers he didn't suffer fools but Dora adored him and he had endless patience teaching her without being either harsh or sarcastic. Beneath his bark beat a sentimental and poetic heart. He was supposed to be running a business but hated people asking him silly questions about gardening, or not taking care of the plants he nurtured, calling them 'time wasters'.

One of the regulars Jack hated most was Mrs Pryce- Jones. Every summer like clockwork – she would call in just before the local horticultural show. He knew quite well she would buy his prize blooms and then exhibit them as her own. Seeing her coming up the path, he would hide in the back shed while she cooed, 'Oh Mr Roberts, dear Mr Roberts.'

Dora would be sent out to tell barefaced lies, 'Bore da Mrs Pryce-Jones, I'm sorry you've just missed my father. He's gone to make a delivery.'…..'No, I'm sorry I don't know when he'll be back.'

But what Mrs Pryce- Jones lacked in gardening skills she certainly didn't lack in persistence. She would forage about drooling over first one bloom then another, and only leaving eventually and unwillingly, still armed with her enormous list and promising to return later.

Her father would break cover cursing and cussing, 'Blast and damn that woman, I swear I'll hang for her one day. I'm not providing her with any more of my plants so she can win even more cups. That's an end to it. I feel like reporting her to the Committee.' He would then determinedly close the Garden – padlock the gate and with Dora running behind him slowly bicycle back to Baker Street. They enjoyed this time together. Dora could run like a boy, and often wished she'd been the son she thought he'd really wanted.

Her father knew everyone in the town and on their journey home would be hailed by old mates,

'S'mae Jack?'

'S'mae Gwilym.'

Dora would be shuffling from step to step but knew once they started they wouldn't be hurried.

'Going to the club tonight?'

Jack would respond, 'Na, not at the moment, I don't want to leave Sis on her own we've so many visitors.'

'Want to buy some raffle tickets – it's a good cause for the Legion, though I expect you've already got some books yourself to sell.'

'Never mind, give me 5 books then,' Jack delved into his back pocket and brought out a handful of change, 'count how much is there or I'll have to owe you.' Dora knew that Sarah wouldn't be pleased. Her mother kept a tight grip on the budget allowing Jack only spending money but her father generous to a fault would never ignore the old soldiers giving his last shilling to the Legion.

'Well, Dora and I must be going we're both wanting our tea, hwyl Gwilym,' and off they went. Dora like a rabbit let loose from a trap, racing to keep up.

One evening, Jack came home late as usual, stony faced, handlebar moustache bristling and frown lines etched even deeper into his forehead, and said, 'Sis, do you know what that damn fool Reid said to me today – that it wasn't right for Dora to be running behind my bike. What the hell's it got to do with him anyway?'

'Calm down Jack -I did warn you. Dora's far too old to be running like that. She's growing up now you know, and it isn't done. She needs to be more ladylike.'

This was something that Dora didn't want to hear, as she loved running and trying to keep up with her father on the bicycle. She didn't care how old she was, this was something she and her father both enjoyed. Who wanted to become ladylike for goodness sake?

But this time even her beloved Gran betrayed her, agreeing with her daughter and saying, 'Dora, your mother's right, you're growing up now and need to act more in keeping with your age.'

Dora felt stricken. Surely she wasn't going to have to float around in a gentile manner in longer skirts with her hair piled on her head?

Barely hearing the rest of their conversation, she felt miserable. Jack noticing her glum face, suggested, 'What about buying a bicycle for Dora? It would be handy for me for the Garden, particularly now I've taken on this agency with the Liverpool Victoria and have all those insurance cards to deliver.'

Sarah said, 'I don't know Jack – who on earth is going to teach her to ride, it's years since I've been on a bike and you just don't have the time.' Dora brightened up immediately – this sounded better. A bicycle of her very own!

But Gran was far more conservative, 'In my day few young ladies bicycled. It was frowned upon- especially when they began to wear those bloomers and knickerbockers. It hardly seems at all the right thing for Dora.'

However Sarah, always happy to disagree with her mother declared, 'It's certainly worth considering. It's practical and it'll help us all. Jack if you find a suitable bike, I'll take on the teaching and by the end of a week or two I'll make sure Dora can ride safely.'

Dora was definitely not at all sure about that, not with her mother teaching her. This could be purgatory. How on earth would they get on but Sarah thorough as ever, soon had Dora on the bike with her running and holding on to the saddle.
She was surprisingly patient, not at all unpleasant, seeming to enjoy the exercise, and complimentary, 'Dora, you have a good sense of balance. I think you're ready to go it alone. I'll give you a push off and then see if you can pedal on your own.'

By the end of the week her mother said, 'Let's show your father and Gran what you can do.' The three of them congregated on Baker Street doorstep – whilst Dora rode up and down the street with them cheering her on.

Eventually the Miss Lewises from next door came out to see what the ruckus was about.

'Well done Dora, you're a natural.'

Amazingly Sarah smiled and laughed, 'I think I deserve some credit too as the teacher.' Sarah was always one to take pleasure in a job well done.

Though missing the running, the bicycle gave Dora freedom. Able now to go further afield, sometimes she managed to escape for an hour or two into the countryside delivering insurance cards. Long plaits swinging out behind her, Dora would peddle like mad until she reached the outskirts of Aber relishing the fresh air; freewheel down the hills, wander round the cottages delivering, munching on bread and cheese and imagining living in some of the prettier homes.

The one she liked the most was at the end of a lane in the village of Llanbadarn Fawr, a house called 'Sunnyside'. Sitting on the gate opposite and swinging her legs,
Dora tried to imagine herself living there – coming to the door in her apron, waving her husband off to work and her children off to school. Of course there'd be a dog to walk, and maybe a cat, and when they all sat around in the evenings after a big roast dinner, she would tinkle some tunes on the piano and they would sing and all four of her children, would dance, and dance.

10

1932 - Death Intervenes

It always seemed to Dora thinking about it afterwards, that it was an evening like any other evening. Yet it proved to be the forerunner of a series of life changing shocks. Afterwards life was never the same. In later life, she would often put her early life into boxes labelled, 'Life with Gran' and 'Life after Gran.'

Gran, having reached the grand old age of eighty, would take to her bed during the winter months, suffering badly with bronchitis. Dora loved this time as she could spend every evening with her reading their favourite books together even the Bible. Dora was not thrilled with the Bible but prepared to compromise, as long as they had a chance to read something more exciting as well. This particular evening, her mother called as usual, 'Dora, take the tray up to Gran.'

Carrying the tray and carefully balancing a candle, a dish of porridge and brandy milk, Dora negotiated the dark stairway. She could hear Gran coughing hard. Pushing open the door with her foot, Dora met Gran's lively blue eyes. They seemed to light up when they saw her; always making her feel wanted and loved.

'I thought it was time for you, Dora. I don't think I feel like porridge tonight. Just leave it on the dresser there's a good girl, and bring me the milk.'

She patted the bed for Dora to sit close. Behind the wrinkles and lines, now and then Dora could see the much younger Gran. At times, they would giggle and laugh together so much they nearly cried. This was always frowned upon by Sarah who found these emotions excessive, commenting 'there'll be tears before bedtime, mark my words.'

'How're you feeling, Gran?'

'Just fine, Dora, just fine.'

However ill she was, Gran would never let on. This harked back to the days when she'd lost her husband and given in to grief for years. She would say to Dora that looking back on that time, made her feel ashamed of herself and the damage she had done her young family.

'Dora, read me a few verses from Psalms whilst I rest my eyes.' She leaned back closing her eyes.

Dora started reading Psalm 23 Gran's favourite: 'The Lord is my Shepherd; I shall not want.' By the time she had got to, 'and I will dwell in the house of the Lord forever,' the only sound in the room was the odd crackle and spit of the coal fire, making Dora lower her voice to a mere whisper.

Stretching her neck and arching her back to a more comfortable position, Dora looked over at the bed. She suddenly felt very odd. It was if the room was holding its breath. Gran gave a strange croaking noise, a gurgle and a sigh and then there was complete silence. Dora snapped the Bible shut. An unfamiliar feeling of panic seemed to rise inside her. Gran's eyes were closed as if she was sleeping, but surely there was something different about her.

Dora shook her gently then a lot more vigorously, calling 'Gran, Gran can you hear me- wake up, wake up please.'

But there was nothing, no response at all. Dora couldn't help herself, she screamed and screamed. Her father rushed up the back stairs – took one look at her pale face, tears pouring down her cheeks, the prone figure on the bed and hurried her on to the landing.
Her mother followed him up the stairs, saying, 'What a noise! What's happened? Do pull yourself together, Dora. You're hysterical,' and administered a sharp smack on Dora's streaming cheek.

Jack came out of the bedroom – his face grey and looking directly at his wife, shook his head. He said as gently as he could, 'Dora, Gran's gone.'

Dora stammered and stuttered, 'What d'you mean, where's she gone?'

'She died in her sleep, bach.'

Her mother chimed in, 'It's for the best. Eighty was a good age.'

But Dora couldn't take it in – how could she have gone – died just like that with no warning and no time for goodbyes. Taking to her heels like a person possessed Dora ran crazily down the back stairs saying to herself over and over, 'She can't have gone. Not just like that. I'm not ready. What'll I do without her? How can I go on living? No, this isn't right, it can't be true.' The darkness of abandonment rolled over her. More and more tears rolled down her face, as she buried her face in the rough comfort of the roller towel. Gran had always made Dora feel safe.

When she was very, very young, she would run home from school with wet knickers sticking between her legs, and sidle quietly up to Gran and whisper in her ear. 'Not another accident, Dora. You must learn to put your hand up in time,' Gran would murmur kindly.
A clean pair of aired knickers would magically appear, and Gran would surreptitiously wash out the wet ones without breathing a word to her mother. Once she was older, they were like fellow conspirators with Gran baling her out of trouble, listening to her tales of woe, or marvelling at every little achievement.

Now there would be no Gran to turn to, to mop up her tears, hug and console her and tell her 'that everything would be alright.'

Her mother called down the stairs to her, 'Dora, pull yourself together. Come back up here this instant. You need to go in and kiss Gran, before we ring the undertaker. No more tears, you're not a child anymore, and much too old to cry.'

Dora, feeling like her body no longer belonged to her, climbed the stairs, dragging her feet along the landing. Her mother was busy drawing the curtains and covering the mirror. Hesitantly Dora bent over the still figure on the bed, trying to reassure herself that 'This isn't a dead person. This is Gran,' but the forehead she kissed was stone cold, and didn't feel at all like Gran, just an empty shell.
Things would never be the same again.

∞

The next few days went by in a flash. Gran had been very clear in her instructions for her funeral. Dora would overhear her mother and father discussing it all:

'I don't know Jack, how we're going to afford it. Ma always wanted a traditional funeral with black horse and plumes pulling the carriage but it's going to cost such a lot in any case, just to take her back to Birmingham to be buried next to Pa.'

'What about Walter?' Jack queried, 'He could afford to pay something. After all he's never done anything for his mother. In fact none of them have.'

Sarah tried and tried reasoning with her brothers but they all came back with excuses. It seemed that everything was going to be left to her and Jack as usual. Jack finally sorted out the arrangements with the local undertaker, an old mate from the War, and it was agreed to go for something much simpler.

Sarah worked morning and night running up full mourning clothes for herself and Dora. 'Sis you're working yourself to death,' argued Jack, 'I don't want you following Ma just yet.'

'Jack, we can't let the neighbours and family see us in anything but the right clothes. Ma would be horrified. If we can't afford a lavish funeral this is the least we can do.'

The trip to Birmingham was painful for them all. Sarah nearly gave way at the burial when she sighted her father's headstone, 'Oh Jack, he was so young to die – much younger than I am now. I miss him so much. He was the only one who understood me and loved me completely.'

Jack protested, 'But Sis, I love you, so does Dora, doesn't that help?' But Sarah seemed deaf to everything except her own memories harking back to her childhood home in Bracebridge Street.

That evening after the wake, Sarah imbibing more than her usual single sherry, let down her guard and began to talk freely for once. Utterly unaware of her husband or daughter being in the room, Sarah seemed immersed in reliving the day her father had died. She sat hunched over, with her arms wrapped round herself, rocking gently and murmuring:
'It was such a cold day. The fog was worse than usual and it was bone cold. I'd been up since five you see. I didn't mind, I liked to make sure my Pa had hot tea before he set out. I wrapped the last of the stale bread and cheese up in that old chequered kerchief I'd embroidered for Christmas, and put them in his haversack. He had such a bad cough. Working in that pipe factory day after day, was wearing him out. He looked so thin and tired when I waved him off, my heart turned over.'

Jack, afraid to interrupt this tortured outburst, whispered gently, 'Please don't go on, cariad, it was such a very long time ago.'

Sarah didn't seem to hear him so immersed was she in her past.

Dora wondered what on earth was happening to her usually hard-headed, unsentimental mother.

Sarah continued ignoring everything about her, as if she was forced to live through it all over again, 'I was just about to shut the door, when I heard a terrible crashing and galloping of hooves, then a high pitched scream. I dragged on my shawl and ran full pelt down the street. There was a huge crowd of people, but I pushed and shoved my way through. On the ground was what seemed like a bundle of rag and bones. It took me minutes to recognise my Pa. He was broken---- his body was completely broken. I knelt beside him. A man in the front of the crowd tried to pick me up and pull me away from Pa's body, but I fought like a tiger until he let me go. I wanted to hold my Pa's beloved face one last time but when I looked into his beautiful sky blue eyes, there was no life or spark there. The men brought him home on a door, and laid him on the kitchen table. It haunts me every day of my life. If only he'd lived how different things would have been for me – I could have been so happy, and now Ma's gone as well.'

She shuddered and put her face in her hands.

Dora could feel her mother's pain as sharply as she felt her own, and stood there uncertain about what to do next. There seemed no way to breach the gap between them. This was a time when they should have come together with their suffering and Dora wanted to be able to comfort Sarah but didn't know how to, or even whether any form of affection from her would be welcome.

Her father quickly left the room, returning with a brimming glass of brandy. He gently lifted Sarah's head and helped her sip the spirit. For once Sarah acquiesced like a child, all her usual fight knocked out of her.

'Now Sis, you need to sleep. It's been too much for you- bringing back such painful times.

Dora will get a brick for your bed, and make you comfortable. We'll be going home tomorrow, back to Baker Street. You'll see. Everything will be alright there. Dora, off to bed as well, and I'll sit with your mother till she nods off.'

Dora slept fitfully wondering what to make of it all. The next day she couldn't wait to leave. Her father was right. Once they were back on the train and pulling away from Birmingham it did feel easier.

But returning to Baker St, the memory of Gran was waiting for her. Dora wished she could find a big dark hole to crawl into and clutch her grief close to her chest. But there was no respite. That warm all embracing feeling of being loved, wanted and secure had disappeared altogether. Now tiny tentacles of ice and cold pierced her heart, leaving feelings of fear and anxiety. It was if there was something dark and secret waiting in the wings to overwhelm her.

11

1933 - Coming of Age

'Life after Gran' made everything in Baker Street feel different. Nothing felt the same. She had kept the house on an even keel, acting as peacemaker between her daughter and Dora, and able to intercede and influence her son-in-law. Over the years, even her daughter had developed a grudging respect for her, although there was never much love between them.

Life in 'no 8', and the Garden went on as before, but things were changing, and not for the better. Dora felt she was stuck in the middle, between her mother and father. Many times she felt she had done something to upset one or other of them? It was like tiptoeing over broken glass. You never knew who you'd upset or where you'd gone wrong. It was bound to come to a head at some point, but when? Surprisingly enough it was Dora herself who turned out to be the catalyst.

Since the fashion of the 'Flappers' had started to influence everyone, Dora would fantasise what it would be like to have short shingled hair. When she was cleaning, she would sing to herself, and if there was no one around would practise the Charleston, pretending that she had a shiny bob, bouncing round her head.

The problem was that Sarah thought that feminine beauty lay in one's hair. When she'd first met and courted Jack her husband to be, her head was piled up with fine curls. He would say 'Never get your hair cut Sis, it makes you look so beautiful.'

But Dora didn't care about this so-called version of beauty.
She wanted to be liberated from her long, thick hair and the torturous washing and ragging every Friday night and inadvertently an opportunity came her way.

∞

Since working at the Queens' Sarah had kept in touch with the other live-in maids from that time. In a way they were her family. Many times she would take their advice before Gran's or even Jack's, and Dora was encouraged to call them all 'Auntie'. They would get together at Baker St. for a cup of tea and a gossip. Dora had never heard her mother laugh so freely as when Annie and Florrie came round. Florrie could be vulgar but Sarah would shrug it off affably, not with one of her cold looks but in a far more tolerant manner.

Dora usually kept her distance from these gatherings particularly since the incident with the painter. About six months earlier, Dora had answered the door to Len Harris, all done up in his 'whites'. A painter by trade, he was a great mate of her father's. Before she could say that Jack wasn't around, he'd cheekily made his way through to the back kitchen, where all the ladies were having a gossip.

'What have we got here then? A mother's meeting?' he joshed.

Dora could see her mother stiffen but for once let it lie.

Not getting the response he wanted, he turned to Dora, 'My word Dora – you are growing into a beautiful young lady. Come and give your uncle Len a kiss, why don't you.' Dora edged closer to the tea table but he was determined to have his way, cutting off her retreat. 'Don't be shy Dora - this'll be good training for you when the right young man comes along.'

Annie protested, 'Do leave the poor girl alone, Len. Come and sit down and have a cup of tea, and behave yourself.'

But there was no hold in him now as he moved nearer and nearer to his prey. Dora felt her temper rising and rising, hating to be humiliated in front of her mother's friends.

Before she had time to think, she'd picked up the nearest cup of hot tea and thrown it all over him, leaving his once impeccable white overalls brown, dripping and steaming. His shocked face said it all. He went beetroot red with embarrassment.

Annie and Florrie were doubled up with laughter, 'Serves you right you dirty old Casanova.'

But Sarah was beside herself with embarrassment, 'Apologise immediately Dora, and go to your room. Len – let me have those overalls, I'll make sure they sure they're washed, and pressed and get them back to you.'

For once Len had nothing to say murmuring, 'Don't worry Mrs Roberts,' and rushed out of the house, before Dora could even say she was sorry.

Jack laughed heartily when he was told later, not in the least put out, 'Well done Dora – he's had that coming a long time. That'll teach him not to try to kiss young girls!'

'Jack, please don't encourage her. I don't think Len meant any harm, Dora needs to control that bad temper or it'll be her downfall.'

∞

The next time Sarah and her cronies were all ensconced having afternoon tea, Dora was battling with her wayward hair as usual as she made her way down the passage to the kitchen, when she heard her name mentioned.
Stopping for a moment she heard Auntie Annie say, 'It'll be Dora's eighteenth soon. What's she going to do about all that hair?'

Dora heard Sarah reply, 'Put it up of course, like any other young lady of her age.'

'Don't be silly, Sis. It'll weigh her poor head down. It's far too thick; she couldn't possibly get a hat on top of all that. Why don't you let me cut it, and give her a permanent wave for her birthday?'

Dora, still lingering and eavesdropping, knew that Auntie Annie owning Aberystwyth's most prestigious hairdressing salon, had just taken delivery of one of the first permanent wave machines.

'Look Sis, you would be doing me a favour too. Dora's hair would be ideal for a trial on the new machine, and a great advert for me,' Annie pleaded.

'Well I might think about it,' Sarah said, never able to resist Annie's charm for long, and of course, always impressed that she'd married well.

Dora left it a few days and waited to see how things would develop. She was helping her father in the Garden the following week when he said, 'Your birthday's coming up soon, Dora, and a special one at that. What do you want for a present?'

Dora knew that whatever happened in the house between her and her mother, Jack always insisted on treating her birthdays as something special, making sure she had the present she most wanted. This was about the only time he overrode his wife.

Taking her courage in both hands Dora said, 'Dada, I'd like to have my hair cut short, and perhaps one of these new permanent waves.' She stared straight at him, her fingers crossed behind her back.

Jack was thoughtful for a moment. His soft heart could never resist Dora's pleading, 'Well, Dora, I'll have to talk to your mother. You know how she values your beautiful hair. I don't know what she'll think.'

Dora thought that's some progress at least. It was never any good going head to head with her mother, as she always came off worse. Now she was getting older, Dora tried hard to work out how Sarah's mind worked, but was never able to come up with any answers or the right approach. Sarah was such a complex woman, with a whole range of different moods, all of them desperately unpredictable, so it was hard to gauge her reactions.

There was after all the saga of the of the 'grey gauntlet gloves'. When she was a lot younger, she and her father had planned a surprise for one of her mother's birthdays. Jack had said, 'Tomorrow Dora we'll go out and buy your mother a really special birthday present because she's been working so hard. You can choose, and I'll pay.' They went round to Ellis' in Terrace Road, a fine new department store, stocking everything that was up to date in fashion. Dora fell in love with a pair of beautiful grey leather gauntlet gloves. Dora was beside herself with excitement. They'd included Gran in their secret, and she kept putting her finger to her lips, every time Dora was bubbling up and dying to give the surprise a way.

A few days went by and just before the birthday, Dora found herself on the wrong side of her mother, having upset her in some unimaginable way. It was something to do with Dora's behaviour but she was not quite sure what.

The day of Sarah's birthday dawned and Dora, having carefully wrapped the precious gloves, presented them with a flourish to Sarah. But her mother reacted violently, shaking her head, and saying, 'I don't take presents from naughty girls, refusing to accept them.

Jack and Gran were appalled, 'Oh, come on Sis, it is your birthday after all. Surely you can forget the last few days, Dora chose these herself. She's been looking forward all week, to giving them to you.' Sarah was deaf to their appeals. The gloves remained wrapped and were put away in a drawer never to be seen or worn again.

A few days after the conversation with her father about 'the coming of age' present, Dora realised that Jack had already broached the subject of her hair with Sarah. Daily life had become a series of long cold silences and stony stares. The dam finally burst one day when Dora and her mother were on their own.

'I suppose you think you've been very clever going to your father behind my back. How'd you know about Annie's offer of a permanent wave? Have you been eavesdropping? The one thing I despise is a devious, sneaky person.'

Dora kept her mouth tightly shut. It was no good responding as that would only be taken as cheek.

Sarah continued, 'As you both seem to have ganged up on me, do as you like. Take advantage of Annie's offer by all means. I want nothing more to do with it.' Turning away, she said to herself almost under her breath, so quietly that Dora had to strain to hear,   '--- it just shows, take someone strange into your family- -----no idea how they'll turn out – bad blood will out.' Pulling herself together and suddenly aware that she was giving vent to her thoughts out loud, Sarah turned away brusquely and continued with the ironing.

Dora was shocked. It was as if the air had been sucked out of her lungs. What did all that mean? There was no pleasure in besting her mother, not with this amount of bad feeling. Where had all this bile come from? It completely took the shine off her birthday.

What had Sarah meant by, 'Strangers being taken into the family—and bad blood?'What was that to do with her? No longer having Gran to talk to and with Sarah in no mood to enlighten her further, the only thing to do was to leave the matter well alone and try and ask her father about it all.

∞

The next few weeks Dora mulled over every word that had been said but couldn't make sense of it. Was Sarah's tirade aimed at her or someone else? After a while Dora decided it was no good getting so distressed about it as there were no answers forthcoming. The only thing she could do was to forget it for the time being and enjoy becoming eighteen. For once Jack had gone out on a limb and backed up Annie's offer of the permanent wave, so now Sarah was barely communicating with either of them.

The day before her birthday, Dora entered the luxury of Auntie Annie's salon. It was like being in a dream and hard for Dora to believe that she'd finally made it. The last weeks had been a nightmare. Perhaps by completely immersing herself in this whole experience the bad memories would fade.

Auntie Annie's was the epitome of chic – everything of the most up to date and modern. The black and silver décor had a sleekness giving a feeling of richness, luxury and pampering, all at the same time. The embossed mirrors, with little pink shaded lights framing them, were set at angles reflecting the light, and making you look far more beautiful than you really were.

Sitting in front of the sparkling mirrors, Dora could hardly contain herself. The scissors cutting through all that hair made a satisfying crunch as the hair plopped to the floor, and the pile round the chair grew and grew. Dora felt free and lightheaded. She was euphoric and exultant all at the same time. No more horrendous Friday hair washing nights.

'Do you want to keep your hair Dora? Perhaps as a memento, it might come in handy as a plait added to your own hair later?' asked one of the assistants breezing round the floor in pristine white cover-ups.

'No, I want nothing more to do with my hair,' Dora said firmly, 'it's been the curse of my life so far and I want it all gone.'

By now Dora was feeling a little queasy about what was to happen next. They wrapped her in an enormous black gown, placed a rubber collar round her shoulders, and walked her across to the centre of the floor. She felt as if she was going to her own execution. Sitting gingerly on the edge of the big chair, Dora felt self conscious with all the clients and the assistants watching.

Auntie Annie bustled in like the magician in a show, 'Make yourself comfortable Dora and do relax. You look frightened to death, child. Sit back, and let me do my work.' Annie carefully rolled Dora's now much shorter hair into tight curlers, covering them in a very cold lotion, and attaching tubular pieces hanging from the ceiling to the curlers. There was a deadly hush in the salon. Once the machine was turned on, it was as if everyone was waiting for the explosion. Dora herself was finding it hard to breathe- she was taking in air in tight short pants.

But Auntie Annie, confidant as ever, smiled broadly saying, 'You can let go and breathe now Dora. You'll need to be patient this is going to take some time. Do you want some magazines or something to drink?'

Dora shook her head too frightened to move a muscle. She spent the next hours trying to think of something pleasant, and considering what Gran would have made of it.

Gran would have laughed at all this fuss to make hair curl and wouldn't have been too thrilled with what she called the 'the new fangled electrical inventions'.

Five hours later Dora emerged from her steel helmet, with a tight feeling round her forehead and the start of a headache, but with a fabulous head full of glossy dark curls dancing round her head. The clients and the assistants cheered.

Auntie Annie took a bow, saying, 'Dora you are such a wonderful advert for my perm. That thick hair of yours has taken so well. Hold on, I'll have to take a photograph before you go home. Your mother will be absolutely amazed.' Dora doubted that, but smiled all the same, thanking Annie for everything.

Dora kept preening herself in front of the mirror, and shaking her head up and down to see if the curls would fall out. Skipping all the way home and tossing her shiny new locks Dora couldn't wait to get home and show her mother. Surely Sarah wouldn't still be cross with her and must have got over it by now – would she still be holding a grudge, could she?

Once in the house, Sarah hardly acknowledged her, giving Dora barely a passing glance and saying dryly, 'At least I won't have all that work on a Friday night. I suppose that's something.' After that she ignored Dora for the next week, just imparting orders. Dora didn't care this time. She was used to being out in the cold. Her new hair delighted her and she never tired of looking in the mirror.

12

The Secret

Once her birthday was over, and all the excitement of the new hairdo had lessened, Dora began to feel distinctly uneasy again. Her mother's anger at being out manoeuvred had blown over, but there was still something brewing. Her parents seemed to be having intense whispered conversations that stopped as soon as she came into the room. Unusually they were even disagreeing. It had to be something important, as her father always bowed to her mother's authority in the house and generally they got on well.

Dora decided to keep her head down and get on with her work in the house and the Garden. Perhaps things would sort themselves. But it wasn't to be, one evening after supper, her father said, 'Come and sit in the front parlour Dora.' This was ominous in itself as they hardly ever used the room – certainly only for business or visitors.

Dora sat tentatively on the edge of one of the highly polished chairs. Looking at both their faces, she knew that she was about to hear some bad news. She hoped it wasn't about the music; after all she had passed all her exams up to now and loved her lessons. Or perhaps it was about Judy – had she chewed the slippers again or made a mess?

Her father began with a lot of throat clearing and nervous knocking out of his pipe, 'We've something important to tell you, Dora. Gran asked us not to talk to you, whilst she was alive and we respected her wishes. But now she's gone and you're getting older, we thought it important we tell you.'
Continuing he said, 'Dora, whatever we tell you now, you must still know that we love you as a daughter.'

Dora couldn't think where this was all going after all she was their daughter, what else could they tell her?

Jack began chewing fiercely on his unlit pipe not seeming to want to say any more.

'Oh, do get on Jack,' Sarah complained, 'or we'll be here all night. I would like to get to my bed at some point.'

Jack frowned at his wife but gamely carried on, 'Dora – there's no way to explain this any better,' and came out bluntly with 'you see cariad bach; we're not your real parents.'

Dora gulped. There seemed to be a massive lump in her throat, and she could barely swallow. What did he mean? What about her beloved Gran? Did that mean they weren't related? That wasn't possible – look how very close they'd been, and hadn't people commented on how alike they looked, the same eyes, the same smile. Dora could barely take it in.

Jack soldiered on, 'It was during the War, that Sis – well – your mother (he gestured to Sarah) – answered an advert to look after a baby, and that baby was you. I was abroad. There was just your mother and Gran in that tiny flat in Terrace Road. Your mother didn't know when I'd come back or if I'd come back, and she wanted a child. So this was the next best thing.'

Sarah impatiently picked up the story, trying to move it along, 'I looked after you during the week with Gran's help. Your real mother, Margaret, brought you every morning and collected you every night. She was a cleaner at the Workhouse, and lived near Clarach, and that's all we knew about her.'

Dora finally, trying to pull her wits together stammered out, 'But where is she now, why aren't I with her?'

Sarah said rather shortly, 'If you'll let me carry on – I'll tell you.' Baldly she said, 'You'd been with us about six weeks, when one Friday night your mother arrived to collect you, full of cold. Gran and I suggested we keep you over the weekend to give her time to recover.

On the Monday night, we had you ready for her collect but she never turned up. We weren't too worried at first as we thought she was still sick.'

Jack took up the story again, 'Sis ---, Sarah, --- your mother went to the Workhouse to look for your real mother but no one had seen her or knew much about her. They were very vague in those days about keeping records.'

Sarah decided to omit the details of her visit to the Workhouse. It was an experience she'd put to the back of her mind and one she preferred to forget. The Workhouse then had been in a part of town that decent people hardly frequented. Tied cottages, dirty drains and barefoot children playing in puddles of muddy water hardly recommended themselves. The Workhouse itself was an imposing Victorian building with six foot high iron railings

Sarah made enquiries first with the porter and then with the matron. The matron, a severe uniformed rambunctious woman had towered over her. 'Margaret Goules? I hardly knew her. She was just a casual cleaner, that's all ---- no, we don't have an address ---and no, she hasn't come in this week ----- there's no depending on people like her--- they come and they go---.' This was the only response Sarah could get. Trying to talk to the inmates gave no joy either. Most were sickly, underfed on the thin gruel that was their main nourishment, and only able to give her the benefit of blank stares.

Returning home Sarah had looked down at the sleeping child. The baby was thriving after its shaky start. Well dressed now and well looked after by her and Zipporah, she was becoming quite bonny. They might just as well keep her, otherwise who knows where she'd end up.

Zipporah was of a different opinion, 'You've no business, Sis, keeping the child. What if her real mother comes back later?

You should at least let the authorities know,' callously adding her well rehearsed homily, 'If Nature had meant you to have children, you'd have had them,' but once Sarah's mind was made up there was no going back.

Seeing Sarah lost in her own thoughts Jack carried on with the story, almost begging Dora to understand. 'You see cariad, your mother wrote to me in Egypt, saying that she and Gran had taken you in. I was so pleased that she had.' Jack had written back, in his stilted English saying,

'My dear Sis,
I had your letter last Friday night. I was very pleased to get it and to hear that you and Ma are alright. You ask about the little girl you have taken. By all means stick to her. Get it made right that she can't be claimed again by anybody. I take your word for all, if you like her, I shall, you bet. I am very pleased she will engage your mind, and amuse you in many ways, and will amuse me as well when I come back
Your loving husband, Jack.'

Jack went on again, 'There seemed to be no one to claim you and we were delighted for you to grow up as our own daughter. We changed your name in order for you to become part of our family.' He patted Dora's hand, 'and we're so glad we did, aren't we, Sis?' he said tenderly, looking across to Sarah for confirmation. Sarah barely made an acknowledgement.

Dora stuttered, 'But my name--- what's my real name?'

Jack suddenly looked uncertain, looking to Sarah for help.

Sarah said directly without any shilly-shallying, 'Your mother's name was 'Goules', whether she was married we don't know, probably most unlikely. No doubt no better than she should be, I expect. She called you 'Catherine Jane'.

But I thought 'Dora Roberts' would be a better name. You'd have your father's and my surname, and that way no one would ask any difficult questions.'

Dora was stunned. It was as if everything she had ever known and depended upon had evaporated into thin air. It was the same feeling she'd had when Gran died – one of bereavement and loss. Who was she then, someone who didn't even have her own name? Where was her mother now? No wonder she and Sarah found it difficult to get on. But Gran and Dada---- plaintively she said to herself- if only they could have been my real family. I love them so much. But no, they weren't her family either. Now she really was alone. She'd have to learn to fend for herself and quickly.

Dora tried to find her voice but all she could manage was a croak, 'Did my real mother ever come looking for me?'

Sarah and Jack looked at one another, 'There was that one time when you were a child at school----,' Sarah's voice drifted off into the distance, and Jack started to say, 'and of course there was that time when you were thirteen------,' but he seemed to think better of it and stopped abruptly, rubbing his hands together as if to comfort himself.

Dora didn't seem to notice their stopping and starting. Countless thoughts and uncertainties piled up in her head, none of which she could form into proper questions. Horrified by the shock of their revelations, all Dora wanted to do was to get away from them, escape to somewhere safe on her own where she could try and take it all in.

Abruptly she said, 'I think I must go to bed now.'

Jack nodded his head wisely and reassuringly, 'Probably for the best– you've had a terrible shock. Just know we love you very much. You can talk to us in your own time. Things will look better in the morning.'

With a heavy heart Dora lit her lamp and climbed the stairs to her room. She quickly undressed and slid between the ice cold sheets – stubbing her toes on the warming bottle. Her mind had gone a complete blank. She wanted to forget everything that had happened in the last few hours and pretend it was just a dream. At last exhaustion lulled her into a deep sleep.

The morning came quicker, sharper and bitterer than ever and Dora woke with a dull sense of apprehension. Snippets of last night's conversation replayed in her mind. It felt as if she had been subject to a battering that had left her breathless, dazed and cowed. Lying there trying to think of what to do next, she rapidly made up her mind. Her mother always said, 'It was no good feeling sorry for yourself you must get up and get on.' Oh for goodness sake, she was even quoting Sarah now, but Dora needed to spur herself into action.

Determinedly forcing herself out of bed– Dora washed swiftly and put on her Sunday best dress, got together some of the rest of her clothes and folded them neatly on the bed, needing some sort of bag or suitcase to pack them in. The big brown case in the loft looked like a possibility but she'd have to collect it later. Then it hit her, it was all very well packing and preparing, but where could she go? Dora sat down with a bump. Suddenly feeling shaky she tried to calm herself, but felt so mixed up. Of course, in time she could get a job; maybe something live in, perhaps as a maid. She'd certainly had the training for that.

But leaving home - the only place she'd ever known. What would become of her? Who could help her? Perhaps one of her friends would put her up? But she'd lost touch with so many of her old school friends as Sarah never allowed any of them to come to the house.
There was always Auntie Annie of course. She'd gone out of her way to make a great fuss of Dora, giving her the most wondrous presents for Christmas and her birthday.

Look at this perm. But then Annie wouldn't want to upset Sarah as their friendship went back such a long way.

It was such a muddle. Dora decided to leave everything and go down for breakfast. Sarah would certainly be able to sort it out and put her straight. Pulling herself together and shaking out the newly bobbed hair which had caused such trouble, Dora smoothed her dress and walked purposefully into the kitchen telling herself, 'I can do this, I really can.'

Sarah busying herself with the breakfast barely registered her. But noticing something was amiss took a good hard look at Dora, and frowned, 'What are you doing in that dress missy, on a weekday? '

Dora responded bravely, 'I thought with all you told me last night you'd want me to leave straight away. I've just got to pack my case and then I can go.'

'Don't be a silly girl. We want nothing of the kind. I've no time for idiocy. Once you reached eighteen we decided to tell you about your background in case someone else did. Now go upstairs and change immediately we've a lot to do this morning.'

And that was that. No reassurances of how much she was loved or wanted. Life was expected to go on as normal. It seemed as if Jack and Sarah having got everything off their chest had no further need to discuss her parentage. Jack himself made no further mention of her background, making Dora reluctant to broach the subject with him. It seemed as if they wanted to brush everything under the carpet, and go back to treating her in the way they thought a daughter should be treated.

But it wasn't the same for Dora there were far too many unanswered questions.

She was not at all sure about her feelings for her parents anymore, if only it had been Gran who'd told her. She'd have known how to make it alright for Dora and help ease this terrible emptiness in her heart. Now her position in the household seemed fragile and vulnerable, not like the place she'd taken for granted for so long.

BREAKING OUT

13

1934 - Guiding

'Dora, have you done your piano practice yet today, - there's still the bedrooms to change, Judy needs a walk, and you might have to take your father's tea down early – he's going to have to work late again.' Sarah's voice cut roughly into Dora's peace and quiet.

Since that dreadful night when her life had been overturned in a moment, Dora had decided that she must carve a life for herself in the outside world. No longer being sure of who she was or how secure she was, she decided she must find another way. Her life in Baker Street could collapse at any time, and then where would she be then? With no friends, no home, and no one who cared about her. When she'd left school, Dora had joined the Guides. With the constant difficulty of finding friends of her own, the Guides had given her an escape and companionship. Every summer Dora would go over to camp in Clarach. Finishing all her household jobs, she would run over the Golf Links to join the camp for the night.

Sarah thought she was completely mad saying, 'I really don't know why you want to spend nights under canvas, after a hard day's work here.'

Dora adored it. It was the lack of restrictions. Nothing could beat cooking sausages and baked potatoes over the fire, with lots of laughter, fun, friendship and singing. Jack was all for it. Anything with a tinge of the military, with uniforms, rules and regulations went down well with him. When he'd returned from the Great War, Dora was still very little and he'd had a miniature swagger stick made for her. Striding out on a Sunday morning, Regimental Sergeant Major Roberts and Private Dora would march up and down the Promenade.

He would laughingly say, 'Now Private – keep those shoulders back. I'll make a soldier of you yet.' People would be laughing and tittering behind their hands, but Dora didn't care. She adored being with him, doing anything he asked.

∞

Dora now 19 was a fully fledged Guide Captain herself, with her new company of guides in Penparcau, a village outside Aberystwyth. It had not been easy being the youngest Captain. Attending the District meetings, many of the old hands would look down their nose at her and make snide remarks about 'new brooms— inexperience –green as grass-won't last the pace.' Dora was hardened to sarcasm and contempt, after all for goodness sake, she was used to plenty of that type of thing at home. None of them would ever be in her mother's league. How weird was that thinking? Fancy actually taken pride in Sarah's acid tongue! What a thing to be proud of! Who would have seen it as an advantage in life, that being on the receiving end of all that nastiness on a regular basis could develop character and toughness!

Dora ignored the remarks; it was exciting building her own company of guides from scratch. There had only been one or two girls at the start but word spread and numbers were growing by the week. Most could not afford the uniforms so Dora would beg and borrow ties and bits of uniforms for them to wear so that even new recruits could feel part of the group.

One particular morning walking through the town, she spotted the local brewery dray turning the corner with a rough unshaven man driving the Shires. Dora recognised him at once. Never fazed when there was a good cause, she hailed him down.

He pulled up with a start tugging hard at the reins and growling, 'What d'ya think you're doing missy, out of my way before my horses do for you?'

Dora moved back but stood her ground, 'Your two girls------'

'What about them? – what've they done now?' he fired back.

Swallowing hard Dora said, 'They joined my Guide troop last week but said they wouldn't come back again, as they'd no uniform and felt out of it.'

'What d'you think I am Miss What-sit?-A bottomless pit of money- me with six mouths to feed and another one on the way.'

Dora ploughed on, 'But that's why I stopped you. I think I can find them ties to start with. Then I'll look for some second hand uniforms. It would be a shame if they stopped coming.'

'We don't want your charity Missy or some second hand uniforms. Only the best is good enough. If you think I can't look out for my girls, do right by them you're------' (he let loose a string of swear words that made Dora flinch), they'll be there next week even if I've to bring them myself. --- Now be off with you. Let me get on, and earn my living.'

The next week two newly uniformed girls presented themselves, 'Miss, Miss --- I don't know what you said to our Da – but he marched us out last week and bought us these.' They fingered their ties and belts in awe, 'We've never had so many new clothes at one time –he says we must look after them, so the youngies can have them after, when they're old enough to join.'

∞

Dora was always scrounging supplies 'for her girls. Jack would bend over backwards to help, 'Come down to the Garden tomorrow Dora –I'll let you have some veg. and tomatoes.

But it was Sarah who astonished Dora when she'd say, 'There's a few sprouting potatoes left in that sack you can have, or I've made an extra pie you can use for your girls.'

Teaching the girls to cook and camp had surprising results. Occasionally a girl would say, 'Do'ya know Miss, since I've been coming to Guides I've never been hungry and me mum lets me do some of the cooking now. We're eating ever so much better.' Dora was thrilled. It was good to feel that all those gruelling days in Baker Street kitchen had not gone to waste. Being appreciated however momentarily made up for a lot.

In the November of their first year, Dora proudly told the pack, 'We've been invited to march in the Armistice Parade. This is a singular honour. We mustn't let anyone down. We'll practice marching over the next few weeks. Make sure all your badges, belts and shoes are polished and your uniform ironed ready.'

On the Sunday Dora shepherded her troop into place taking up the lead with the standard, and feeling a great surge of pride to have achieved so much in such a short time. All her hard work had paid off and she was proud of 'her girls'.

Her father marching with the old soldiers from the Legion passed her, giving her a quick wink and a smart salute. Dora was thrilled to actually be marching with him again, just like their old days on the Promenade – but now as ex- R.S.M Jack Roberts and Captain Dora Roberts.

14

Treading the Boards

'I don't know where you get all this energy from, Dora,' Sarah would remark ironically. 'What with Guides, Chapel, swimming, the piano and now gym classes, surely you get enough exercise running up and down stairs and cycling to the Garden? You seem to be out all the time these days. Mark my words miss, it'll catch up with you. You can't burn the candle at both ends.'

Sarah always started the day with two aspirins and a cup of tea and once the midday meal was finished, she would retire to bed promptly at two o'clock, leaving Dora in charge. Dora loved these afternoons. This was often when she missed Gran the most. In the past they would have enjoyed themselves gossiping or laughing at the wireless and Dora's terrible jokes. Nowadays, Dora would put her feet up and read a book, other times she would be memorising her part for a play, or singing and dancing round the kitchen to the latest Bing Crosby on the wireless. This was time to relax and be herself.

Dora's one day of freedom was Sunday. Work in Baker St and the Garden went on relentlessly seven days a week, but attending Chapel three times on a Sunday Dora could temporarily break away from the routine and meet other people of her own age. Sarah and Jack never went to church. Sarah had been brought up English High Church and Jack Welsh Baptist, so they could never agree on where to go.

Jack would say laconically, 'God's the same – wherever you worship.'

Dora often thought that he treated the Garden as his place of worship. In the far potting shed, opposite his workbench Jack had clipped out a verse–now almost faded, tacked on a rusty nail. It read:

The kiss of the sun for pardon,
The song of the birds for mirth,
One is nearer to God's heart in a garden, than anywhere else
on earth.

This seemed to sum up everything he believed. But it was agreed by her parents and Gran that Dora was to be brought up from the start as God fearing. To begin with she and Gran attended St. Michaels' together. Once Gran found it difficult to manage the walk, Dora was allowed to go first to the Sunday school at the Wesleyan Chapel with the little girls next door, and eventually as she got older to the Chapel services.

Having very little idea about Methodism however, her parents were taken aback when Dora, aged thirteen came home and announced, 'I went up on the stage today and took the Pledge.'

Jack choked on his tea and said, 'D'you know what that means, Dora?'
'
No - isn't it something to do with drink?'

Even Sarah cracked a smile when Gran on her high horse, said, 'Well I've never heard anything like it- fancy asking a mere child to take the Pledge when she's never had anything stronger than a cup of tea. It's just as well you didn't send her to the Baptists – or we'd be facing her complete immersion by now.'

When Dora was very small, Sarah would take it upon herself to deliver Dora to the Sunday school and collect her later. On one occasion the teacher asked Sarah if Dora would recite from the pulpit the following Sunday morning.
Sarah said, 'Good heavens. I really don't think so. She's only five you know! I can't teach her all those verses by Sunday I've a house to run. Anyway it would be too much for such a young child.'

'Don't worry Mrs Roberts;' said the teacher, 'I catch her mouthing the words to all the hymns as she learns them. She'll surprise you, you'll see.'

The following Sunday Sarah reluctantly went along to the service with Dora decked out in her best velveteen dress. On the way there, Sarah said, 'Make sure you behave, Dora. Don't show me up. No crying if you forget any of the words. I'll stand nearby and prompt you.'

When the moment came Dora bold as brass mounted the pulpit, never giving her mother a second glance and clambered on to the box provided. All that could be seen was the top of her head crowned with a large white bow, but once the minister introduced her there was no mistaking her loud clear voice ringing through the chapel proclaiming the first verses of Genesis, 'In the beginning God created the heaven and the earth---- .'

She was word perfect and carefully stepping down, gave a perfect curtsey. Sarah was astounded. The congregation was so amazed and delighted that in unison they rose to their feet and applauded. At the end of the service they gathered round to offer congratulations.

'It's nothing to do with me,' Sarah said shrugging it off, 'I don't know where she gets it from, she's a bit of a show off, I suppose.'

∞

Once she was older, Dora had joined the Chapel's Drama Club. It was fun to dress up and pretend to be someone else, especially not knowing who she was anyway. Most of the younger members of the Chapel joined whether they could act or not.

There was always a gang of them ready for the next play. Violet and Mona would take on the costumes between them, whilst Dora, Sian, Ruby, Jenkin and Henry would vie for the main parts.

Many of them had day jobs in Aberystwyth. Dora would bump into them round the town when she was running errands: Ruby worked in the chemists', Violet, the bakers', Jenkin was training to be a surveyor and Henry was doing his articles as a solicitor. Besides the cast, there were others willing to paint flats and scenery or do lighting. They even had a director- a retired man who'd been a bit of a thespian in his youth.

One Tuesday evening the director took her on one side, 'Dora, we are going to do a Shakespeare play next – Hamlet, I thought and I'd like you to play Hamlet.'

Dora was shocked, 'But Mr Page it's such a major role, there's so many speeches to learn, I'd never do it, and won't people think it funny for a girl to be playing the part?'

'Shakespeare used boys to play girls' parts so this is no different. You always know everyone's lines as well as your own. That's what comes of having a photographic memory. I guarantee you'll have no trouble with the words. It's the acting we'll have to concentrate on.'

'But Mr Page – it's such a big role. Will I be able to do it?'

'Of course you will Dora. I've every faith in you. You've got the talent. You just need more confidence in yourself.'

Dora went home, her mind in a complete dither – but thrilled and proud to have been chosen for such a part. She couldn't wait to tell her parents. Perhaps her mother for once might even be pleased with her. But it was not to be.

Sarah was not the slightest bit impressed complaining, 'I suppose you'll have your nose in that play book even more than usual.' Always one to focus on the practicalities, Sarah continued, 'What about your costume? Wearing all black you say? I haven't got any time to get the machine out at this time of the year.'

Dora responded tightly, 'You won't need to. The Wardrobe Mistresses sees to all our costumes.'

Jack of course loved the idea, 'Well done, Dora. What a part! Perhaps I can help with something.'

A few weeks later Jack came home with a fine wooden sword he'd made and painted grey and silver to give it a touch of realism. 'Will this do Dora? Do you think it'll look genuine enough from a distance?' He made Dora go to the end of the passageway, 'Now raise your sword and run towards me as if you were going to stab me.' Jack brandished his old RSM baton and they indulged themselves in a mock sword fight until they both burst out laughing.

Dora remembered how good he'd been when she was a child. He'd said to Sarah one summer, 'Sis, what about entering Dora in the town carnival?'

'But Jack, what could she go as?'

'With all that hair of hers, I was thinking of Lady Godiva. I think I can get a white horse from somewhere.'

Sarah and Gran were scandalised, 'What on earth will people think?'

'What does that matter?' he retorted 'Everyone will know who it is. She's just a child. It'll be a winner you can bet on it,' and he went off chuckling to himself. There was no restraining him.

In the end Gran and Sarah capitulated. Between them they ran up a pink woollen flesh like garment that Dora was poured into, and with her hair pouring down her back she looked the very image of Lady Godiva. Jack proudly led the horse round and round the town, with Dora loving all the attention and smiling fit to burst. There was no question but she'd get First Prize. They all congratulated themselves on their original idea. However in retrospect when Dora looked back on the occasion it seemed as if Sarah and Jack appropriated the prize as theirs by right, rather than allowing her to bask in any of the glory.

Dora hoped that playing such a prestigious part as Hamlet would mean that Jack and Sarah would at last take some pride in her, and come to see her perform. So far neither of her parents had attended any of her acting performances perhaps this one would be different. If only Gran was still alive, she would have been sitting in the front row applauding with all her might.

Smugly Dora presented her parents with the very first printed programme, her name emblazoned in big black letters on the front, and gave them two complimentary tickets in prime position in the front row.

Jack was impressed, but immediately looked at his wife who said, 'If we have time Dora, we'll be there, but no promises,' and that was the best she could get out of either of them.

On opening night, Dora sat in front of the mirror backstage. Her bobbed hair was tied back tightly and her makeup was in place as she pulled on the black tights and black velvet doublet. Studying herself in the mirror she certainly looked the part despite the flutter of nerves.

Mona came rushing in, 'Let me take a last look at you Dora. Don't forget to buckle on your sword.'

Henry, who was playing Horatio, bobbed in, 'Don't worry Dora you'll do fine and I'll be there to support you remember.'

The director ducked his head round the door, and said, 'Ready Dora, break a leg.'

'Thanks Mr Page. Any sign of my parents?'

'Fraid not Dora but I expect they'll get here soon. They wouldn't want to miss your debut, would they?'

Dora was nowhere near as sure about this as him. There would be new orders at the Garden and fresh visitors arriving at Baker Street but surely on this of all nights, they would really try to make time to come. However, it was no good dwelling on it. The first bell rang, and the call came, 'Beginners Please.' She was on.

The play flew by. As Dora was on stage most of the time, she barely had time to register the two empty seats in the front row. Before she knew it there were bows to be taken, a standing ovation and calls for 'Hamlet'. It was such an honour to take so many curtain calls

Dora was fizzing with excitement and adrenalin. She was presented with a beautiful bouquet from the company, and everyone gathered round, patting her on the back and praising her performance.

But when the realisation of those two empty seats hit home, it was as if the bottom had fallen out of her world. She felt again that sharp pain of rejection, and aloneness. No Gran, no one in her family to take an interest in her achievements, always this lingering sense of disappointment that there was no one to share her victory with. Returning home should have been a triumph but instead dragging her feet as if they weighed a ton, and still clutching her giant bouquet,

Dora let herself into Baker St. All was deadly silent even for eleven o'clock at night. There was a note on the kitchen table from her mother, 'Have migraine, gone to bed early. Your father's been called out, pie in larder if you're hungry,' with not even a postscript to hope that everything had gone well for her.

There was nothing for it – but to put her flowers in water and go to bed. Carefully carrying the vase and a lamp, Dora crept upstairs to her room placing the flowers on her dressing table so she could see them first thing in the morning. At least she was proud of her triumph, if no one else was!

15

1936 - Love and Rejection

What was happening to her? Dora felt the Pier ballroom swirling and dipping around her, mirrors splintering, and hanging lanterns on fire. She was sinking into a white hot furnace.

'Take it easy there, young lady--- can you hold her other arm-she's as white as a sheet. Lie her down gently, and run to the cloakroom for smelling salts?'

'What's happening – what's happening to me?' Dora heard her voice whisper echoing into the far distance as if it didn't belong to her.

'Don't take on Miss; your friend has gone for the salts. You fainted. Perhaps it's too hot in here? Did you get overheated dancing?'

'No, no,' murmured Dora, 'we only just arrived.'

'No more talking there's a good girl – just rest. Take a sniff – it'll do the trick.'

Dora numbly sniffed up the salts, which hit the back of her throat making her cough violently.

'Better out than in' came the tough but sympathetic response from her saviour, 'you'll be as right as nine pence in a minute. You should think about going off home though. Where do you live? – is it far?'

Rosie spoke up for her, 'She lives round in Baker St. I'll take her home.'

Dora thought resentfully, I don't need anyone to take me home. I've never fainted in my life before. I'm not fainting – how weak is that? Perhaps it was the shock of seeing Norman again? He'd not even acknowledged her. She lay back trying to pull her shattered thoughts together.

∞

She'd met Norman at one of the dances. Dora loved to dance, picking up any rhythm from the band. Young men would queue to whisk her round the floor because she was so light on her feet.

On the Pier when the sea was rough, you could hear it seething, boiling and splashing against the iron balustrades below, giving the sensation that the dance floor was on the move. Dora thought it was like being afloat on an ocean liner heading for faraway lands.

To her credit, her mother always insisted she have a new dance dress each season. The last few years, Sarah had said, 'You're getting much too big Dora for me to make you anymore dresses. You'd better pick out some material and go up to the dressmaker.'

Dora would pick out her beloved pink or blue, and get the dressmaker to make her dress as different as possible to other peoples' with a touch of trimming or embroidery or different collars or sleeves. Several times at the weekly dance when Dora had been touching up her hair in the cloakroom, a girl would come and stand beside her. The strange thing was they always had on the exact same colour and pattern of dress, even though each of their dresses was new for the season.
They would look at one other and grin, 'How is it we both have the same dress every time?' The other girl would say, 'I made mine myself you know, and I never expected to see another like it.'

Dora would say, 'I went to the dressmaker for mine, yet it's strange that our dresses are the same every time.'

Although Dora joined in the laughter she wondered to herself, if this could be more than just a coincidence. It was almost as if they could read one another's minds. She knew the other girl came from the country, but how was it they were dressed alike each season in a brand new dance dress? Was there some possible link? Maybe they were even related, cousins perhaps? Dora would have loved to have found out more about the girl, but she was far too shy to ask any personal questions and also wary of hearing some unsettling answers.

But returning to the subject of Norman, it was the night she was wearing her new blue satin dance dress with the tiny embossed flowers that Dora had met him first. He was so gallant and gentlemanly seeing her home with just a kiss on the cheek. Before Dora knew it they'd been seeing one another for months. Even her mother had started asking questions. Then all of a sudden Sarah invited Norman to Sunday tea. Dora was of two minds about this. Tea with the parents always meant something serious, and honestly was she really that committed?

Norman would escort her to the weekly dance but once there he invariably drifted off to the bar, making sure that varied of his cronies danced with her all night. Dora worried about his drinking but he never showed signs of being drunk, was always steady for the last dance and seeing her back to Baker St. Possibly Norman himself wasn't serious and being invited to tea wouldn't really matter to him?

To her amazement Norman was delighted with the invite. Sunday arrived and he stood at the front door with a huge bunch of flowers, large box of chocolates and a big grin. He presented the flowers and chocolates to her mother, and strode into the house as if he owned it.

'Mrs Roberts, this is a fine spread.' He teased and flirted with Sarah who twinkled and sparkled round him like a young girl.

Dora felt like a gooseberry. It was so embarrassing.

She'd never seen either her mother or Norman behave like this. She wondered if there was something wrong with her, perhaps she was the one who wasn't behaving normally. Flirting was something Dora knew hardly anything about, preferring young men to say what they meant rather than flatter her unduly. Dora couldn't wait for the evening to be over. Maybe this was a mistake?

Finally, Jack came home from work to join the party and an air of seriousness descended. He proceeded to interrogate Norman about his prospects and his job as a telephone engineer.

Dora felt it was now going to the other extreme. She looked across at her father and he seemed to be nodding and agreeing with Norman – so she took this as approval.

Dora herself wasn't at all sure, wondering if things were moving far too quickly and conveniently for everyone except her.

Sarah had given her the talk several times. It went along the lines of, 'your mother was no better than she should be or she wouldn't have left you with strangers. You have to be careful to behave yourself. I don't want you getting a bad reputation or getting into any sort of trouble that would reflect on us.'

Inwardly Dora always felt indignant at the talk, given regularly now she was growing up, thinking to herself that she always behaved well never putting a foot out of line. Trying to be fair however, maybe her mother had some right on her side. Having no idea about her background or lineage, how could Dora judge?

What if she went completely off the rails and ran off with a soldier or a sailor? Think of the adventures she could have. Dora chortled to herself at the idea. That would certainly give them something to talk about. However Dora knew in her heart of hearts, that nothing of that nature was in her character. She might not know her real birth parents but she was absolutely confidant of her own innate common sense and level head.

For the next few months, the courting progressed. Things however seemed to be escalating. Then Norman went away on a course. He rang Dora every night and she tried to make herself believe that perhaps he was 'The One'?

She would fantasise about becoming Mrs Norman Lloyd, practising writing her new signature 'Dora Lloyd'– and thinking about the house and the family she would have. But somehow, however hard she tried to convince herself, none of it seemed to ring true.

Her parents were now waiting for an engagement announcement, and her mother yet again took the opportunity to take Dora on one side and say, 'You must tell Norman about your background before you get engaged. We have no idea where you come from, and he would want to know the family he's marrying into. He might well change his mind when he knows your situation.'

During Norman's time away, Dora continued attending the Saturday dances but always coming home alone, or with a girlfriend. Going to chapel three times on a Sunday could become arduous especially in the spring and summer when the weather was fine. On these occasions Dora would skip Sunday school and walk with her friends on the Promenade. Linking arms they would parade up and down past the bandstand and on to kick the Bar at the bottom of Constitution Hill.

The last few evenings before Norman was due back, there'd been no phone calls. Dora wondered if something was wrong.

Surely he would ring her to let her know when he was coming back. Even Sarah remarked on the lack of calls.

A few days later when he should have returned, she bumped into one of his friends on the street, 'Hullo Bill, is Norman home, he hasn't rung me yet.'

'He doesn't want to have anything more to do with you,' Bill mumbled and hurried off.

Dora was shocked, not knowing what to think or do but certain she had to find out what all this was about. Norman owed her that much at least. Doggedly Dora walked round and round the town until she spotted one of the stripped tents put up by the telephone engineers. Norman was there alright.

Dora called across to him, 'Norman, why haven't you rung, or let me know you were home?'

He looked surprised for a moment, even stricken. Accusingly he said, 'A mate saw you out last Sunday with your friends.'

'That's right. What about it? Are your friends spying me or something?'

He retorted, 'I need to know what sort of girl I'm courting. He said you were out with that Betsy – she's no better than she should be and got quite a reputation round the town,' and continued pompously, 'that's not the sort of company I want my future wife to keep.'

Dora was aghast, it sounded exactly like something she'd heard before, but last time it was from her mother. Sure enough Betsy was a bit flighty but she never meant any harm. Her kind and generous heart probably did more harm to herself than to others. 'She's my friend I like her and there's no harm in her, whatever you may have heard about her.'

111

'Then that's it – it's her or me. You make your choice – but I won't have my girl hanging about with that -f-----slut.'

He turned his back on her and walked off, leaving her standing alone in the middle of the street –mouth agape.

Dora had had enough and headed for home with a sinking heart. This was a side of Norman she'd never seen before, and could see she'd never truly known him. If this is what he could do or say about just a friend of hers, what would he have thought of her lack of parentage and family? Perhaps it was a lucky escape, though it hardly felt like it. Returning home, Dora said nothing– but continued to live as before.

When her parents finally mentioned his name, 'What's happened to Norman, Dora? We don't seem to have seen him around lately?' Dora rather mutely responded, 'It didn't come to anything. We'd different ideas about what we wanted.'

Her mother said only, 'That's a pity; he seemed a nice enough chap.'

But her father had more to say, 'Honestly, Dora, I didn't think he was right for you. I think you can do a lot better. There's plenty of time. You're only young. Take your time, and the right man will come along, you'll see.' In some ways, it seemed as if both her parents were relieved that everything could go back to normal with just the three of them.

For the next few Saturday nights Dora stayed in. Finally she plucked up the courage to go to the Pier dance with Rosie. The first person she clapped eyes on was Norman, propping up the bar as usual. He looked straight through her, as if he'd never seen her before in his life.

∞

By now Dora had recovered from the faint. The smelling salts had definitely helped. Rosie said 'Come on Dora your colour's better, I'll take you home.'

Dora had never fully realised how much her feelings had been involved when Norman had turned on her. It had been a blow. It wasn't just her pride that'd been hurt, it was the rejection and being tossed to one side like a piece of rubbish. Dora swore to herself that she'd never let herself be hurt this way again. In the future she would be the one in control, never letting her feelings overwhelm her in this way, nevertheless Dora couldn't entirely ignore that tiny inner voice continually asking, 'Will I ever fall in love? Will someone love me just for myself? Will I ever have a home and family of my own?'

Arriving back at Baker Street after this disastrous night, Sarah looked up from her crocheting remarking, 'You're back early from the dance?'

Dora replied, 'Yes, I felt tired and thought I'd get an early night,' not wanting to explain what had happened. It was all too raw. She was only glad that she'd never got to the stage of telling Norman about her background. Being that judgmental about her friends, he would have had even more reason to discard her if he knew she was a 'foundling'. What a stupid word that was anyway. After all she'd never 'been found' just 'left', not the same thing at all.

16

1938 - Introductions

Dora decided that after the Norman disaster she'd have nothing more to do with the opposite sex. Just enjoy the dances and partner young men, but no more relationships. She was happy enough on her own. Now with different sets of friends, her life outside Baker Street was full to overflowing. But a few weeks later at the Saturday dance, things were set to change.

Sitting chatting to her friends, a voice stammered, 'Would you like to dance?' interrupted her discussion. Dora turned her head, and was confronted by a very good looking young man with a bright red face, shuffling from foot to foot.

Dora quickly said, 'No I'm sorry I don't think so.' Inwardly she thought, he's definitely had too much to drink, and I don't want a repeat of Norman.

The young man looked so sheepish and dazed at her refusal and just kept standing there shuffling from foot to foot, that she suddenly felt sorry for him, and relented, 'Perhaps one dance.'

Dora moved into his outstretched arms. He was barely an inch taller than her, and seemed to have two left feet and couldn't seem to speak and dance at the same time – looking down constantly and apologising every time he stepped on her toes. Dora was glad when the music finally stopped, and mumbling a quick thank you, rapidly made for the exit with her friend. Flicking a quick backward glance on her way to the cloakroom, she saw that he was still in the middle of the floor, a stunned expression on his face

She said to her friend, 'I'm not sure if he's all there. Maybe he's just drunk too much and needs to go home and sleep it off.'

A few Sundays later after chapel, Jack Hargett stopped her at the door. Jack was one of the ushers, and always knew everyone and what was going on. 'Dora, I've got someone I'd like you to meet. He's a good friend of mine from the Territorials and he's very keen to meet you. Can I introduce you? Look he's over there. Let me call him over.'

He pointed to the red faced drunk she had danced with a few weeks previous. But this time he looked a lot less rosy faced, and seemed to be smiling inanely at her.

'I don't know Jack I met him at the Pier dance. He's a terrible dancer, trod all over my feet. His face was so red. I thought he'd had too much to drink, or that he was a bit gormless.'

'Don't be silly Dora, he hardly drinks at all, and as far as I know he's got all his marbles. He's very, very shy and blushes a lot, that's why he's goes red in the face but he's a sound chap.'

And that was Dora's first official introduction to Arthur Hamer.

Once Dora could see past the stammering and the blushing she realised what a gentle, sensitive soul he was. Arthur told her he came from Llanidloes and had been in Aberystwyth since he was sixteen working for the Star Grocers round the corner from Baker St. Dora thought how marvellous it was to meet someone from outside the town. She was constantly afraid of bumping into someone from her original birth family? What if she went out with someone who turned out to be a relative, a brother even? How catastrophic would that be! Another plus for Arthur was that he came from a big family and this was just what she herself wanted. Maybe she could enjoy becoming part of his family instead.

This time, deciding to keep her personal life private, Dora did not mention Arthur's name at home.

Every Saturday night, she would quickly wash, change and race round the corner to meet him from work. Her mother was used to her going to the dance on a Saturday so never gave it a passing thought.

Arthur would say, 'I'm not much of a dancer, Dora, what about us going to the pictures tonight instead?'

On their way to the Coliseum, they'd stop at 'The Bonbon' on Terrace Road. Arthur always asked, 'What sweets would you like tonight?'

Dora would look longingly at the sugared almonds or the Walnut Whips, but knew after paying for his digs and his clothes Arthur had very little money left.

'Why don't we buy a quarter of cream toffees to share?' she'd suggest.

His face would light up, 'If you're sure.' Dora absolutely hated toffees, spending most of the time ungluing them from round her teeth, but for some reason she always felt she wanted to make up to him for things he'd never had.

They both loved adventure films, mysteries or comedies. In their early days of going out together, Dora would wait to see what type of mood Arthur was in, and whether he would flare up like her father. As much as she loved Jack, his temper and outbursts could be frightening. But Arthur's moods seemed to be on an even keel, and Dora was able to say and do what she liked when she was with him. One Saturday night, while they were watching 'The Lady Vanishes' and contentedly sucking on their toffees, Dora felt someone constantly kicking her seat. She tried to ignore it and concentrate on the film but it was too distracting so she was forced to whisper to Arthur, 'There's someone kicking my seat.'

Holding her breath and waiting for some sort of scene when Arthur would turn round and shout at the person. Dora was pleasantly surprised by his response when he passed it off by saying, 'Let's move further forward.'

Dora found she could be comfortable and relaxed with Arthur all the time. At home it was if she was continuously waiting for an explosion from Jack or a change of mood from Sarah. Sarah's moods were so variable it was hard to keep up with them. All Dora really wanted was a quiet life. On Sundays, Dora was still skipping Sunday school and hoping no one who knew her parents would spot her and instead walking on the Promenade or the Castle with Arthur. He loved to sit and contemplate the sea.

On one of these Sundays he told her a story about his adolescence, 'When I was 13, I used to carry out for my grandparents who were butchers. I saved every penny I could and told my mother I was going for a week's holiday to Aberystwyth. I found lodgings up in Crynfrin, bought a bus ticket, and spent the whole week down here on the beach. After that I was determined to come and live here by the sea.'

Dora was taken aback, 'Was'nt your family shocked? What did they think?' She'd never have been allowed to do anything like that even if she'd had the money.

Arthur grimaced, 'They barely noticed I'd gone. No one was interested in me. I spent most of my time with my grandparents. They were such kind people, and really loved me. My father was quite ruthless and told us all, that as soon as we reached 16 and had a job we'd have to move out, be on our own and fend for ourselves.'

Dora was upset to think that someone's real father could treat his children so callously, but then she herself had been deserted by her real mother so what was the difference?

In many ways, Dora began to understand that she and Arthur had a lot in common. Both had difficult home lives, and were often left to their own devices; both were quite lonely and looking for love and security. Maybe this was one relationship that could work out. Arthur badly needed a home and she would be glad to find a different one to the one she had.

17

Courting and Obstacles

Six months had gone by, and Dora felt that she and Arthur might definitely have a future together. However there were a few 'flies in the ointment'. Sarah had at last noticed that there was a young man on the scene, though Dora had been very guarded about him. Arthur would wait for her down the street leaning against the doorway of Lloyds Bank. Unfortunately in a small town like Aberystwyth, there was always going to be someone who would see them and delight in passing information back to her mother or father.

Finding out through Jack, that it seemed Dora was seriously courting again, Sarah confronted her, 'I hear you're seeing another young man. If this is serious, I think we should meet him, don't you? I don't want anything underhand happening behind my back. Bring him to tea on Sunday next.'

Dora was not pleased, and not keen to have a repeat of the last Sunday tea with Sarah and Norman. She wanted to protect hers and Arthur's blossoming relationship, and didn't want to expose him to her parents too soon. She knew Arthur was far too shy and wouldn't dream of flirting with Sarah, but it would be like feeding him to the lions. Dora prevaricated, 'I think he might be going home to see his parents on Sunday.'

But Sarah was not to be put off, 'Make it the following Sunday then, and I'll make sure that your father is here as well.' This apparently was an order, so there was no way Dora could get out of it.

Arthur, very different to Norman, was far more reticent and certainly had no charming patter at his fingertips. On the Sunday in question and with no sign of Jack, by the time they had worked their way through the cold ham Sarah had questioned him thoroughly.

Arthur had reached the stage of becoming practically monosyllabic, giving one word answers only and stuttering with nerves, bright red to his ears:

'Where does your family come from, Arthur?'

'Llanidloes.'

'What does your father do?'

'He's a timekeeper.'

'How many brothers and sisters do you have?'

'I'm one of seven.'

Dora could see her mother weighing him up and finding him wanting, and Dora's hackles began to rise. All her maternal instincts came to the fore but before she could spring to his defence, her father arrived home and saved the day.

Sarah got distracted from her interrogator role and hurried about getting Jack's tea. To Dora's relief her father was in one of his sunnier moods. He'd had a good day at the garden, free from customers, just pricking out seedlings.

Her father's presence seemed to relax Arthur, who was by now desperate to escape Sarah's attentions. Jack started, 'I hear you're in the Territorials Arthur,' and before Dora knew it, they were away discussing and comparing their time as part-time soldiers.

Quietly congratulating herself that they were getting on so well, she gave herself a metaphorical pat on the back for having reminded her father about Arthur's signing up for the Territorials.

After Arthur had left, Sarah said, 'I can see what attracted you Dora. He's certainly very good looking, (Dora waited patiently for the 'but' and then it came) but he doesn't have much to say for himself, or have much about him.' She sighed and shrugged her shoulders 'anyway as long as he suits you I suppose----'

But Dora was far more interested in her father's opinion. Getting him on his own later she said, 'What do you think, Dada?'

'He seems a hardworking decent lad. If you're happy with him Dora, I am too.'

The fact that Arthur had signed up for the Territorials voluntarily probably went a long way in gaining Jack's respect. Dora had the good sense to omit Arthur's real reason. The Star was not known for being generous with holidays so Arthur had thought that two extra weeks' paid holiday with the Territorials would be a bonus. What he hadn't taken into account was that two weeks spent under canvas, training, was hardly a benefit.

After passing the initiation of the Sunday tea, Arthur was now able to come to the house to call for Dora, who felt quite smug that she had at least overcome yet another of their obstacles, but there was still another looming on the horizon.

Arthur turned up one Sunday and said, 'I hope you don't mind Dora, Mona's at the end of the street and would like to come for a walk with us.' Mona was his landlady's daughter and she had definite designs on him. However, being totally unaware of this and wanting to keep his landlady happy, Arthur had agreed to her coming.

After a few Sundays of this Dora decided enough was enough.

The following Sunday, when Arthur stood at the front step with Mona hovering down by the bank, Dora said clearly, 'I won't be coming out today, or any other day with you if she comes along,' and shut the door firmly in his face.

The following week, a somewhat shamefaced Arthur arrived as usual but this time armed with a box of her favourite 'Black Magic' and announced, 'Mona won't be coming again.'

Dora never asked how he'd managed it. But for such a shy unassertive man it must have been difficult. It made her see that he'd made his choice, and that she was important to him after all.

One of Arthur's drawbacks was that although he had this very steady temperament – he loved to argue and debate about world affairs or politics- even religion sometimes. He could be very expansive about what was happening in Germany, and would continually ask her opinions. 'Dora what do you think of this fellow Hitler, do you think he's a good leader or a dangerous man? He seems to be taking over more and more countries. He may set his sights on crossing the Channel? There could be the possibility of war for us, don't you think?'

Not caring enough to argue, especially about world affairs, Dora was far more pragmatic only really interested in what was happening on her own doorstep. Once she'd heard enough of the discussion and his various theories, she would walk off, leaving him mid sentence saying, 'Go and have a pint and argue with your mates at the YM. I'll see you on Saturday.'

Wondering if Arthur would get angry about her lack of interest, Dora was concerned they were entirely suited. Of course they couldn't be exactly alike, how boring would that be! But Arthur never batted an eyelid when she up and left him sitting there, only laughed about her indifference.

He would teasingly threaten her saying, 'What will you do Dora, if Mr Hitler turns up in Aberystwyth and throws you bag and baggage out of Baker St?'

Tossing her head she almost blurted out, 'That's nearly happened to me already, and there was no Mr Hitler around then.' But she kept her thought to herself and chuckled with him as they enjoyed their ice-creams. It seemed to Dora that there were so many things they agreed on they could afford to accept their differences.

Dora was used to hearing her father giving forth on his views about the world and politics. Jack would have made a great explorer. He loved his adventure stories and tales of mayhem in far flung corners of the globe. Avidly reading 'The Wide World Magazine', he would pass on exotic tit-bits over the tea table. Sarah would turn her nose up saying it was all make believe anyway, who would ever think that anything realistic came from that magazine. Dora was very much in accord with her mother on this. Perhaps it was a male thing Dora thought, having no experience of brothers or close male relatives. Possibly men felt they still had to prove themselves, true to their caveman genes. Well, let them get on with it, they were welcome to it all, as long as it didn't involve her.

GROWING UP

18

1939 - The Engagement

'Dora, Dora, there's a telephone call for you – hurry up.' Her father's voice sounded curt and impatient, 'Don't be too long. I'm expecting a call about new plants.'

Dora was in shock, to actually have a call herself and nearly dropped the receiver, 'Who is this please?' she asked timidly.

'Dora, it's me Arthur, Mr Putt kindly let me ring you. I need to see you tonight urgently.'

'But it's Tuesday – you know Mom isn't keen on my going out mid week.'

'Seriously, Dora, I've been telling you for weeks it looks like war. Now I've heard a rumour that the Territorials will be called up first. We may not have much time.'

Dora hung up the receiver her hand shaking. She'd only been half listening to Arthur talking about the possibility of war.
Surely it couldn't really be happening. Things were going so well between her and Arthur. She felt at last this was someone she could depend on, someone just for her. Now it was as if everything would be blown apart, all the plans they'd make and the future they could have .Deflated and dragging her feet towards the kitchen, her mother took one look at her long face and said, 'What's the matter? You look like you've lost a shilling and found a penny?'

'I have,' Dora said miserably, 'it's war.'

'What do you mean 'war'? I haven't heard anything on the wireless. Your father certainly hasn't said anything.'

'Arthur's heard a rumour and the Territorials will be called up first,' Dora explained glumly.

'I suppose they would be. They were certainly called up first in the Great War with your father being one of them and we were only just married. Once he shipped out to the Sudan I didn't see him for years.'

For once Sarah looked at her with sympathy, 'Go and see Arthur tonight, and find out the facts. I'll ask your father to make enquiries at the Club. Last time, we had months of a 'phoney war' before anything really happened,' she continued reassuringly.

Later that evening, Arthur said, 'With times as they are I'd like to give you some money to buy a present from me, some sort of keepsake.'

Dora was amazed. Arthur was never mean, but he was cautious with the little money he earned. To her astonishment and delight he said, 'Give me your hand' and he carefully counted out some of his wages from last week, and a small amount he'd been saving, and tenderly closed her hand over it all.

Bemused Dora wondered what he was intending. Was this to be a farewell present? It felt final and that certainly wasn't right. She wanted beginnings not endings but putting a brave face on it, she asked hesitantly, 'what sort of keepsake were you thinking of?'

'I don't know, maybe jewellery,' Arthur suggested, 'but I'll leave it entirely to you. I'm sorry I'm going to have to go now, or I'll never get up in the morning,' and with that he shot off back to his lodgings.

They arranged to meet the following Saturday, so Dora had less than a week to buy something suitable.

On the way home, she thought long and hard. They'd been courting for just over a year. Was she sure this was the man for her? Granted Arthur liked to argue and debate world affairs a lot but Dora didn't mind that, at least he didn't get drunk or lose his temper. He was a quiet, kind, peace loving man, compared with her tempestuous father, who could go off like a rocket losing his temper over trifles, and ending up shouting and yelling loudly. Dora knew in her heart that her father was all bark and bluster. There was never any malice or malevolence in it. But, she longed to live in a calm harmonious home, where she knew what expect, no surprises, no bad moods for days on end, no sarcasm, criticism or unkindness.

If only Gran was there to talk to– her advice would be so welcome, or if only there'd been a sister or brother to discuss it with. But this was a decision that Dora would have to make on her own. She would have to be brave and seize the moment or it might never come again. Once she felt strong enough, Dora gathering her courage marched into the local jewellers and made her purchase.

All through the week when she had a minute, Dora would sneak upstairs to her room, carefully take the velvet box out of its hiding place and stare in awe at its contents. She just hoped she'd done the right thing. The following Saturday, though her knees were knocking and her heart pounding, once she caught sight of Arthur's handsome, sweet face, she knew she'd made the right choice.

Arthur asked casually, 'Did you manage to buy anything, Dora? Was there enough money? I could manage some more this week if it wasn't enough?'

'No, it was plenty. Would you like to see what I bought?'Dora asked boldly, trying to appear a sophisticated woman of the world.

Arthur bent towards her eagerly. With a touch of flamboyance and a flourish, Dora peeled back the glove from her left hand revealing a tiny diamond chip ring on her third finger. 'Ta—da--- what do you think?' she said proudly.

For a second, Arthur was taken aback. Then on closer inspection he asked, 'Does this mean we're engaged?'

'I would think so,' Dora replied confidently and haughtily said, 'I certainly wouldn't be wearing it on this finger if we weren't.'

Arthur for once put aside his shyness and right in the middle of Great Darkgate Street with people milling around and about, pulled her to him and kissed her soundly. Dora was euphoric. Neither of them could stop smiling. It was as if they'd finally conquered all the barriers in their path. Dora was home at last, the War could definitely take a backseat.

A few days went by at Baker Street, and no one seemed to notice the ring. Dora hugged her news close to her chest.
Her mother remarked, 'You seem unusually cheerful Dora, even with this threat of War hanging over us.'

Humming quietly to herself as she finished the beds, Dora didn't let on, this was something private, and she was determined to keep it that way. The only being she confided in was her poor Judy –so crippled now with arthritis in her back legs that she wasn't long for this world.

Cavorting up and down her bedroom, Dora would flash the tiny chip at the dressing table mirror and say, 'What do you think Mrs Dora Hamer? Is this a ring for a queen or what? How do you take your tea, Mrs Hamer? What a lovely family you have. Doesn't that little girl look just like you,' and end up bursting with glee, doubling up and rolling on her bed in merriment.

However one evening when she was laying up for tea, one of the lodgers looked across and caught the sparkle reflected by the lamp, 'Dora you secretive old thing, that's a ring if I'm not very much mistaken.' Before Dora could shut her up, Poppy went on, 'Look everyone Dora's engaged!' They all crowded round her – patting her on the back and congratulating her.

As soon as Sarah came in and before Dora could shut them up they called out, 'You never told us Mrs Roberts that Dora's engaged? Were you keeping it hush-hush?'

'It's news to me. I know nothing about it and am apparently the last to know,' her mother retorted sarcastically.

Dora was forced to come up with some sort of explanation, saying that Arthur was likely to be called up any day and they'd done this on the spur of the moment.

Her mother mumbled something unintelligible under her breath and snorted quietly saying nothing in front of the lodgers. Once in the kitchen though, she was quick to comment, 'I hope you know what you're doing Dora. I thought Arthur would have the courtesy to speak to your father first.'

How old fashioned Dora thought – after all I'm twenty three, quite old enough to know my own mind. It's my life, and I'm going to live it the way I want to. Maintaining a neutral expression, Dora determined to keep cool.. Knowing her father as she did, she knew he loved her and wanted nothing but her happiness and wouldn't mind not being 'asked for her hand' first.

However Sarah now thoroughly provoked into one of her moods wasn't going to give up that easily and thwarted by Dora's seeming detachment brought out the big guns, 'Have you told Arthur yet about your background ? Make sure you do, before this goes any further. He may decide he doesn't want to marry someone with such a questionable past.'

Dora, trying to let off steam without noticeably retaliating, pulled faces and rolled her eyes behind Sarah's back. Was her mother never going to let it lie? Could Sarah just once show approval or take pleasure in Dora's happiness? But this was too much to hope for. On this particular occasion Dora didn't care, she was glowing with happiness and nothing or no one was going to spoil that.

The following Sunday, Dora and her new fiancé were sitting at the Harbour watching the last of the boats bobbing in and out on the incoming tide, with the early evening having a softness and calmness about it that inspired Dora. She decided to pluck up her courage there and then and tell Arthur about her past. There was never going to be a better time, and it was best to get it over with. After she'd explained everything, there seemed to be a weighty silence with Dora wondering what to think.

Rattled by his lack of reaction, she finally blurted out, 'Do you still want to marry me, Arthur? You can back out if you want to, I won't hold you to anything'

'Of course, I want to marry you,' came the reply, 'it makes no difference to me at all. I don't care where you come from, it's you I love, (he tightened his grip on her hand) you I'm marrying -not your background, or any long lost family.'

Dora had never heard him make such a declaration before. She was moved, feeling the pinprick of tears welling up in her eyes, and quickly gulping them back trying to control herself. Finally it was as if this was the person she'd been waiting for. This would be the start of her family and she couldn't wait.
Exactly like her parents before, Arthur never mentioned the subject again. Whereas Dora always felt Sarah and Jack were ashamed of the 'secret' they had kept all those years, and were perhaps faintly embarrassed about her and her antecedents or lack of them, she realised Arthur wasn't in the least concerned.

The mysteries of her hidden beginnings were of no account to him. Arthur was not one for discussing his feelings and rarely mentioned his own family except for his mother, so perhaps he himself saw this as a fresh beginning for them both.

As she'd got older, Dora at times would have liked to have been more open and talked about the little she knew about her past. Sometimes it was tantalising not to know much about her forebears. Why should she be made to feel ashamed about the mother and family she'd never known?

But Arthur had more pressing matters on his mind. War was imminent and more than likely a certainty, with Hitler moving rapidly across Europe. Everything depended on Chamberlain and the Peace Talks, and he said, 'I know you don't want to think about it Dora, but any day now war could be declared and I'll be one of the first to be called up.'

Dora, ever hopeful, said, 'It may not come to that – perhaps it's just a storm in a teacup. The Prime Minister will surely come to some agreement.'

Arthur continued, 'It might be best not to think about marriage yet. I wouldn't want you to be left a widow or have to bring up a child on your own. We must be sensible Dora.'

But Dora was adamant, 'Whatever happens we'll get married. I want a home of my own and a family. And no war is going to get in the way.' But it would be easier said than done, particularly in the dark days to come.

19

War Work in Holyhead

The sound of the 'Alert' took Dora by surprise. There was no time to get to the cellar. All she could do was crouch, dry mouthed, under the heavy oak table in the parlour, and hope the bombing wouldn't last. Sensing that she was breathing in time with the bombs dropping, she let out a big puff of air, biting down hard on her tongue and tasting the metallic flavour of blood.

Nothing like this had happened in Aberystwyth, so much for thinking that the war wasn't going to interrupt her life. It was hard to believe it was only a month since the announcement, and only six weeks since she and Arthur had got engaged. She, her parents and the lodgers, had huddled round the wireless at Baker Street, to hear Neville Chamberlain's ominous tones, proclaiming:

"I am speaking to you from the Cabinet Office at 10, Downing Street. This morning the British Ambassador in Berlin handed the German government a final note stating that unless we heard from them by 11.00am.that they were prepared at once to withdraw their troops from Poland, a state of war would exist between us. I have to tell you that no such undertaking has been received, and that consequently this country is at war with Germany."

The heavy weight of the words sounded like doom and it was as if everyone had been struck dumb. Trying to lighten the mood Sarah said to Jack, 'Well here we go again. Twice in one lifetime is once too many. At least Jack, this time you are too old to fight.'

Dora kept thinking that no sooner had she found her husband to be, than her future happiness was to be snatched away from her. It really wasn't fair. How dare Hitler interfere with her plans!

In no time at all Air Raid Wardens were calling for blackouts and everyone was carrying gasmasks. Arthur's company was, as he thought, the first to be called up. He had very little time to say a proper farewell. Obviously, there was a good reason for his departure, but Dora still felt the pain of desertion. There was always that familiar ache of saying goodbye to someone she loved. Would it never ease?

It certainly didn't help when a worried Arthur said, 'Perhaps we shouldn't have got engaged. I mightn't come back. We don't know how long this war will last, or how long you'll have to wait.' He murmured, 'I should really give you your freedom.'

'Don't be silly,' Dora said, 'I'm glad we're engaged. I love you. I don't want be free. Anyway I'm not giving you the ring back – so there,' and put her tongue out at him.

That made him laugh, it was rare to see him smile these days. He seemed to have the cares of the world on his shoulders. Dora was concerned how such a sensitive man would cope as a soldier, but never voiced her fears.

Trying to sound more positive, she said, 'Anyway, the newspapers are saying it'll be over by Christmas. We'll soon be together again Arthur, you'll see.'

At first, Arthur was sent to Llandudno for training, and Dora decided that she should be as near to him as possible during these dreadful days. Contacting the local YMCA in Aberystwyth, Dora answered a vacancy for a maid in a seamen's' hostel in Holyhead, and was accepted.

For once Sarah was sympathetic, 'You may as well see as much of Arthur as you can. No doubt he'll be shipped out soon enough.'

Jack however, didn't approve saying forcefully, 'I think you're making a big mistake Dora – you can bet your life the bombing on the coast will be bad.'

Now ending up hiding under a table whilst Holyhead was bombarded night after night, Dora wished she'd taken more notice of her father. Not only that but the hostel itself was a tough place to work, with the matron Miss Mates or Ma Mates as everyone called her, a crabby elderly woman, believing in working her staff into the ground. Very few stayed long. The minute she clapped eyes on Dora, she said, 'There'll be no skiving here miss. Don't come up here with all your West Wales airs there's hard graft to be done. Don't forget, I'll be watching you.'

Dora thought surely it couldn't possibly be harder than Baker Street and her mother's eagle eye?

The hostel was packed to the rafters with Dutch sailors, who'd lost their ships. Any families they had were left behind in occupied Holland. Dora felt great sympathy for them. It was as if in some ways they were kindred spirits. Hans and Johann in particular, would address her in broken English, 'Come sit Dora – so tired, such hard work. Look, hier ist mijn little Anna and Henrik– they will be big by the time I get home,' and they would each produce crumpled, water stained photographs and lovingly unfold them for her to see.

Always smiling and willing to help in any way, Dora knew the chances of them seeing their families again were not good now Hitler had overrun Holland. But she kept up the charade doing her best to bolster their flagging spirits. On her one night off she sometimes went to the cinema with several of them. They treated her like a much loved younger sister, 'Dora, you pick picture. We don't understand much, but love pretty girls, and hear news.' During the Pathe News, they would whisper to her if they saw a shot of their country and ask what was happening.

Dora did her best to keep up a running commentary, which they would pass along the row from man to man. Their sadness affected her deeply-wondering what it must be like to not only to be without a family but a country too.

Opportunities to see Arthur were few and far between. One Sunday–they met at Llandudno. The promenade and beach was mined and sealed off. To shelter from the freezing wind, they found a small milk bar that was open. Arthur sat down heavily on one of the wooden chairs, 'I'm glad to give my poor feet a rest for a few hours, all that square bashing in new boots is giving me terrible blisters.'

'I don't see why you have to do all that marching. After all didn't you train hard enough in the Territorials?'

'The Regular Army doesn't rate the Territorials, those hard bitten career soldiers think we were just playing at it,' Arthur replied.

Dora smirked, 'They'll have a real shock when those raw unfit recruits turn up, won't they?'

They grinned at each other. Dora thought how lucky she was to have him. He was still her Arthur– even if his handsome face was thinner his beautiful grey eyes looked the same. Her heart turned over with love, and she leaned forward to kiss him on the cheek.

He blushed, 'Not here Dora, someone might see us.'

She laughed out loud, 'Don't be silly, there's no one here but us.'

The owner shouted from the back, 'I'm closing up in a minute.' But when he came out and saw the soldier with his girl he patted Arthur on the shoulder, 'Take as much time as you like mate, I'm not in any hurry.'

They wandered arm in arm back to the bus station, and putting her on the bus, in usual Arthur fashion, he barely pecked her on the cheek, patted her arm to say goodbye and with a parting, 'Look after yourself, Dora,' hurried back to his barracks.

Dora felt lighter on the journey home- even Ma Mates was not going to get to her. Thank goodness for Sarah and all her training or she wouldn't have lasted a week. The hostel had gone through five maids in the last six months. They had either left because of the workload or because of the vileness of the matron. It was a bit of a tossup.

During Dora's next few weeks, Holyhead was not spared. German bombers would drop any remaining bombs on the North Wales Coast, as they made their way home. Night after night was spent in the cellar or under a table. Dora started to suffer heavy nosebleeds every time the siren went off. Her sleep suffered, her weight dropped, and she felt chilled and edgy all the time. Eventually her periods stopped. Finally she was forced to visit the doctor and he diagnosed, 'A type of shock. It won't do you any good to stay with all this shelling, if you don't have to. Go home to Aberystwyth. Get some rest, peace and quiet and good food into you.'

There was certainly no point in carrying on with her health deteriorating rapidly, particularly as Arthur had just received new orders. Who knew where he would be sent next?

There was nothing for it – but to return to Baker Street. Dreading ringing her mother Dora was uncertain about her reaction. Luckily her father's gruff voice answered and without any hesitation he said, 'Come home at once cariad, I'll tell your mother to air your room. We'll be glad to have you back. We've missed you. Have you money for the train? Find out the time and I'll meet you.'

Dora had yet to break it to the matron, and knew what she'd be in for. The onslaught was as expected, 'You're a lazy good for nothing- you're no good to me anyway. Be off with you – the sooner the better.' Dora took it all on the chin. This was 'water off a duck's back' compared with Sarah.

On the train back to Aberystwyth, Dora thought back over the experience. Apart from when she was a child this was the longest she'd ever been away from home as an adult. She was glad to have seen Arthur, but the Hostel work was a nightmare. She would miss the Dutchmen though, and they were plainly sad to see her go insisting on having her address so they could keep in touch. For them Dora was like 'a younger sister' or a 'daughter' and they were loath to part with her. However it would be good to get back to Aber and some much needed silence.

Jack's familiar, wrinkled face, moustache bristling expectantly through the steam at the station was a welcome sight. Dora knew without a doubt that he was pleased to see her.

A few weeks later, the lady from the YMCA who had recommended her to the hostel stopped her on the street, 'Dora I wanted a word with you. Miss Mates from Holyhead has sent me a rather libellous letter about you saying,
'You were no better than you should be, and that you were lazy, also that you were over friendly with some of the Dutch sailors, when it was obvious you were already engaged.' I just couldn't believe it, knowing you as I do.'

Dora was horrified – to think that her compassion for the sailors could have been so badly misinterpreted, and went on to explain the situation.

The lady from the YM said, 'I thought that might be the case, I've heard some pretty bad things about that matron and the way that hostel is run. Don't worry Dora, I'll write a sharp letter back and report her to my superior. You don't need to worry you'll hear no more about it.'

But on the way home Dora did worry about what had been said, as there was really no one she could confide in. Sarah would probably say that it was her bad blood coming out and Jack would be on her side, but probably make a big stink about it all and make matters even worse. Feeling hurt and bewildered Dora began to question herself, wondering why in her innocence, she was so badly misjudged by people. Perhaps she was to blame in some way. All she wanted was to love and be loved, and to help as many people as she could along the way. What was so wrong with that? When would she ever find people who would accept her?

20

Meeting the Hamers

'What a lovely smile you have Dora. Your whole face lights up.' Confounded by the compliment Dora looked across the tea table to check if this was sarcasm. But looking into Mary Jane's bright blue eyes she could only see sincerity.

'Thank you,' she stammered so unused to compliments about her looks, even Arthur only ever managed to get out, 'You look nice today.'

His mother was obviously cut from different cloth, unlike her own mother. Sarah's best form of compliment was to look her up and down and say, 'You'll do.'

Dora had been nervous about meeting Arthur's family, but amazingly Sarah had come up trumps insisting she had a new hat and making over one of her own suits. It was difficult with rationing, but seeing Arthur's face when he met her off the train in Llanidloes made it all worthwhile. He beamed proudly and kissed her right there on the platform, tucking her gloved arm through his and striding out like a Colossus.

Arthur was keen to show her Llanidloes though truthfully there wasn't a lot to see. An ancient black and white Market Hall standing at the crossroads of the four main streets tended to dominate the town and its tiny population. Dora was intrigued to see that they could walk round the whole town in well under fifteen minutes.

'They've laid on a special tea for you,' Arthur said in a rush, 'Mam has been saving coupons for the occasion,' as he rushed her down Long Bridge Street, 'Eddie's home on leave, but otherwise there's only us and Mam and Dad.'

Dora did her best to hold back her nerves-what if they didn't like her, what if they thought Arthur had made a mistake. All these concerns buzzed round and round in her head.

But thank goodness on meeting Arthur's mother, her earlier anxiety disappeared, 'Call me Mam or Mary Jane everyone shortens it to 'Mar' Jane' whichever is best for you Dora,' this sweet faced rather rotund little lady said. Dora could see immediately how like his mother Arthur was especially when he bent down to kiss her cheek so tenderly.

His father though was quite a different kettle of fish, 'You can call me Dad, now you're official,' he announced pompously. He was a rather severe looking little man, full of self importance despite his lack of stature, with just the remains of a few strands of red hair on his bald pate. Dora really didn't want call him anything, but she could see he was trying his best, 'I hear Dora, from Arthur that you're very musical. Perhaps you'd play for us one evening. Our old piano probably needs tuning though – as there's no one here to use it nowadays.'

'I'd be delighted,' replied Dora, 'I don't get the chance to play for an audience these days, as so many of our boarders have been called up or gone off to do war work.'

They all sat down to tea formally in the front parlour. At once Dora could see how lame Mrs Hamer was and wondered what was wrong with her, but no one made any allowances for her or went to help as she struggled to lift the heavy silver tea tray on to the table. Dora sprang up immediately to help her – but received not a trace of acknowledgement or even a smile. It seemed as if this was definitely the wrong thing to do.

Eddie however, Arthur's younger brother, was a charmer in his RAF uniform. He had a shock of fair curly hair which stood straight up on his head.

Dora took to him immediately. He set to, offering her sandwiches and home baked scones, and cutting her a large slice of Bara Brith. Each of them bombarded her with questions from, 'How was your journey?' to 'Where do you and your family live in Aber? What do they do? What do you think about the War? Where will you live after the War?'

Dora could see that their questions they were trying to show her that she was already accepted as one of the family and tried to relax. She was glad the rest of the brothers and sisters weren't all there as well. Now that would have been an ordeal. Unexpectedly Dora started to calm down and feel more and more at home. Glancing across at Arthur, she could see he was grinning from ear to ear and nodding in agreement with everything she said. Yet there was a palpable tension between him and his father.

Companionably washing up after the meal, Mary Jane said, 'I love you hat and veil Dora. It makes you look very chic and Parisian.'

'Oh please, do try it on,' said Dora generously.

'I don't like to. I might spoil it,' Mar' Jane responded.

'Go on, you know you want to,' teased Dora.

'Pull the kitchen door to then Dora I don't want those boys laughing at me.'

After lots more merriment, Mary Jane put on the hat, tilting it this way and that and preening in front of the mirror.

'You'll have to buy one,' said Dora standing back to see the whole effect, 'it suits your face so well.'

'There's no point. When would I ever wear it?' her future mother-in-law said, pointing to her leg, 'You see I never go out because of this.'

'What happened to your leg?' Dora asked without thinking, immediately wishing she'd had the sense to hold her tongue as perhaps this wasn't the best of times to ask something so personal.

To her surprise, Mary Jane didn't take offence but went on to explain, 'It happened when I was very young and sent to train as a milkmaid on a farm. I got kicked by a cow, and the wound never seemed to heal. I've put dressings on it every day of my life since.'

This revelation opened the floodgates, and over yet another cup of tea they sat companionably on either side of the kitchen table whilst Mary Jane filled Dora in on the rest of the family. There seemed to be an endless numbers of Hamers living in the town though Mary Jane assured her that most weren't related to them. Despite this reassurance, it still looked like Arthur had a quantity of elderly aunts and cousins who required visiting whenever he was in Llani.

All through the evening Dora kept thinking about how this poor woman had become a cripple over the years, and nothing had been done about it. Later when she and Arthur were on their own, having a last walk round the town, she brought up the subject but the only reaction Dora could get out of him was, 'It's best not to mention it, my father wouldn't like it. He does have someone come in to help my mother with the heavy work. That's how it is, he thinks he knows best and he certainly won't thank you for any interference, in fact he would probably be extremely unpleasant if you said anything.'

Dora was dying to ask how a man who seemingly loved his wife could burden her with seven children when she was so badly disabled, but thought better of it.

This could be risky territory. It was much too early in hers and Arthur's relationship to comment on his father's strange behaviour.

All her life Dora had wanted to be part of a big family and one of Arthur's many attractions was that he came from such a family and yet even there, despite the warmest of welcomes, were signs of troubled undercurrents and secrets. Dora was starting to believe that all families had something to hide.

21

Working in Hove

'Push harder Dora, she's nearly in,' Pom shouted urgently, and they all but fell into the Anderson Shelter in a heap. The rather large lady they were busy pushing, was panting and puffing but still smiling after all their efforts. They all burst out laughing to release the tension. This was the first time Pom and her neighbour had had to use the shelter. It was a very snug fit for the two slim girls let alone their alarmingly bulky neighbour.

'I hope we're not here for the rest of the night,' said Pom thoughtfully, 'with any luck there'll be an 'All Clear' soon.'

Dora thought, 'Is this to be the sum total of my war experience? First of all bombed out in Holyhead and hiding under a table, and now stuck in a tiny shelter in Romsey.'

∞

Dora's debacle in North Wales had left her feeling far from confidant about herself and her judgement. Even the successful trip to Llanidloes to meet the Hamers hadn't really helped.

Going out and about in the world brought home to her just how sheltered life in Baker Street had been. Gran or Sarah had always been there to tell her what to do and Jack was always on hand to fight her battles. Certainly Dora had met and mixed with lots of visitors and lodgers over the years, but life particularly in wartime seemed uncertain and testing, and she was starting to wonder if she was up to the challenges to come.

Just in time to restore her flagging spirits, Dora received a lettercard from Arthur training in Hereford. Though he was not a person for flowery words, Dora treasured the few compliments he gave her as they always were so genuine.

He wrote,

*'Dear Dora, I cannot tell you in words how much I appreciated your
letter. I have always told you how thoughtful you are of other
peoples' feelings. It would be great if you could come on Sunday,
mind you it is a long journey and tiring in a bus. I do not like to ask
too much of you. If you come I will wangle off all duties.*
*Dora, I want you to enjoy yourself while I am away. I do not want to
be selfish and jealous, I know you love me and I can trust you,*
Love Arthur.'

Reading this gave Dora a feeling of warmth and security,
encouraging her to find the strength to go on.   Here was
someone who not only loved her but approved of her. Her old
optimism came flooding back and later when Arthur was
posted to Hove she decided to follow him.

∞

One of Baker Street's old lodgers, Pom.was living in Romsey
just up the coast from Hove and currently running a butcher's
shop She had written to Dora several times, asking her to
come and stay and help out in the shop. This seemed a great
opportunity with Arthur now posted nearby. Maybe this was
the change Dora needed to take a break from Baker St.

Once she arrived, Dora for the first time in her life was able to
enjoy the freedom of sharing a flat with another young woman
near her age. On her days off she was able to get up when she
liked and go where she liked. At last it was like being a grown
up, though Pom treated her like a younger sister, by turns
spoiling and teasing her. They would chat till the early hours
and struggle complainingly out of bed in the morning just in
time to open the shop. Dora loved it. There wasn't always a
lot of fun or even chit-chat in Baker Street as the volume of
work in the house was so intense.
Dora thoroughly enjoyed working in the shop, meeting
customers, and doing different things to home.

The queue round the shop front seemed to go on forever each day, but there was a good spirit 'of we're all in it together,' that helped.

'Pretty young lady,' they would shout to Dora, 'give us a bit of that offal to make up the ration – I hope it's not some dead dog's innards!' and the whole queue would explode in laughter.

Dora loved the cut and thrust of it all. From being shy and reticent to start with, she soon felt at ease and could giggle and make cracks with the best of them. There was never a chance for this sort of repartee in Baker St, Sarah would have been outraged. The more hard-boiled landladies of the town could give Dora a difficult time, spinning yarns and lying through their teeth, 'When I got home last time, ducks, I was short of a chop, I want it made up today.'

Dora would challenge them, 'How would I know that? Where's your evidence? Did you bring the chops back?'

'No, we ate them of course what d'ya think? It's my hubby that's short of a chop.'

'And what else?' someone piped up, 'What about a brain?'

'And that too', the crowd shouted and they all shook with laughter. They were as good as Tommy Handley and ITMA - definitely a case of, "it's being <u>so</u> cheerful as keeps me going."

Each day Pom would dole out the work, 'Dora your first job of the day is to make the sausages- don't be too generous with the offal, it's got to go a long way.' Sausages not being rationed were in great demand. Dora never minded mixing the sausage meat and the rusk, though there was generally more rusk than meat, but feeding the mix into the skins was a tricky business.

At least there was no one standing behind her telling her what she was doing wrong. Being a fast learner, she soon took over the whole responsibility for the sausage making. The regulars would call to Dora in the back room as she filled the skins, 'Hey sausage lady, mind there's more than a sniff of meat in my sausages, or there'll be hell to pay with my old man.'

Arthur often rang the shop for a chat and to find out how she was coping. This particular time, he said he'd be free the following Sunday and would skip Church Parade, and meet her in Hove.

Dora could hardly contain herself. She complained to Pom, 'I wish I had something else to wear instead of that blue dress. Arthur must be tired of seeing it by now. I've worn it that many times.'

Pom, a marvellous seamstress remarked, 'I've got a remnant in the back of my cupboard. I'm sure it'd suit you, Dora. Let me run you up a new dress, Arthur won't know what's hit him.'

On the Sunday, Dora took the bus to Hove, immediately spotting Arthur, smart in his uniform, pacing up and down and blushing nervously.

Before she could open her mouth, he said, 'I'm afraid this wasn't a good idea, Dora. There's barbed wire all along the front, and the beach is mined. We'll just have to wander round the town, and hope there's a café open somewhere.'

They wandered disconsolately arm in arm from street to street. Nothing was open and being Sunday morning there wasn't a soul on the streets. It was like a ghost town. In due course they arrived back at the main street, and were slowly sauntering down it when, out of nowhere they suddenly heard the sound of rumbling. It sounded a lot like trucks, tanks and marching feet.

Arthur instantly paled, 'Oh good grief, quickly Dora, into this doorway. There's some sort of parade coming. I'm not supposed to be here.'

'What do you mean Arthur? I thought you had permission.'

'I did, but at the last minute they cancelled all the leave. There was no way to let you know, and I couldn't let you down after you'd come all this way. The gang's supposed to be covering for me if they can.'

They cowered into the doorway as they far as they could, trying to be pretend to be invisible, but it was difficult with no one else on the street. The noise of the tanks rolling forward began to surge over them in waves as they came nearer and nearer. Dora whispered, 'What'll you do? They are definitely on this street, and any minute now they're going to pass us. Will you be in bad trouble, Arthur?'

'I'll just have to bluff it out I suppose,' Arthur replied shamefacedly.

The parade finally drew level, so there was no chance of getting away with it now. The men in the second tank, supposedly his mates from the platoon smiled and waved when they spotted Arthur. They shouted, 'Hamer you're supposed to be with us.' They were laughing fit to burst.

Arthur beetroot red was forced to move out of the doorway on to the pavement and stand and salute, and keep standing and standing to attention until the whole convoy had passed including the colonel of the regiment. Dora, lurking just behind him, thought the parade would never end. Poor Arthur, now the colour of a pillar box was a solitary figure of a soldier on the street with his girl, and had to endure more and more catcalls and ribaldry.

Afterwards Arthur was beside himself with embarrassment,

'I'm so sorry Dora, to have put you through all that. Will you ever forgive me?'

'Don't be silly Arthur – it was much worse for you – some mates you've got.'

'Oh, they were just jealous because I'm with a pretty girl and not on parade that's all. There's no malice in them really. But I don't know about the adjutant. I mightn't get off so lightly. Let's hope it's not jankers for a week.'

The next day when Arthur was marched in front of his adjutant, he was laughingly reprimanded with, 'I think you had enough punishment yesterday Private Hamer, standing to attention for so long on that street. I've never seen such a red face. I'll let you off this time. Don't let it happen again though.'

Not long after this when they were able to snatch a few hours together, Arthur confided in Dora that he thought they were being readied for embarkation, 'Seriously Dora, I don't know what to say about **us**.'

'I do,' replied Dora 'I think we should get married and the sooner the better.'

Arthur wasn't so sure, 'Perhaps we should wait a bit longer and see what happens.'

'No,' said Dora adamantly, 'I think we must go ahead. I'm not letting that fellow Hitler get in our way. He's already ruining our lives. I'm not letting him stop us getting married.'

That said, they agreed on a date at the beginning of March with Arthur putting in for leave straightaway. But who knew whether it would be granted or even where he might end up next.

Dora being an incorrigible optimist decided to leave Romsey and return to Aberystwyth to prepare for the wedding. She was sad to leave Pom and all the freedom behind but it was no use staying if Arthur was on the move again. There wasn't long till March 9th and with rationing there was a lot to do.

22

1940 - The Wedding

Returning to Baker Street early in the New Year, Dora decided she had better break the wedding news to her mother, ' Mom, Arthur's company will be leaving shortly to go abroad. We think we should get married before he goes.'
'
You're not expecting are you?' was Sarah's immediate response.

'No, of course not nothing like that,' Dora said indignantly. Trust her mother to think the worst of her.

'That's alright then,' Sarah continued, saying to Dora's amazement, 'maybe it's not such a bad thing. At the beginning of the last War, they said it would be over by Christmas but it dragged on for another four years. It was lucky your father and I had married just before. Once he was stuck in the Sudan there were no trips home from that distance,' adding callously, 'unless of course he'd been injured or sent home in a box.'

Dora never got used to her mother's harsh way of expressing the facts, however at least it seemed as if she was taking Dora's news in her stride. It was always better to leave things for a few days, and feed information to Sarah on a 'drip by drip' basis. When Dora was in a calm frame of mood, she knew this strategy worked well but most of the time she was too impatient or excited, wanting things to happen quickly and inevitably rubbing Sarah up the wrong way.

However this time on her own initiative, Sarah said, 'I suppose we'd better get on with organising this wedding then as we haven't much time. There'll be a lot to do, dresses to sort out, food, photos, guests.' Sarah was practically rubbing her hands together in anticipation.

Meekly Dora mumbled, 'I was hoping to make it a small wedding, just a few friends and family.'

'Why would you want that?' her mother retaliated, 'You don't want some poor affair when there's nothing to be ashamed of. Don't worry, your father and I'll see you out in style for sure. It'll be a chance to show those neighbours of ours, what we're made of.'

Dora knew that for many years her mother had put up with slights and put downs from the people in the street. Not being Welsh, they'd often ignored her, talking in their own language to Jack, and treating her as if she was an alien. Sarah's nose had inched higher and higher - whilst they all gossiped about her 'airs and graces'.

There was nothing Sarah relished more than getting 'her teeth into a big job.' There'd be no hold in her now. She would take charge of it everything down to the last detail, with Dora relegated to the background as a mere bit player. This really wasn't what Dora wanted, however it was worth keeping mum just for a quiet life. There was no point in kicking up a fuss at this stage, as all Dora wanted was to get married, plain and simple.

The next two months sped by. With no Arthur on the scene, Dora was completely at the mercy of her mother and the dressmaker. Visiting the dressmaker in Crynfyn Row was as bad as being on the frontline. Sarah had clear ideas of what a fashionable wedding dress should look like, studying 'Woman and Home', and 'Cambrian News' cuttings of the latest weddings in the area. 'Now Mrs Hopkins these leg of mutton sleeves won't do,-so very dated-Dora must have sleeves in the Gibson style narrowed down and buttoned all the way to the elbow so they come to a point. This is a far better use of material in these times, and there's far too much material in the skirt-smaller gathers to the waist please.

Dora's not small, but she's got a neat waist and needs to show it off to its best advantage.'

'But Mrs Roberts, I've already cut out the pattern like this ---,' Mrs Hopkins would protest, and away they would go scoring points off one another. There was really no contest as Sarah always won. Whether Dora should wear white lace gloves, or whether the veil should be short or to the hip and what about the headdress.

Dora began to wonder whose wedding it was. She knew that Sarah herself had had a very plain unadorned wedding at the local Registry Office. Gran had regaled her with tales of their marriage before the Great War, Jack smart and erect in his Territorial uniform, waiting to go to training camp, and her daughter in her best dress edged with crocheted lace. Florrie and Jack's best friend John Davy had stood up for them and then they'd all gone for a sit down meal at the Queens.

According to Gran, Jack had said in his inimitable way, 'To hell with the expense. My bride deserves to be a guest at this hotel after all the hard work she's put in here.' Later the four of them went on to the Music Hall at the Coliseum to see the shocking sight of Vesta Tilley dressed as a man.

Dora tried her best to be patient about the wedding arrangements, but with her mother imposing her opinion on every detail, not hearing from Arthur regularly, and with lots of little things going wrong, it was difficult not to be apprehensive about the big day.

Then there was another setback as at the very last moment. One of the bridesmaids was taken ill. Dora with a dress half made for the girl, had to have the dress refitted for herself supposedly for a going away dress, though any chances of a honeymoon were practically nil. Thank goodness the other bridesmaid, Mary being a dressmaker, could make her own outfit.

Her mother seemed keen to prove, not just to the neighbours, but to everyone in Aberystwyth that they were 'someone'. Even her father was determined not to miss out and was in his element, seeing it as a chance to call in favours from old mates and wanting his daughter to have the very best day possible though this also meant inviting many of his cronies to the wedding.

He said to his wife, 'I'll talk to old Davies at the Talbot. He'll do us a good spread, and Pickford will take the photos. Of course I'll do the flowers. We'll need a car for the bride. Everyone else can walk from the Wesleyan to the Talbot. Is there anything else?'

'There's the cake', Sarah added. 'Dora and I can make a plain cake. I'll get Sian at the Bakery to ice it. It'll just be the one layer though. We'll have to make use of those cardboard tiers and pillars, to make it look the part.'

Dora was thankful that her parents had thrown themselves into all the preparations, but as usual she felt pushed to the side, as if it none of it had anything to do with her. Twenty four people had been invited to the reception, most of whom were Jack and Sarah's friends and acquaintances. Dora thought about all her friends from Chapel, the Drama Society, and the Guides, all of whom meant so much to her and wished that she could have at least invited a few of them. But after all she wasn't paying. She was only allowed Mary, one other friend, Arthur's father and two brothers, and of course his best man.

Protesting weakly on one occasion she said to her mother, 'It would be nice to have some of the Guides or some people from the chapel don't you think?' The only response she got from her mother was, 'Your father's got a business remember, so he needs to invite some of his best customers, and as for my friends, you've grown up with them. You can hardly expect me to leave them out.'

Dora wondered whether things would change once she was a married woman. Perhaps her parents would stop treating her like a child or a possession. Maybe she would have more say though she doubted it.

It would have been so much better to have married in peacetime, and been able to set up a home with Arthur straight away. But it was never going to happen at this time. How long would she have to wait for that? Both her parents were such strong personalities and with Arthur away at war, what chance did she have to lead a different life?

Even with Arthur's army pay, Dora saw no chance of affording to live anywhere else unless she could find a job, but what could she do in terms of work? She was only trained for domestic work. At this time women were taking over more and more of the men's' jobs but what could she offer in the way of skills and what if Arthur didn't come back? Sometimes Dora felt very much on her own against the world, questioning whether it would have been any different if her real mother had been around. Then of course everything would have been altered and she might not have met Arthur.

Of course, the changes to come were exciting but also frightening and then again would they transform her daily life that much? With a slight shiver Dora forced herself to be positive. Maybe, this was just a case of wedding jitters? It was only a week till the wedding and then she'd be Arthur's wife. Dora made up her mind to focus on taking good care of her new husband and making sure that he always knew how much he was loved. There was nothing else to concern herself with for the moment. Let everything else happen as it may.

23

The Big Day

'Dora, you're going to have to wear that long sleeved chemise under your dress to keep you warm, it's such a sharp day.'

Dora thought she was still asleep. Surely her mother wasn't still going on about that dreaded chemise, or perhaps she'd heard it so many times now that it had permeated her dreams. Wasn't it her wedding day? She must have nodded off to sleep again. Jumping out of bed, Dora tiptoed across the freezing boards and peered through the curtains. This couldn't be March weather surely, it was more like January. At any rate there was a tiny glimpse of sun and not a spot of rain in sight.

Breathing a sigh of relief Dora felt the beginnings of nervous tremors in her stomach. Sitting at the dressing table she tried to calm herself, but suddenly catching sight of a shadow in the corner of her eye she started involuntarily, saying, 'Mom, I'm just coming,' then became aware she was talking to her own wedding dress hanging on the wardrobe door. Its white figured satin folds seemed eerily to have a life of its own; gleaming in the early morning light–satin shoes lined up beneath-beckoning her towards her new life.

'Dora, you need to be down here and having your breakfast. We can't have you fainting in front of the minister.' This time it really was her mother at the door her voice sounding strident and edgy.

Trying on the orange blossom headdress and billowing veil, Dora looked at herself in the mirror, hardly believing that she would be a grown up married lady by this time tomorrow.
She didn't appear to look any different. Shaking herself and trying to bring herself back to reality, Dora wondered how Arthur was feeling.

He'd only arrived the night before. At one time they thought he'd never make it. The Army had waited till the very last minute to turn down his application for leave. Then with Arthur and the whole of no.8 panicking, the Army chaplain had intervened, getting him an emergency 48 hour pass.

Downstairs Sarah was more abrupt than ever, 'Don't forget that chemise, or you'll catch your death.'

Inwardly Dora felt she was on fire. Her whole body was steaming despite the weather. How on earth was she to fit that bulky woollen garment under such fine satin, surely every bulge would show. Wasn't she hot enough already. But it was no good arguing especially today.

After breakfast, getting ready took no time at all as Dora's hair had been permed weeks before, a present from Auntie Annie, so there was only the dressing. Sarah kept fussing about saying she should help, but in the end Jack hustled her along saying, 'Sis, you've done all you can – off to the chapel now. Leave the poor girl some breathing room. Mary will sort Dora out.'

Her bridesmaid took one look at the dreaded chemise and said, 'Definitely not–not on your wedding day even if you freeze to death. You look pale though. I'll give you a touch of makeup.'

'I don't think they'll approve,' Dora protested, 'Dada hates what he calls 'war paint'. He thinks it's only for floozies not decent women.'

'Dora you're a grown woman just about to get married, a little colouring is neither here nor there.' Mary carefully made up Dora's face with a minimum of face crème, powder and lip rouge, blending some of the rouge into her cheeks.

'There I'm done, it's only a very slight touch, they won't be any the wiser.'

Dora could hear her father calling up the stairs, 'Are you ready Dora? Everyone's gone to the chapel .The car's here. We should make a start.'

Jack never appreciated being kept waiting and was always running on military time. Standing ramrod straight at the bottom of the main staircase, he looked up and beamed from ear to ear when he saw her. Dora herself thought she'd never seen such a lovely sight, his weathered face cracked into a thousand wrinkles. For a moment, she thought she glimpsed a stray tear but it was brushed away and gone instantly.

'Dora, you look a picture, and so beautiful. I'm so proud to walk my daughter down the aisle on her wedding day.' Dora loved the sound of 'my daughter'. It was something she never heard enough perhaps this was recognition at last. Taking his arm, they paraded towards the car-Dora holding on tightly as well as clutching the shower bouquet of pink and white carnations, he'd made that morning.

With Mary in the front seat when they reached Shiloh Chapel, her father told the driver, 'Go round the block again we don't want to be too early.' Passing Shiloh for a second time he said, 'Well Dora–now's the time if you want to change your mind or you're not sure — we can always go home.'

Dora was shocked, 'No Dada, I am sure, I've never been as sure of anything in my life. I'm marrying Arthur today and that's that,' she said with resolve.

It seemed for a second as if her father sighed heavily and looked a trifle downcast but maybe she was imagining it. 'That's my girl. You'll make Arthur a fine wife. He's lucky to have you. There's no doubting that.'

The ceremony itself was plain and simple. The only break in the seriousness of the occasion being a subdued titter of laughter when Jack Hargett the best man rummaging around in his pockets for the rings–produced a gold sweet wrapper instead. He was such a joker sometimes, Dora was never sure whether he'd done this on purpose to ease the solemnity of it all, or it had really been a mistake. Finally with a show of his usual audacity, he located the rings and placed them on the minister's outstretched Bible.

The only other break in the ceremony that gave Dora pause for thought, was when the minister asked the congregation 'is there anyone here present who knows why these persons may not be married, declare it now? '

Dora felt her stomach tighten, and for a second anxiously waited to see if anything from her past would surface. But the service moved on, and she gave a great sigh of relief, feeling the reassuring grip of Arthur's hand.

The minister finally pronounced them man and wife saying, 'You can kiss your wife now, Arthur,' and with Arthur gently pecking her on the corner of her mouth, it was soon over.

Dora's friend Henry Miles from the Drama Society boomed out her favourite 'Trumpet Voluntary' on the organ, whilst the bride and groom processed down the aisle, husband and wife at last. The two of them stood on the steps of the Wesleyan, Arthur blushing and proud in his uniform, his forage cap at just the right angle with Dora in her beautiful figured satin. Guests showered them with rice, calling out – 'Go on Arthur kiss your bride again,' knowing he would be too shy and self conscious. But Dora didn't mind in the least. It was such fun being the centre of attention for once and turning her head she kissed him thoroughly herself.

Hardly believing they were married and laughing together, they rushed off to the photographers.

Dora could hardly contain her fits of giggles, as old Pickford tried to get her new husband to smile, 'Go on smile Arthur, this isn't an execution!' Dora gave him a quick peck on the cheek. He was so red by now that the old photographer quipped, 'It's lucky this is in black and white.'

Then it was on to the reception. To Dora's complete surprise, her Guides formed a Guard of Honour to greet them on their arrival at the Talbot. Dora was touched they'd made such an effort, 'Arthur here's my Penparcau pack, what a surprise!'

'Miss Roberts, we meant to be at the Wesleyan, but you were too quick and we missed you. Your mother suggested we catch up with you here.'

'Thanks so much girls, but no more Miss Roberts, this is my new husband. I'm Mrs Hamer now.'

Dora could hardly believe she was 'Mrs Hamer' and a wife. Was this what it was like to be a grown up? It seemed only yesterday that she was running full pelt down Baker Street with her plaits flying out behind her, but this wasn't a day for looking back. Today was such an important occasion, hers and Arthur's special time to enjoy and make the most of it as who knew when they'd see one another again.

Jack and Sarah had gallantly found lemonade and cake for fourteen excitable little Guides, and included them in the celebration. The wedding party presided with panache at the top table as Arthur's best man Jack and his brother Eddie took turns to read out the telegrams. Dora was thrilled to hear from so many of the summer visitors and all the Birmingham crowd – the Sims from Belcher Lane, The Jeffries from Smethwick, Stroud Green and all eight of the Thorpes from Nottingham. It was so unexpected to be remembered by so many old friends from the past.

Then Eddie with his usual easy charm moved on to give the toast, 'The beautiful bride and her groom.'

Arthur by now even more of a blush, stammered a response trying manfully to start with 'My wife and I', whilst the whole room erupted in clapping and cheering. Guests congratulated them on their pluck for embarking on marriage at such a difficult time. Everyone was enjoying themselves, even Sarah managing to raise a smile or two and Jack was well away with his old comrades telling jokes and laughing fit to burst. It was a chance for everyone to take a break from the war.

With the constraints of war there was no room for dancing or even music but Dora's heart was beating to its own rhythm.
She felt whole at last with someone of her own and was constantly touching Arthur's hand to make sure he was real. Leaning across talking to his youngest brother Bobby, he fleetingly looked back at her smiling and mouthing 'you alright?' and she immediately felt protected and loved.

Later in the evening something came about that threatened to tarnish that happiness. Dora had noticed that Arthur's father had had little to say all day. He had spent most of the time with Jack though they had little in common. When he saw she was on her own, Mr Hamer came over, 'I am pleased Dora, that Arthur's married you. Mar' Jane is so happy too, and sorry she couldn't come because of her leg.' Dora smiled back, delighted to have satisfied her new in-laws. But there was more to come.

'It's the first sensible thing Arthur's ever done. I've tried my best with him. I got him a job as a telegraph boy with the Post Office when he first left school. That would have given him the start of a good career, but he got stranded in the blizzards and I had to take over his delivery. Then he got a dead end job as a grocery assistant job at the Star in Llanidloes himself and transferred here. The boy's got absolutely no ambition or drive. You do realise he'll never make anything of himself.'

Dora could hardly believe her ears that someone's actual parent could talk so badly of their son. It was difficult to show anger with other guests within earshot but she wasn't going to have her new husband derided like that and retorted, 'He's a gentle, decent man, fighting for his country. He works hard and I love him. You should be ashamed of yourself, talking about one of your sons in that way,' and turning her back on Mr Hamer, Dora walked off.

Dora thought about whether she should say something to Arthur but noticing that he and his father hardly spoke, she decided to forget all about the conversation. Why was it that families were so difficult? Surely there were some families somewhere who got on and loved one another? Anyway she was going to make sure, when she had her family that they were all close and loving.

At last the day came to an end. Dora had found it exhilarating but hadn't realised how tired she was. Her face muscles ached after all the smiling and her head throbbed, where the headdress had dug into her scalp. It was hard to believe after all that planning it was over so fast. Once everyone had said their goodbyes and good lucks, there was nothing for it but for her and Arthur to return with Jack and Sarah to Baker St, with no honeymoon in sight.

'I'm so sorry Dora, this wasn't the way I wanted our wedding to end,' Arthur said, 'we should have had more time together. I could have watted you away in that beautiful blue suit you'd bought.'

Dora was disappointed about the leave but said reassuringly, 'Arthur, we'll have all the time in the world one day to be together. Let's enjoy ourselves as much as we can.' Their first night as a newly married couple was spent at the cinema watching 'Waterloo Bridge', and going back to Baker St for cocoa and an early night, with Arthur leaving for the Battery early the next morning.

Dora was understandably nervous about their first night together as Sarah had always insinuated that Dora's real mother's morals and behaviour were questionable but with no further explanation. There'd been a lot of talk over the years about Dora being a 'good girl' but nothing about what that meant, or any clarification about the facts of life. Dora lying expectantly in bed in her pristine handmade laced nightdress earnestly hoped her new husband knew more than she did. However she needn't have worried as on this first night Arthur seemed content to just hold her, whilst they fell into an exhausted sleep together.

Two weeks later Arthur rang, 'Dora, you'll never believe it. They've given me a fortnight's leave. Trust the Army. I'll be back in Aber on Friday- so perhaps we can go away for a few days, maybe go home to Llani. What do you think?'

Dora was over the moon. After the fuss of the wedding it had been a bit of an anti-climax not to enjoy the start of married life together. Though her father-in-law's words had left a bitter taste in her mouth she had become very fond of her mother-in-law. Knowing that Arthur would be eager to see his mother, she wrote her to tell her the news. Mary Jane replied with a beautiful letter inviting them to stay and was avid for news of the wedding.

A week later sitting comfortably in the back kitchen at High Street exchanging wedding gossip over cups of tea with Mary Jane, Dora looked at her new mother-in-law's kind face full of love and interest and thought why isn't my relationship with my mother like this, so easy, cosy and comfortable?' But there wasn't an answer; however many times Dora asked herself the question.

INDEPENDENCE

24

1941 - Joining the War

Not long after their wedding, Dora knew she was going to have to play some part in the War whether she liked it or not. It was becoming more and more probable that conscription for women would become compulsory. Rationing was well under way – they were even taking down the railings from Bethel Chapel opposite, to be melted down and recycled for tanks.

During this time Arthur was waiting to be posted overseas and all leave had been cancelled, so Dora wasn't likely to see him for some time. Being a newly 'married' woman made Dora think about her new status. Did she really want to go back to the life she had before the wedding, and reconcile herself to just being a daughter living with her parents, and not a wife living with her new husband. Everyone had to make sacrifices at this time – but why oh why did it have to be her and Arthur? It really wasn't fair.

Weighing up the possibilities, Dora thought at first that she might find work in one of the munitions factories in the Midlands, despite the fact her parents thought she was mad to even consider it.

Sarah would say, 'Jack, I can't see why you can't pull a few strings to get Dora into some reserved occupation and then she could stay at home. A lot of your mates are doing that for their daughters.'

'I couldn't possibly do that, Sis,' replied Jack, who would never dream of being swayed when it came to any sort of preferential treatment for his nearest and dearest, especially when it came to the honour of serving one's country. 'I must say I'm not in favour of the munitions factory, Sis either.

163

I know they earn good money – but they deserve it, it's extremely dangerous work. Dora'll just have to make her own mind up- whether it's that or the Services.'

In the next weeks, Dora joined a group of women bussed over to Birmingham for a tour of one of the factories. If any of the women decided to work there, they were to be billeted in a local hostel. The wages were astounding – far more then the meagre pocket money Dora earned in Baker Street. But before they even entered the main factory, the noise hit her in waves of drumming reverberating through her head. This factory was making tanks and the foreman showed them the machines they would work on to make the parts.

Taking them outside to the factory yard to get away from the din, he addressed them all 'We are doing good work here, valuable work for the War. You ladies could learn skills which would stand you in good stead for the future, as we don't know how many of our brave lads will return. Who's going to be the first to sign up then?'

Dora could barely hear him though they were outside. She wondered how she'd ever cope with that level of noise every day, having already being deafened by it. No, it definitely wasn't for her; all the money in the world couldn't make up for losing your hearing. Refusing to sign any papers, she determinedly got back on the bus, ready for the long journey home.

There was still plenty of work at Baker Street with her mother and the few lodgers left, some of whom were going to be there for the duration of the war. Her father was now splitting his time between the Garden and the newly formed Home Guard, so there was plenty for Dora to do as well as knitting endless socks for the Red Cross and rolling bandages.

But soon there would be no choice. Married women without children were to be called up next.

Dora decided it was probably better to 'bite the bullet' and volunteer before conscription became compulsory but the options certainly weren't great. There was the W.R.N.S(rather elite),the A.T.S (deemed rather common),the W.A.A.F(with nothing vaguely relating to flying),the Land Army(girls in breeches working as farmhands),or the Women's' Voluntary Service(with most 'plum' positions already allocated locally to so-called pillars of the community).

As it turned out, once Dora had registered at the Aberystwyth Labour Exchange, she was offered nothing but the W.A.A.F and that was it. Shyly she suggested, 'Perhaps I could apply to become a Physical Instructor. I've got this letter of reference from the YWCA and I've done a lot of P.T.' The woman in charge took a cursory look at the letter and immediately dismissed it out of hand, 'The majority of your experience seems to be in cooking and cleaning and there's plenty of scope for that in the kitchens.'

Dora groaned inwardly, not more cooking – would she never escape Baker Street. It wasn't as if she felt any great urge to serve her country, but at the very least they could provide her with more prospects than cooking up great vats of custard and gravy again. Memories of her childhood indoctrination to those two wonderful liquids were coming back to haunt her.

Even joining the W.A.A.F had its drawbacks. Everything in Britain at this time revolved round matters of identity, the correct paperwork and the bureaucracy that had to be followed to the letter. As if, out of nowhere the sorry question of Dora's birth reared its ugly head yet again-and the question of her non-existent Birth Certificate. Dora had presented her Marriage Certificate to a rather officious clerk but no, this wasn't enough as she must also produce a full Birth Certificate.

'But I haven't such a thing,' Dora protested.

'You have to have the right documentation,' she was told, 'there's no question of you joining any of the Services without it. You could be an enemy alien for all I know.'

'Don't be silly,' Dora gasped 'Do I look like an enemy alien to you? You know me, at least you know my father Jack Roberts. He's in the Legion with you, and we live up the road in Baker Street.'

'I'm sorry Mrs Hamer, all I know is I have to follow the system, or where would we be?' The clerk softened slightly, 'Bring your Certificate back next week and I'll move you to the head of the queue.'

'But honestly,' Dora pleaded, 'I really don't have such a Certificate? Where can I get one or who can I ask?' But there was no help forthcoming and the clerk moved on towards his next victim.

By now, Dora was nearly in tears. What was she to do? The Wesleyan Minister hadn't even asked for such piece of paper when he'd married her. Of course he'd known her since she was a child and wouldn't have realised that her name wasn't her own, just Sarah's made-up one and not her rightful one at that. Well, she'd been married as 'Dora Roberts' so possibly even her marriage wasn't legal. Who knew? She couldn't bear to think about that now but what was she to do about her existing dilemma?

Back at Baker Street and wondering how to broach the subject with her mother, Dora decided it would be wiser to wait till her father came home. Once they were all sitting round the tea table, Dora said, 'I went to register for the Services today.'

'How did you get on?' Sarah enquired.

'They offered me the W.A.A.F?'

166

'That's good Dora, they'd be lucky to have you,' said her father.

'There's a problem though Dada, a serious problem. Before I can be signed up I must produce a full Birth Certificate.'

There was sudden quiet and Dora's statement was left hanging in the silence. The three of them avoided catching one another's eye. Jack was completely nonplussed, clearing his throat and gazing at his plate.

Sarah for once seemed shaken and for once shamefaced, her words spilling out in a rush, 'I'm so sorry Dora–there really wasn't much paperwork to be found when your mother disappeared all those years ago. Any old records I got from the Workhouse later I put on the fire as I didn't think you'd ever need them. There seemed no point in keeping anything as you were going to live with us and be our daughter. I do know there was no sign of a proper Birth Certificate and took it for granted your mother had never bothered to register your birth.'

This was the first Dora had heard about there being any papers of any kind. Neither of them had mentioned anything like that, when they'd first told her at eighteen. What if there'd been an address for her mother or another family member, Dora might have been able to track them down, and find out why she'd been discarded in such a way.

Jack, always trying his best to help and seeing the glisten of tears in Dora's eyes, reached over and patted her hand, 'I'll make some enquiries cariad in the next few days and find out who you can contact about all this. Take heart I'm sure we can find a solution.'

Her father, true to his word, managed to find the name of the local Registrar at the County Offices in the old Queens Hotel building.

'Dora I've made an appointment for you to see this chap Thomas Davies. He's supposed to be a bit of an expert in the area of Births, Marriages and Deaths. Perhaps he can shed some light on this. Do you want me or your mother to come with you?'

Dora noted that Sarah didn't seem at all keen to go with her and thought it might be best to do this on her own. 'No, Dada, I'll be fine.' Her father was so well known in the town, it might be embarrassing for him if people found out that she wasn't his real daughter.

The Registrar was a kind man, and once he'd listened to her halting explanation of her birth he reassured her saying, 'Don't worry Mrs Hamer there are many people in the same boat as you. Years ago, no one worried about official paperwork. Often relatives took in next of kin children without notifying the authorities at all. Leave it with me and I'll do some investigations and see what I can find out.'

In the days that followed, Dora found herself more and more preoccupied with her early life, trying to understand how a mother could desert her child and leave her with complete strangers. It was something Dora herself would never do however hard things might become; her children would be everything to her and she was determined to give them the best possible life.

Back at the Registrar's a week later, Mr Davies smiled broadly at her, 'Come in, Mrs Hamer and take a seat. I think I might have some good news for you.' Dora felt some signs of hope after her soul searching week.

'Yes,' he said consulting his papers, 'I've been successful. Your real family name 'Goules' is so unusual I was able to trace an entry for your baptism on June 30th 1915 at Llandre Church. Do you understand what this means?' he queried, looking quite elated.

Dora had no idea what he was getting at.

Seeing her puzzlement Mr Davies explained, 'Your parents must have married properly or a Welsh Church wouldn't have allowed anyone illegitimate to be christened, that means you're legal and you'll have been registered at birth. With these details, I can send to London for your Birth Certificate,' and with a flourish, he presented her with a paper with details of her baptism signed and certified by him.

Dora didn't know what to think and felt absolutely stunned; whenever Dora had thought about her birth mother at all, it was always along the lines that the woman had got pregnant, been unmarried, abandoned by the father, and then dumped her baby. Sarah had always been in the background, implying that Dora might end up the same way as her unmarried mother, and hinting that Dora was no doubt a bastard.

A great sense of relief rolled over Dora. She might not know her real mother but she was legitimate, had an official place in the world and a certificate to prove it. She felt like shouting it from the rooftops.

If only Arthur was there to share this, though he'd probably not have been that perturbed. Having roots and a family lineage himself, he found it hard to understand how Dora had always suffered about her questionable beginnings. At long last Dora felt like a butterfly emerging from a dark cocoon, to be a person in her own right with nothing to hold her back or be ashamed of.

'I'm so grateful Mr Davies, for all your trouble. I can't tell you how much this means to me.'

'Off with you young lady,' he laughed delightedly, 'I'm glad to have helped.'

169

On her way back up the Promenade, Dora wondered what she was going to tell them at home. An edited version would be best. There was no point in going into all the details or to enlighten her mother about the baptism and her legitimacy. As long as she herself knew who really she was that, nothing else mattered. Just telling them that she was able to get a Birth Certificate would be enough. Then of course, there would be the W.A.A.F to look forward to and another getaway from Baker Street!

25

1941 - Life in the W.A.A.F

Once initiated into the W.A.A.F, Dora was dismayed to find the experience not at all to her liking. It had seemed the lesser of evils when she had joined up after all she was used to wearing a uniform with the Guides, marching and doing things 'by the book'. But this was something different. There were so many petty rules to be aware of and so many jumped up officers who thought their rank placed them next to 'God'.

The only advice Arthur had proffered was, 'to keep your head down, and never volunteer.' It was alright for him, he was an old hand at all this saluting and square bashing. The summers he'd done in the Territorials had stood him in good stead. Dora wished she'd been able to see him before leaving for Cardiff, but his unit was still readying to leave for overseas.

For once both her parents were there at Aberystwyth station to see her off on that hot August day in 1941. Her father proud as punch said, 'They'll soon recognise your officer potential, Dora. This is a great day. You'll be a corporal before you know it.'

'Honestly Dada, I'm quite happy to remain an Aircraftwoman, I really don't want to order people around.'

Dora was afraid she was never going to measure up to her father's exacting military standards, whereas her mother always the realist said, 'Just do your best Dora,' and with her usual sting in the tail, 'do be careful who you make friends with and who you confide in and trust,' but finishing more reassuringly with, 'the war will be over soon enough and then you can get back to normal life with Arthur.'

Arriving on the bus at St Athans, Dora and the other raw recruits were rushed through the medicals and on to the line up for uniforms.

Two grumpy male sergeants catering for all the shapes and sizes, shouted out in turns, 'Move along, there move along.' Using rough estimates of build and size they matched the women as best they could. There was no chance for pleading for better fittings or any form of special requirements.

The sergeants hands on hips, would mimic the smarter city girls who looked in disgust at what they were given, prancing about on tip toes and saying sarcastically, 'We don't do posh here your ladyship, you'll have to consult your tailor.' In next to no time, each recruit was piled high with air force blue great coats, uniform coats, skirts, shirts, ties, caps, shoes, polishing materials and the obligatory gas mask.

There was no time to chat or even make a friend. NCOs herded everyone into groups and straight into the Nissan huts and dormitories. By now it was late in the evening and with no hot food forthcoming except wilted cheese sandwiches and builder tea, there was nothing for it but to go to bed.

The beds were definitely not intended for comfort. Basic iron bedsteads with three horsehair 'biscuits' (blocks lined up as mattresses),freezing cold calico sheets, three gray blankets that had seen better days and pillows filled with straw. Trying to sleep with sixteen women in one room was never going to be easy. There was the snoring, the grinding of teeth and of course the muted sobbing from the youngest who'd never left home before. Dora herself felt close to tears as she tried to warm up her ice block feet and to think this was the height of summer. Oh for the luxury and warmth of those enormous feather beds in Baker Street, she'd never complain again about all that daily turning and shaking.

Before Dora knew it, it was 6am and Reveille. 'Rise and Shine you lazy lot,' shouted the corporal, 'twelve minutes for showering and dressing- then line up here for breakfast and no time for gossiping.'

The ablutions were outside in an open ended hut, just a stand-in shower and a few basins with barely enough time to splash water on the appropriate areas as they struggled into the unfamiliar uniforms. The pants were enormous from knees to chest and there was much amusement about being drowned in pants. Skirts had to be sixteen inches exactly from the ground, and ties were an unknown quantity to most. At least Dora had experience tying ties, and helped out where she could.

Under the corporal's beady eye, they formed a wavy uncertain line and were promptly marched down to breakfast. 'Get plenty of stodge inside you girls,' she warned, 'you'll be glad of it later.'

One of the girls next to Dora whispered, 'My name's Cathy, what's yours? What do you think of it so far?'

'I'm Dora. I don't know yet.' Trying to see the positive, she added, 'I expect we'll get used to it once they stop shouting and know what we're supposed to do.'

She was rapidly to regret her words. The day ground on and on, consisting of hour after hour of marching up and down the parade ground, turning first right, then left, then at attention, then at ease. There was always someone out of step or moving in the wrong direction. Keeping hands and feet in time caused near fatalities, with arms bumping heads and noses behind, and feet kicking insteps in front. The new shoes squeaked and rubbed in unimaginable places.

Cathy, who was next to her mumbled out of the corner of her mouth, 'I'll never stand all this.'

'Me neither, I could certainly do with a sit down,' said Dora. To think she'd been so proud to be marching with the Guides in Aberystwyth on Remembrance Sunday. Now she realised how poor their efforts had been.

'No talking in the ranks, eyes front. Stand to attention for the officer.'

By the end of the day, they could hardly wait to be dismissed before chasing off to find bowls of hot water and salts to soak their feet. The days seemed to merge into weeks for Dora. Finally when the squad was thoroughly miserable, exhausted and beaten down they made it to the passing out parade and leave and postings. Escaping back to Aberystwyth for a few days, it was bliss to sleep in a proper bed and enjoy home cooking.

Jack was beside himself with pride walking round with his uniformed daughter, though Dora would have much preferred being in civvies. 'Dora, you must stay in uniform after all you volunteered. Be proud to be 'doing your bit' in the Services, and not a 'conchi'.'

'Don't be silly, Jack,' said her mother, 'not everyone is as keen as you to get into uniform. Now Dora's home she should relax and wear her own clothes. Soon enough, she'll have to do all this ridiculous saluting, bowing and scraping to some jumped up little NCO with a chest full of medals who's never been near any sort of war.' For once it was good to have Sarah's backing.

Dora would laugh to herself about her parents' varying wartime viewpoints. They both vividly remembered the Great War. Whereas Jack had relished and sentimentalised the comradeship, the heat and dust of the Sudan never affecting his love of all things military; Sarah on the other hand, had seen the aftermath of it all and the terrible toll it had taken on soldiers' broken bodies, minds and families.

Dora did so wish though that Arthur could see her in her full uniform. It was true that her parents were being very supportive at the moment, but it could never be the same as coming home to an adoring husband.

Jack and Sarah seemed to be proud of her despite showing it differently, and adult life with them seemed far easier than when she was younger. But Dora still felt like an intruder in their lives–always on the outside of their relationship–a bit like a 'cuckoo in the nest'–a kind of add–on.

Dora wrote to Arthur every day but it was hard not sharing the small moments of their daily lives. On receipt of the latest photograph of her in uniform, he wrote back teasingly, 'I don't think you're supposed to wear your cap at that angle, Dora – you look more like a bus conductress. Trust you to make the uniform your own. The W.A.A.F will never tame you though they might have a very good try.'

Returning to St Athans again was a wrench particularly to a posting in the kitchens, cooking with great aluminium drums, and gallons of the 'orrible custard and gravy. It was a salutary lesson for Dora remembering how much she'd complained about all the cooking in Baker St. That would be child's play now. If there were such a place as heaven and hell then she must be in hell's waiting room, Dora would think, as she dropped exhausted into her bunk at night. Her dreams were full of floating seas of gelatinous browns and yellows.

The only bonus was that she'd made friends with Cathy who was working with her. Occasionally when they were delegated to work in the officers' mess kitchen, she would whisper to Dora, 'Let's make life a bit more interesting, shall we?' and together they would swop round the sugar and the salt–so nothing tasted right. The furore it caused delighted them both whilst they stood smugly by, looking the pictures of innocence.

They even went as far as doctoring some of the less pleasant NCOs' meals with powdered laxatives. This however had far more serious repercussions with the whole of the kitchen staff lined up and threatened.

One of the Warrant Officers strode up and down barking and screaming, 'I'm going to find out who's responsible and when I do they won't know what's hit them. They'll be on jankers and suffer till the day they die, mark my words.' But nothing came of it no one ever gave them away. The kitchen staff looked after their own each one smirking and giggling at the officer's impotent rage.

Despite the fun and the friendship Dora felt frustrated, wasn't there a more worthwhile role for her in this war? She'd already spent sixteen years of her life so far slaving away in a kitchen. Why couldn't she do something more exciting like parachuting into occupied France, or plotting map positions - or even a cushy job sitting in an office answering telephones would be acceptable.

Determined to escape the toil of catering, Dora searched and searched for alternative postings. Finally she got lucky. There was an opening for a bat woman to an officer. Of all places it was in Harrogate – hopeless for getting back to Aber, but very near to Arthur, who kept being moved round the country. She was so excited and couldn't wait to tell him.

'I don't know, Dora, we're still waiting to be posted overseas, it seems to drag on and on. Is it a good idea to come all this way when I mightn't be here long?'

Dora felt deflated to receive such a 'wet blanket' response, 'It's too late Arthur, the posting's already gone through, and I can't do anything about it.' Sometimes it was hard in their relationship when she was always the enthusiast and he the pessimist.

Perhaps once the war was over things would be easier, and they would balance one another out.

Trying not to be discouraged Dora plodded on, 'At least we'll have a little time together and I'm finally escaping the kitchen, still having to do cleaning and housekeeping of course, but nowhere near as much as at Baker Street,' doggedly she added, 'I'm so looking forward to seeing you and Yorkshire and a change of scenery.'

26

A Posting to Harrogate

'Atten- shun!' the voice boomed.

Dora shot to her feet, looking down from her superior height of 5 foot 3 and a half inches on to the sandy haired head of the miniature warrant officer. He was busy pulling himself up to his whole four foot nothing, as if his spine had any more stretch in it and putting on a pair of clean white gloves, 'Ready for inspection, Aircraftwoman Hamer?'

Dora took a pace or two back whilst he busied himself with running gloved fingers along wainscotings, and the backs of cupboard humming to himself. Reaching the six foot wardrobe he looked up and hesitated then continued pompously, 'I take it you've cleaned thoroughly up there.' He gestured with his head.

Dora could hardly conceal a grin, as she meekly proffered a chair. She could hear him grinding his teeth, and continued to bite down hard on her lip, whilst he hauled himself on to the wonky legged chair. He still had difficulty leaning over the front parapet of the wardrobe to reach the back, all the time the chair creaking ominously under his weight. Dora felt a bubble of laughter rising from her stomach, and had to quickly turn away to control it.

Getting off the chair, he landed heavily on the floor trying to suppress a barely muffled groan.
Dora bent her head to look down at him. He knew he'd been bested, but he said gruffly, 'Good job, keep it up, we'll make a corporal of you yet!' Heavens above, Dora thought inwardly, not if I can help it.

However the new job had its perks. At least now she could work independently. Of course being the Services, there was always a price to pay.

Her officer was no trouble, a kind mature woman who was grateful for any little thing but Dora had also inherited this miniature warrant officer who was on her trail day and night trying to catch her out. He wasn't a major problem just an annoying mosquito she had to flick out of the way every so often. Years of 'ducking and diving' around her mother had helped.

One of the other perks of being in Harrogate was being able to meet up with Arthur after so long and they managed to wangle a few days leave together.

Visiting nearby Knaresborough and Mother Shipton's Cave, Arthur said, 'I wonder what she would have prophesied about the war, if it will ever end and if we can get back to some sort of normal life?

'I don't know love. There seems to be no chance of that at the moment. I suppose we'll have to make the most of every second we spend together.' Yet there was never enough time.

Trying to get back home to Aber was no joke either, as most of a forty eight pass was spent getting there. Her father wrote regularly keeping her in touch with things at home since Sarah had recently injured her right hand.
Dora couldn't help but giggle when she received Jack's latest epistle as he seemed to be spending his time in the Garden talking to everyone who knew Harrogate and trying to find things for her to do in her time off, as if she was there on holiday!

Her father's letters were so meticulous with their carefully looped handwriting and quaint back to front English that she missed him more than she knew. It was if he was right there talking to her and she could touch his arm and tease him gently.

'It's a very funny thing Dora, how small the world is. To the garden the other day came an elderly lady ordering a wreath to be sent to her solicitors in Harrogate to be put on her sister's grave. She is living on the Buarth, you know Dora, Mrs Lloyd Jones' old house,' and then later in the same letter, 'I mentioned you were at Harrogate and she said her brother owns the Grand Hotel – but the family have moved out now and live in a house nearby called 'Little Grand' – perhaps you might visit them and tell them about their sister in Aberystwyth.'

There were more suggestions of the same type in the letter, Dora wondered how he managed to get any work done but she knew it was genuinely meant and he was doing his best to stop her missing home.

Unpredictably and inadvertently a chance came to get back to Baker St. In the early hours of one morning Dora found herself being shaken awake by one of the officers, 'Hamer, wake up. Quickly and quietly get dressed and come through to the office.' Wondering what all the fuss was about and worrying in case something had happened to Arthur, Dora presented herself in the office.

With no explanation the officer gave her a telegram. Instantly Dora's heart dropped. First of all she could hardly take it in and then she couldn't make head nor tail of the message,

Come quickly Stop Father dead Stop Funeral Friday Stop Love Arthur Stop'

The colour must have drained out of her face as the officer quickly proffered a chair, and poured her a glass of brandy, 'Put your head between your knees my dear. It's the shock. Try and drink a little, it will help. I'm so sorry, there's never an easy way to break bad news.'

Dora could hardly believe it. Her beloved father dead! Not Jack surely. He was in the peak of fitness when she saw him last, setting out on manoeuvres with the Home Guard and she'd only just finished reading his last letter. Why would the telegram come from Arthur and not her mother? How would Arthur have known? Perhaps they'd contacted him first.

The officer was speaking again and Dora could hardly make out the words, 'Here's the telephone. Call your home. I'll wait outside and then I'll make arrangements for transport it's Aberystwyth isn't it?'

Dora nodded numbly. She rang Baker St in dread. The telephone was answered almost immediately, 'Baker Street 350, Jack Roberts speaking.' Dora was stunned, not able to speak. Her father's impatient voice continued, 'Is there anyone there, is there anyone there?'

Finally she was able to stammer out, 'Dada it's me Dora- are you alright? Are you alright? What's happened?'

'I'm fine Dora. Nothing's happened – are your ringing about your next leave?'

Dora quickly pulling her wits together realised that the telegram was not about her own father but about Arthur's. She shook herself, and very quietly said, 'Arthur's father's died. There's been a telegram. I think I may be coming home today. I'll let you know the train time later.'

'I'm so sorry bach,' Jack said, 'but we'll be glad to see you all the same.'

Almost as soon as she'd replaced the receiver the officer was back telling her that she'd arranged everything. Without another word, Dora was bundled into the back of a lorry, equipped with special warrants to get her back to Aber.

With a week's leave in her pocket, it seemed ungrateful to tell them it really wasn't her father who'd died, as they would never have considered compassionate leave for an in-law. But it was an opportunity to get back to Aber and even better to see Arthur, though not under the best of circumstances.

Arthur had already arrived in Baker St by the time she got there. They were to stay the night and take the milk train to Llani for the funeral. It was shocking to think that his beloved mother Mary Jane had died only two weeks before and Arthur hadn't been allowed leave to go to the funeral as his company was on manoeuvres. And now it was his father. Taking his mother's death hard, Arthur's suffering showed itself in his face and he looked ill and gaunt.

Dora didn't know what to say or do to comfort him. The only utterance he seemed able to make was, 'I just wish I'd been able to go Mam's funeral.' It was unbelievable that in a matter of weeks he'd lost both parents.

'Had your father been ill?'Dora asked, trying to help her husband release his feelings.

'No, that's the funny thing he was as fit as a flea. Once Mam died he went downhill quickly. My sister Gertie said it started with a bad cold and then it was like he'd given up and that was it. I honestly never thought he loved my mother that much. You know what he was like. When he wasn't working he spent most of his time at the library studying history, and never had time for any of us, but I suppose we don't know what goes on in other peoples' marriages.'

'What about your brothers?'

'Only Bobby's coming, as he's in training. Eddie's unit is being deployed, and Gwen has only just joined the W.R.E.N.S so I don't know. I don't think Eric will bother as there was never much love loss there.'

The chapel funeral in the Wesleyan in Llani was short and sharp with little pomp and ceremony. It was a freezing cold day and the few mourners didn't linger at the burial. Gertie had provided a rationed tea at the house in Great Bridge Street with only a few elderly neighbours and relatives present, as many of the younger cousins had been called up and it was a gloomy gathering. Dora was glad when it was time to leave.

She was worried about Arthur as he'd been so quiet through the service. But back on the train and warming up a bit, he seemed to want to talk. 'Gertie says there's very little money from the house but what there is she'll divide between us. The only other thing of value was the silver tea service but I don't know where that's gone. I'd have liked you to have had it Dora, d'you remember that first time you came to stay and Mam insisted on serving you tea from it? It was her prize possession, and she'd spent all the previous evening polishing it. She'd never done that for anyone else – not even Gertie when she got engaged.'

'It doesn't matter about the tea service, Arthur; I genuinely loved your mother. Do you know, she wrote to me every week after we got engaged as if she was my own mother and was so kind and thoughtful I'll miss her terribly.'

'She thought the world of you too, and was always telling me how lucky I was to find you.'

Dora wished there was some way to console Arthur. It was surprising that his father's death had upset him so much. Understandably, his mother had meant everything to him, but he and his father barely exchanged a word. Perhaps the one shock coming straight after the other had proved too much for him. Wanting to help her husband find something good to think about Dora said reassuringly, 'We've got this week together. You can have a good rest, some sea air and some reasonable food.'

During the week Jack and Sarah tried hard to make him feel at home in Baker Street.

Jack would say, 'Come on Arthur - leave Dora to chat to her mother. Take a turn on the front with me. The beach is all wired off but we can still breathe in some good air. Give you a chance to see the sea before you go back.'

Their time was over before they knew it. Dora just wished Arthur was in a better frame of mind to go back – but at least they were able to travel together as far as Crewe, though having to say goodbye was painful.

27
1941 - Escaping the W.A.A.F

In their week together talking about what they were both doing, Dora said 'I hate the W.A.A.F, in fact I hate the Services altogether. It was bad enough being told what to do by my mother – but at least she had right on her side – this is all petty bureaucracy for no reason. It's hard to believe that we're fighting a war and how desperate things are, when everything military is tied up in such a lot of 'red tape'.

Dora didn't want to tell Arthur about the daily bullying by the warrant officer despite the fact that handling it was child's play However it was becoming wearing.

'Well there's nothing to be done about it, is there,' Arthur responded baldly, 'Neither of us has any choice Dora.'

'Oh but there is,' Dora insisted 'now if I were having a baby, I could come home.'

Arthur looked perplexed, 'But won't they try and keep you, and make arrangements for the baby?'

'No,' said Dora, 'I've found out all about it. The mother has the final decision about staying and I can opt for a discharge, with the WAAF having the option to reenlist me later.'

'I don't know, Dora. What if I don't come back or was severely wounded how would you manage?'

'Women have always managed,' Dora said airily, 'Look at my mother during the last war coping with me, my grandmother, and running a soldiers' convalescent home to boot.'

'But your mother's tough– she wouldn't let anything stand in her way if she wanted to do something.'

Dora prickled, 'Well I'm not exactly a delicate little flower, Arthur. I may not be related by blood to her- but she's certainly shaped me in her mould, and on occasion beaten me into shape.' There was a sudden quiet. Perhaps their mutual upbringings would always be between them. Arthur was used to his kinder softer loving mother who always gave way to her husband, Dora on the other hand had been brought up by two forthright independent parents, never afraid to speak their mind and who ran their own territories, the House and the Garden, in their own way.

No more was said and they both tried to forget about the strains of war and what it was doing to them and their relationship. Dora felt sad to think they were never going to get the time to get used to one another and sort out their minor differences as most young couples were able to do in the early days of a marriage. They would never have this period back. All they could do was to move on to the next stage of their marriage and think about a family.

Dora hoped she'd at least planted a seed in Arthur's mind. Certainly he wasn't keen to leave her with the responsibility of a baby, but then again what if something did happen to him and she was left with nothing.

Strangely enough it had been her mother who had been instrumental in encouraging her to get married soon after war was declared, and who was now the very person suggesting strongly they think about a baby, 'Dora, don't wait. You'll only regret it if you do. Your father and I got married late, practically on the eve of the Great War, and with Jack going overseas, we hardly got used to married life let along think about children.'

Dora kept going over all the conversations in her head. Of course there were doubts about whether it was the right time or not.

But no, she said to herself, I don't want to hear the reasons why not - even if Arthur is still dithering, war or not, we're going to start our family.

The only obstacle now was the fact that Arthur's platoon had already departed, and who knew when he would come back. Of course there was always the very slightest possibility that she was already pregnant perhaps Fate had intervened and decided for them.

Returning to Harrogate and the daily grind of the W.A.A.F, Dora felt terribly unsettled. It was hard getting back into the routine and the silly little warrant officer hadn't improved. He seemed to be on her track morning, noon and night.

There were no letters from Arthur – it was as if he'd dropped off the face of the earth. It was hard to try and rationalise that the post was probably being held up somewhere like Timbuktu and would arrive in bulk one day. Dora felt more tearful than usual. Her normal ebullience seemed to have completely disappeared and she felt tired and listless and quite unlike herself. Finally she was forced to report in sick and the camp doctor – a rather brusque Captain said, 'Well my dear, I'm surprised at you. I would have thought you could have diagnosed yourself.'

'What do you mean?' Dora said fretfully, 'I've no idea what's wrong with me.'

'Put together your tiredness and your emotional state, with the fact that you're a married lady who's recently spent compassionate leave with a husband who's just lost his mother, and what do you have?'

Dora looked blank.

'Bingo, a sympathy baby of course, we see it a lot these days.'

Dora could hardly believe it. She stammered out, 'Am I really going to have a baby? I hadn't got a clue.' It was what she was thinking about regularly but hadn't considered it was going to happen so quickly.

Fate had intervened in the end. Full of elation she sent a cablegram to Arthur hoping it might catch up with him,

'Baby Hamer on way STOP Write soon STOP Love Dora STOP'

Phoning Aberystwyth to tell them the news, there was a rather mixed reception. Sarah, for once, was delighted for her and started talking about crocheting baby clothes but Jack was a lot less happy about the coming event, 'It's a big responsibility Dora. What about the W.A.A.F? You've hardly been in five minutes. Will you be able to carry on?'

Dora didn't want to upset him but thought hang the W.A.A.F this is my ticket out of here and for the best of reasons. Instead she replied in a conciliatory fashion, 'I do have the option to come home Dada. It wouldn't work for me to stay as I don't want my baby brought up in a Service nursery and only be able to see him or her a few hours a day.'

Jack gallantly replied, 'If you've decided Dora, then come home once you've been discharged and you know we'll help as much as we can.'

Dora knew that being the man he was;-in due course he would take it in his stride. Her next battle would be with the W.A.A.F. They were never going to make it easy for her and over the next tedious weeks she was proved right.

On parade each day and getting bigger by the minute, Dora was constantly reprimanded 'Hamer, your coat's unbuttoned, you're not properly dressed. What on earth is that on your waistband?'

'Sorry, ma'am, I'm pregnant and I can't do up my uniform. I've had to add a piece of elastic so that I can button my skirt.'

'How many months are you then?'

'Just two months ma'am.'

The officer grimaced, 'What on earth will you be like in another 3 months? You better see the captain to decide what arrangements you can make-and for goodness sake get a bigger uniform.'

Dora was definitely <u>not</u> going to get a bigger uniform. There was no way she was going to encourage them to keep her. She made an appointment with the captain, buttons popping and seams groaning, as she was marched along the corridor.

'Hamer, we'd like you to stay on. Your record is spotless and your work is up to scratch. Of course, you'd be put on light duties in the office nearer your time. We have good facilities for having you baby on the base and a first rate nursery at your disposal.'

Typical thought Dora – now I'm like this they are going to give me the office job I've hankered for. But there's no way I'm going to have my baby here. Goodness knows how they look after them in the nursery – it would be all routine, spit and polish and little care and love. This is not going to be a W.A.A.F baby but a Hamer one whatever inducements they offer me!

'Thanks you for your offer ma'am – but I have decided to go for a complete discharge.'

'Of course that's your prerogative Hamer but we don't recommend it. We need every fit and able person in this fight. Don't you want to help us win this war? Things are not going well for us and you could make a difference.'

Inwardly Dora was hardly able to control herself at this last statement. If she'd been doing something important for the war effort there might have been a case to answer, but one Aircraftwoman not cleaning an officer's billet was hardly going to make any difference to the Front Line. Smiling inwardly Dora could visualise Hitler's army advancing rapidly forward because she hadn't cleaned the back of that pesky wardrobe. These days, just like the little warrant officer, she could barely lift her expanding body onto the creaky chair to check for dust.

However this was not the time to voice an opinion or answer back, so with head bent meekly but with a firm and insistent voice she requested her discharge. Even then, whilst stamping and filling out the papers, the W.A.A.F always had to have the last word as the captain reminded her forcefully, 'You do realise Hamer, you will still be on the Reserve and that means we can call you up whenever we need you.'

Dora thought just try and catch me first. She didn't care, at last she was free, stuff their petty rules, she was a civilian again. Hardly able to contain herself Dora forced out one last salute and practically ran out the door thrilled to be able to ring Baker St and tell them the news.

There was still nothing from Arthur and Dora still had no inkling what his reaction to the forthcoming baby was. She just hoped he'd be pleased. There could be some letters waiting for her in Aber.

On the telephone Sarah seemed happy enough that she was coming home, 'I never did like that uniform Dora. We'll have to find some things for you to wear now you're so much bigger. I've let out one skirt for you already.' As usual her mother took a down to earth approach to the events to come, but the question was how would Jack cope?

Dora's very last job in the Services was to hand back the uniform and every vestige of kit down to pairs of well worn, voluminous and scratchy navy blue flannel knickers. Who on earth would want to wear her knickers afterwards anyway? But everything had to be counted and accounted for in the Services, as after all even her knickers belonged to the British Government!

Squeezing her burgeoning frame back into her 'civvies', and armed with a travel warrant, Dora walked out the Front Gate for the last time, back to everyday wartime life but relieved to see the back of the last eight months. Never again would she feel envious of anyone in uniform. The only uniform she wanted now was her pinny over her maternity clothes.

28

1942 - Motherhood

Returning home that April of '42, Dora was pleasantly surprised to find that Sarah and Jack had painted and papered the back bedroom for her. They had even bought a second hand Moses basket for the baby. Jack had cleaned it out and spruced it up, and Sarah had made frilly covers and a tiny mattress for the inside. Most of the lodgers had already gone only the Grogans stayed on. Mrs Grogan had helped out when Sarah had injured her wrist, and they were all buoyed up at the thought of a new baby.

Dora seemed to be getting bigger than ever and felt like a beached whale walking round the town in the daytime in her smocked maternity dresses. It was a pity there was no chance of her going out after dark instead but her eyes had never adjusted to the blackout and she'd already had one fall.

Sometimes on a Saturday, Sarah taking pity on her condition would say, 'What about going to a matinee this afternoon. I see in the Cambrian News that 'The Magnificent Ambersons' are on.'

Her mother loved any sort of family type or romantic film, though Dora would have preferred some blood, guts and adventure, but this was a rare treat and one to be enjoyed. There were not too many treats to be had. Even food was a problem. With her Green Ration Book, Dora could have extra milk and eggs and Jack was able to keep them well supplied with fruit in season and all the root vegetables they could eat.

However all of a sudden Dora started breaking out in hives. 'You better pop down to Dr Evans,' her mother said, 'I don't know what's causing them. They seem to be getting worse every day.'

Even though he was their family doctor Dora had never liked Dr Evans, a large pompous man with a paper thin moustache that made him look rather 'Spivey'. He thought doctors were a cut above the general population and made sure you knew it. Jack thought highly of him because he'd been a major in the last war and was big in the Legion and wouldn't hear a word against him.

The doctor took one look at Dora's face and neck and said rudely, 'What a mess. What on earth have you been doing to yourself, girl?'

Dora had a hard job keeping her mouth shut. What an obnoxious man. Why did she have to have him as a doctor? What was worse they were actually paying him for his so-called services.

Dr Evans could see by her tight lips and glinting eyes that he might have gone too far. Carefully and more considerately he said, 'Please sit down Dora if you can, and we'll find out what's causing all this.'

The culprit turned out to be the masses of eggs her mother was giving her, to supplement her diet. Apparently they were too rich for Dora's blood. The doctor sent her away with plenty of calamine for the spots and orders to limit her diet to not more than one or two eggs a week.

The other difficulty was clothes. There were no maternity girdles to be had. Sarah did her best to make some form of girdles that would stretch, but as the pregnancy progressed Dora found herself festooned in bigger and bigger flowing smocks. In some ways she was glad Arthur wasn't around. What on earth would he think of his slim attractive bride now? She looked more like an elephant these days.

It was six weeks now since Dora had heard from Arthur.

193

At least he knew about the baby as that cable had caught up with him at long last, and he'd seemed delighted when he'd written last – but lately there'd been nothing.

Dora remarked to her father, 'I am worried, I haven't heard from Arthur for weeks now.'

Jack did his best to reassure her, 'In the last war your mother didn't hear from me for six months once. Being out in Egypt it was difficult for the mail to get through. I'm sure there'll be news soon.'

Dora thought about Arthur every day – wondering if he was still alive or injured badly or possibly a prisoner of war. The papers were full of obituaries *'missing believed killed'* and *'missing but mentioned in dispatches'*. Families dreaded the sight of the telegraph boy at their door.

The day came however when Jack came bounding in with a pile of 'flimsies' from Arthur. Dora scanned them quickly, trying to sort them into dates. Apparently Arthur had been seriously wounded by one of his own platoon as they dug trenches at night, a pick axe only narrowly missing his spinal cord. He'd been hospitalised in Palestine, had developed a mild form of diphtheria, been found to be a carrier and had remained in hospital longer.

Dora felt a huge sense of relief. Why, oh why though couldn't he have been sent back to a hospital here where she could have seen him for herself? These days there was always a dark cloud of disquiet hanging over her.

Her mother would say quite baldly, 'Just be glad he's survived so far. You want to concentrate all your energies on yourself and your baby and stop worrying about things you can't control.' Sarah never had much time for self pity. 'Get up and get on' was still her attitude to life.

However as Dora's due date approached and then passed even Sarah started to be concerned. Dr Evans pooh-poohed their anxieties, 'First babies are often late. They like to take their time. If you're still like this next week I'll arrange for you to go in and be induced.'

Dora didn't much like the thought of that, and neither did Sarah who'd only been involved in home births, 'I don't know what's involved in their inducement methods but it sounds grim,' she remarked, 'There's nothing for it we'll have to get you started ourselves, Dora. I'll make up some raspberry leaf tea for you to drink and then perhaps one of your father's hot curries might do the trick.'

In the end it happened much quicker than they thought. Dora's waters broke just after they had had their tea one day. There was only she and Sarah in the house, Jack was out somewhere with the Home Guard and even the Grogans had gone visiting for the evening. Sarah cool as a cucumber, ran down the street to see if they could get a taxi, but there was nothing in sight. Taxis were few and far between. There seemed to be quite a space between contractions so Sarah said, 'There's nothing for it Dora, we'll have to walk to the Maternity Home.' The trouble was the Home was in Caradoc Road on the other side of Aberystwyth.

Leaning heavily on Sarah's slight tiny frame, Dora struggled along as best she could. Every so often she would gasp as another contraction hit her, and say, 'I have to stop for a minute,' finally slumping on the wall outside Paine's grocery shop on Llanbadarn Road.

Sarah gamely kept saying, 'Honestly Dora, you're doing so well it's really not that far,' as they painstakingly inched their way along. Dora never knew how long it took – but it seemed a lifetime.

They finally made it and Dora was bundled on to a bed in the empty Labour Ward, 'It could still take some time,' the nurse warned. Sarah said, 'In that case I'll hurry back to Baker Street, get your case and leave a note for your father. I'll be back as soon as I can.'

Much later in fact forty eight hours full of pain and suffering later, Dora and Arthur's baby boy arrived. By then Jack had found them and the three of them were over the moon. The baby only weighed five pounds but he was fit, healthy and yelling at the top of his lungs. Jack said, 'Dora, Arthur would be so proud if he was here-we must cable him as soon as we can.'

'Definitely,' said Dora, 'I think he'll be pleased it's a boy. I don't know what I'm going to do though. I was so convinced I was having a girl, all I've got is a lot of pink matinee jackets.'

Sarah said, 'Don't worry. We'll get everyone knitting again. He's so tiny a lot of the clothes you've got will be miles too big for him.' They both finally left to go home for some sleep.

The midwife appeared asking, 'Would you like something to eat, Mrs Hamer?'

Feeling much better after her ordeal Dora perked up at the mention of food, 'Certainly, I' m ravenous. I haven't eaten since tea on Monday I'll have anything you've got.' The nurse obligingly produced pilchard sandwiches and a cup of tea, which Dora munched down happily.

Two hours later she went into severe shock and started haemorrhaging badly. By then Doctor Evans had arrived. Seeing the tray on the side, he demanded angrily, 'What on earth possessed you to give her something to eat so soon after the birth?'

The midwives scuttled around making lame excuses, while he set to work on his patient. Dora's face gained some colour at last, and she started to come back to life, but in the meantime her milk had gone. By the end of that week, Dora was never so relieved as to return to Baker St with her new son, all the time wishing Arthur was there to share not only the joy but some of the responsibility.

Jack was beside himself with excitement over the baby as he'd never seen Dora until she was walking and talking. He had a bad habit of leaning over the crib right into the baby's face. His handlebar moustache and gnarled face frightened the baby to such an extent he would scream and scream. Sarah would admonish him, 'Stop doing that Jack. It's hard enough to get him to sleep anyway.'

By now Dora had sent off a cable to Arthur's regiment announcing: '*Baby boy Stop 5 lbs Stop David John Hamer Stop Love Dora Stop*'.
She and Arthur had decided to call a boy *David* as a first name, after Arthur's own first name and the grandfather he'd been so fond of when he was young, and *John* after both the grandfathers hoping to keep everyone happy.

In the days that followed Dora wished being a mother for the first time wasn't so daunting. She seemed to feel nervous all the time and wondered if this was how all new mothers felt. Would she ever get used to it? And she was the one who wanted a big family. Perhaps one was enough. This was when she most appreciated Sarah's experience and toughness when it came to handling babies.

29

Coping with Baby

Baker Street was not a happy place in October 1942. Master Hamer cried if he was hungry and cried if he wasn't. Being small at birth, he had to be fed frequently and seemed to suffer from wind and colic unendingly, making Dora wonder why she'd ever wanted a baby.

The only time he slept soundly was in the well sprung second hand pram that had been passed on to her. Dora and Sarah would take him out every day down the Promenade as the weather was mild. Dora remarked to her mother, 'I don't know what we'll do when the winter really sets in.' Sarah replied optimistically, 'No doubt, he'll have settled by then.'

The only problem with parading him down the Promenade was that people would peer in at the baby and feel free to make all sorts of comments and observations, 'Oh what a long baby. He's going to be so tall,' and 'He doesn't look anything like you Dora,' and then consolingly and purposefully, if they didn't know Arthur, 'He probably takes after your husband.' What was much worse were the ones who did know Arthur and would still say, 'Gosh what a lovely head of curls, but he doesn't seem to have inherited yours or Arthur's looks.'

Indignantly Dora would retort to all the comments, 'Well I can assure you, he is definitely mine and Arthur's baby.' The cheek of it to imply, however subtly, that she might have cheated on her husband, and produced someone else's baby. There was so much of it going on in wartime that everyone seemed to get 'tarred with the same brush'. Unfortunately David's golden blonde curls hardly matched up with either hers or Arthur's colouring. The height thing was going to prove to be even more embarrassing when Arthur came home on leave as between them they could barely summon up more than 5' 3 and a half inches in height.

One of Jack's old friends Mr Pinsent had called round to the house to apologise for missing the news of their wedding, 'I'm so sorry Dora. I'd like to buy you something even if it's a bit late. Come down with me to Morgan the Jewellers and we'll pick something out.'

Dora had never dared venture into Morgan's before, as the exterior had always looked so expensive. After some persuasion, Dora agreed to a set of fine fish knives and forks in a silk lined case dreading to think how much they cost. The price would probably have fed a family for weeks but old Pinsent was so kind, with no children himself, that she couldn't turn down his generosity.

Afterwards on their return to Baker Street there was nothing for it but he had to come up and have a good look at the new baby. 'He's going to be a tall one Dora. If you let me measure him, I'm pretty good at predicting how tall he'll be when he's fully grown.'

Dora was not at all sure about this, but the old gentleman was so excited by now and eagerly sent her mother scurrying about for a tape measure, that she hadn't the heart to stop him.

'Go ahead then Mr Pinsent. It's just as well to know I suppose.'

The measuring was done carefully with David just taking it all in his stride and beaming at them and kicking his legs. Mr Pinsent scribbled down figures and then thoughtfully said, 'Well, by my calculations I would think he'll be at least six feet or thereabouts, and knowing Arthur as he did, he added quite innocently, 'It's very interesting. He's obviously a throwback to an earlier generation–it often happens, Dora.'

Dora was too stunned to know what to say. Obviously the old gentleman had no idea about her background, and she tried her hardest not to show any embarrassment.

All the Hamer men were short of course – the tallest being no more than five foot seven. Mr Pinsent was also aware of the lack of height of both Jack and Sarah, taking it for granted they were her parents. He would have been mortified if he'd had any inkling of the truth, and would have hated to upset her.

All Dora was capable of, was just smiling and nodding and thanking him for his gift as she showed him out, wondering all the time what her real family had looked like. What if David grew more to look like one of them with nothing of her or Arthur, surely she'd suffered enough her own children should inherit something from her.

The only hint she'd ever had about her real family and their looks had come about accidentally. Years before, Dora had been out shopping for Sarah in Great Darkgate Street and in the greengrocers a rather gossipy woman had said casually to her, 'I saw your father last week Dora, driving the brewery drey. What a fine tall figure of a man he is with his blonde hair – Irish isn't he?'

Dora was rattled for a minute and trying to gather her thoughts quickly, retorted, 'I think you're mistaken Mrs Lewis. Surely you know my father, Jack Roberts. He's a very short grey haired man with a handlebar moustache, rides a bike, and has a market garden on Llanbadarn Road.'

The woman pursed her lips and looked away saying nothing further. Dora knew full well that Mrs Lewis knew Jack Roberts and decided she must be troublemaking. This woman and her mother had never got on because of the Welsh, and she was probably trying to stir things up. Dora speculated does she really know something, is she fishing for information, or maybe she's heard some rumours about me.

This had unsettled Dora for weeks as now Gran was gone there was no one to talk to.

Trying to put it to the back of her mind, Dora had succeeded until now but this business with David's blonde features and height brought it all flooding back. Aberystwyth was such a small town with everyone knowing everyone's family and forebears as well as their business. If only Arthur was around to tell her not to worry and to forget about it all, but this was one of those occasions when she wished she knew more about her birth and background.

On top of this David was proving to be a difficult baby and though some way into his first year still crying, never allowing Dora a full night's sleep. He had been examined by both the doctor and the hospital – but to no avail. All they would say is that he would grow out of it when he gained more weight.

The three of them did their best to keep him amused during the day, so that he would sleep at night. It was either she, Sarah or Jack walking the floor with him every night. One night when there was just the two of them and David, Sarah said, 'We can't go on like this Dora. You look exhausted and your father and I aren't much better. Look Jack's not due back till late. What about putting a finger of brandy on his lips? I used to do this with young Tom as a baby and he'd go off like a light. Whatever you do though, don't tell your father as he'd be horrified.'

Sarah tentatively touched the baby's bottom lip with the merest trickle of brandy. Surprisingly, David stuck out his tongue and lapped it up smacking his lips together. There was no more to be heard from him that night.

On Jack's arrival home – he came bounding straight upstairs where they were both hovering on the landing outside the baby's room. He boomed, 'It's exceptionally quiet here tonight? No crying. What are you both doing?'

'Do keep your voice down, Jack. David's finally off and we want to keep it that way.'

The brandy seemed to have done the trick, and broken the cycle. There were to be no more nights walking the floor – though Sarah and Dora never did dare repeat the trick or let on to Jack.

Throughout David's first months Dora would regularly take him round to Pickford's to have him photographed so she could send the photos to Arthur overseas. He was growing into a blonde beautiful little boy before her eyes and she wondered when or even if Arthur would ever see him.

At last there was good news. Arthur cabled to say he was coming home on leave in a few days. The Desert Rats had fought their way through North Africa and were deploying to Italy. Dora was beside herself with excitement. With her limited coupons she bought David some little blue trousers and she and Sarah sewed a tiny white shirt for him made from parachute silk, embroidered with little flowers and his name. Dora could hardly wait for Arthur to see his son.

Arthur arrived later than expected as he'd had to scramble from the backs of tanks to lorries to buses then finally onto the Aberystwyth train. Hefting his kitbag on to the door step at Baker Street he was gaunt and grey with fatigue.

Dora practically ran up the hall, 'Arthur, at last,' and couldn't stop hugging him though he was drooping in her arms. 'Come straight through to the back kitchen. Mom's visiting Lizzie and Dad's at the Home Guard. I've only just put David to bed.' Dora felt herself babbling. It was so hard to take in that he was finally here – even if only for a few days.

Arthur dropped down wearily at the wooden table, barely able to unlace his boots. Dora cut him a slice of Spam which is all they had in the way of meat and cut up a loaf.

She knew she was being far too liberal with their cheese ration, but felt he deserved as much as she could give him.

'I'm sorry Dora --- too tired,' he mumbled '--- need sleep.'

Dora put his arm round her shoulders and helped him up the backstairs. He was like a drunken man weaving his way to their bed barely able to take off his army blouse – before he collapsed in a deep sleep without noticing the basket holding his sleeping son.

Dora felt disappointed after such anticipation and totally deflated. It had been like looking at a stranger. Where was her smart loving young husband? She carefully finished unlacing his boots, pulled them off and drew the eiderdown over him, reassuring herself he would be more like the old Arthur tomorrow, she would just have to curb her enthusiasm and be patient.

Next morning the baby was up early as usual but Arthur slept on. Eventually at teatime, he opened a bleary bloodshot eye and drank a cup of tea. David toddled into the room behind his mother, and Dora said, 'Look David, this is your daddy. Come and say hullo to him.' David, now eighteen months old and a proper little boy took one look at the unshaven unkempt figure on the bed gave a piercing scream and ran from the room.

'I don't think he likes the look of me,' Arthur murmured.

'It's not that, Arthur, he's not used to you yet. It'll take a bit of time. He kisses your photo every night but it's very different from seeing someone in the flesh.'

The days went by slowly whilst Arthur regained his strength; Dora and her mother were understanding and let him recover in his own time. But Jack always the military man, was agog for details on how the war was progressing in the field. Dora could see that Arthur didn't want to talk about the war, and she tried her hardest to protect him and help him disappear when his father-in-law's steps were heard in the passage.

There was still no more than an armed truce between Arthur and his son. Arthur would try tentatively to make contact but David would look suspiciously at him and run for his mother's skirts. Dora supposed they would get used to one another gradually. It was hard for Arthur as he'd never seen David as a helpless baby and was contending now with a young child.

After a few days Dora said, 'Arthur, why don't you take David up the street on your own – he can toddle along if you don't go too far.'

Arthur looked unsure, 'He won't scream will he?'

'No, I think he's over that now–it was just the shock of another man in the house.'

Somewhat reluctantly Arthur, with David dressed in his best coat, made his way towards the front door. 'You do need to hold his hand firmly though. He's not that steady on his feet,' Dora said anxiously.

With Dora standing waiting on the doorstep of no.8, they slowly made their way up Baker Street David constantly turning back to look at his mother. Finally they turned the corner into Eastgate Street and Dora started to come in thinking everything seems to be going alright perhaps there was no need to worry. As they disappeared however there was one almighty bellow and two seconds later Arthur trying to manhandle a squirming red faced infant appeared, only too keen to hand him back to Dora. It was not a good start.

Arthur said, 'I think I'll have to take it a lot slower with him.'

In the little time they'd had together Dora tried her hardest to help Arthur feel he was back to normality with his family–but the leave was really too short for this to have any effect.

Arthur had never been cut out to be a soldier and was more suited to being a family man living in peace and quiet. As the days moved rapidly forward, Arthur's nervousness grew and grew as he became more and more remote, suffering badly with sick stomachs which he put down to the aggravation of the desert sand, though Dora thought it more likely that he was dreading going back to the war, and wishing she could protect him from what was to come.

30

1943 - Home Front

Sometimes Dora felt Aber was so distant from the war it was hard to believe there were people fighting for their lives and fleeing bombed out houses. Her own life revolved around the baby, and in between she worked in the House and the Garden. Relieved as she was, to not still be in the Forces, life at No.8 was very humdrum. It was just as if she was waiting, stuck on the sidelines - marking time for the War to finish so that she and Arthur could finally start living.

Nothing dramatic ever seemed to happen in the town. Most people were in uniform now – there was little food and plenty of queuing for rations. Everything metal had disappeared long ago and been melted down, the days were shorter because of the blackout, and the Promenade had been fenced off completely.

The only time Aber had been near to a scare was earlier in the War. Her father had come home one night from the Home Guard, and said, 'We've been put on Alert. There's a chance the Germans are going to invade Ireland. They may try to land on this coast either at Milford or Holyhead.' At the time Dora had realised with a shock, they might suddenly find themselves on the Front Line. Security and troop movements tightened up all down the coast. But luckily Hitler, concerned about antagonising the Irish in America had other priorities, and had moved on to Africa. Dora hoped against hope that Hitler's knowledge of Britain might not stretch to the little known country of Wales or even Aberystwyth.

As the war progressed there were only a few lodgers; Mattie a reservist at the Post Office, an elderly couple, the Gibsons who had evacuated from Coventry after the rumours of the 'phoney war', and Greta a Dutch lady who'd been a nanny in London and couldn't return to Holland after the invasion.

Greta worked at the Forum Canteen in Bath St. She would come in with bits and pieces of war news she had gleaned from the Service personnel. In her heavily accented English she would say, 'Mr Roberts, I hear a Junker -- crash near Mach. We vill not be safe in our beds. Vat if die German pilots are vandering around?'

Jack would frown and admonish her severely, 'Greta, now, now. Walls have ears, you shouldn't be gossiping about what you hear, you don't know who's listening.' Everywhere there were notices warning people, '*Careless War Talk costs Lives*'.

Greta would sulk and flounce off, saying, 'God in de Hemel, if I had a gun I vould shoot dem one by one and vith lots of pain.' She was very passionate and angry about what had happened to her country, even going round to the Police Station to ask about training in handguns. But Jack had put his foot down at that, refusing to have a gun in the house.

Dora admired Greta's gutsy spirit, and sometimes wished she could talk to her father like that. But with the Garden and his duties in the Home Guard he was already working too hard. Seeing his face strained and tight with worry lines Dora always felt she should try and ease his load rather than add to it. With all his commitments, he never ate regularly, and would take himself off to the back lavatory doubled up with gripes of wind.

Sarah would say, 'Make up some scrambled egg for your father Dora- he'll need something easily digestible when he feels better.'

Dora always saved her one and only weekly egg for these occasions. Powdered egg was never the same as the real thing.

Each week they struggled with the rationing, as juggling everyone's books did some doing.

207

Dora felt as if she was endlessly shopping. Trying to get everyone fed reasonably was a work of art, though there was always the great fall back of Spam or even Snoek. Sarah tried her best to provide one cooked meal every evening and with the Garden they had a plentiful supply of root vegetables and potatoes to bulk out everything, but it was becoming harder for her and Dora to come up with any sort of variety that would stretch to feed so many hungry people.

Sarah was a great devotee of the 'Women's Illustrated' which she would pore over in search of tips and hints about daily life. 'Come on Dora, what about this?' she'd say pushing the paper towards Dora and pointing at an advert on the back, 'How one person's meat ration can make a Meal for Five.' The only problem is we don't have this 'Pyrex' they mention – it looks like it's done in one dish something called a casserole.'

Dora scanning it said, 'It'd certainly save washing up all those saucepans. What about Auntie Annie – she always has the most up to date stuff. With her girls away in the Forces she might have something she could lend you. Let's have a go at it – it might make life a lot easier.' They chortled together over it and with Annie's equipment were able to make a whole range of casseroles using all their vegetables, roots and sprouting potatoes. At these times Dora felt that at last she and her mother were working on an equal basis – there was mutual respect if nothing else. Sarah seemed to relate better to her since she'd married and had David.

The baby was finally well and truly settled and growing fast these days. He loved his mashed up vegetables and there was a steady allowance of milk, orange juice and eggs for him. All those sleepless nights became a distant memory. Chattering away to Dora and singing to himself, David was a joy to be around. Easily occupied with a few wooden soldiers made out of clothes pegs, and a wooden spoon, he would march them round the kitchen table whilst she scrubbed the flagstones for the umpteenth time.

Dora had even begun to wonder what to do with herself, with so much more time to herself and the days dragging by bogged down with dreariness. During her scrubbing Dora would indulge herself in the luxury of daydreaming. What would life with Arthur be like if this war ever finished? It was so long since she'd seen him. Every night when David kissed his father's photo, Dora would stare down at the handsome man in uniform and wonder if she had truly married him, and if he really was her husband. It sometimes seemed like another lifetime.

Nowadays David was walking confidently on his own, but it hurt her that spotting Jack he would run towards him, making 'Dad, dad'— noises, thinking this man in uniform was his father. Of course Jack was delighted and would pick him up swinging him round and round until the poor child was nearly sick.

Dora would protest, 'Put him down Dada – you're too much for him sometimes. He's not a toy you know. You could hurt him.'

Jack however would take no notice and say, 'Dora – he's a regular little boy – a bit of rough and tumble will do him a world of good. You can't have him turning into a mummy's boy.' Dora would bite her tongue. He'd been so good and patient when David was just a baby. But having little experience of small children, Jack always went too far. Dora couldn't have David treated like that. He was a delicate little boy and needed looking after.

Taking matters into her own hands she made sure that David was well and truly tucked up in his bed by the time Jack came home. He would complain loudly saying, 'I never catch sight of David these days. He's either not up when I go out or just been put to bed when I come back.' Dora would look across at her mother and they would both raise their eyes to the ceiling but never pass a comment.

The only break and escape from routine was the pictures. The Coliseum and the Pier cinemas, thank goodness had remained open, except for Sundays, throughout the war. Occasionally Sarah would offer, 'Dora, you and Mattie can go to the Pictures on Saturday evening if you like. I can babysit David. Now he's older and sleeps, there's no problem. I see in the 'Cambrian News' that 'Gone with the Wind' has come back. It's a long picture –but your father and I are always up late anyway.'

Dora's spirits would rise. There was nothing better than a costume picture to take you out of yourself. She and Mattie decided to take themselves off to the early house. Arriving in the cinema in the pitch dark, Dora would clutch on to the back of Mattie's coat until she felt the seat against her legs. It was just the same coming out, with Dora linking arms with her friend as they made their way through the blackout. Afterwards they bought fish and chips eating them straight from the paper as they chatted about the picture. The drama, the colour and the excitement of the picture could keep Dora going for days whilst she relived scene after scene.

Reading, the Pictures and her music were the only things which could nourish Dora's soul whenever things became too hard to bear. She no longer practised on the piano, but still bought the latest sheet music and was always willing to play when they had a singsong.

On the occasional Saturday night, when Sarah was in a good mood after a sweet sherry or two, the whole household would gather round the piano. Dora would let David stay up late sleepily perched on his grandfather's knee. There would be requests and Dora would attempt to keep up with all the ragged singing. Jack with his deep bass voice would say 'Play something military or rousing Dora – what about the 'Keel Row' or 'Men of Harlech'?' and then proceed to sing with all his might.

'Jack – you'll wake the street, do keep it down,' his wife would admonish. But there was no stopping him once he'd started and they would work through his whole repertoire until Sarah put her foot down. 'Play something quieter Dora. What about 'I'll walk beside you' or 'In a Monastery Garden?

The latter always calmed Jack down, as there were no accompanying words, just the chiming of the monastery bell. They would all agree to finish on 'Land of Hope and Glory'. The words meant more to them now they were truly battling for their country's freedom. Afterwards they would all depart for bed, reinvigorated with renewed confidence that the war would end before long and they could return to their old lives.

31

1945 – The End is in Sight

By mid 1944 the war had lasted nearly five years, and was taking its toll on not just the fighting soldiers but on the people left behind. The last Dora had heard from Arthur was when the 8th Army landed in Italy and he'd written about Monte Casino. He never mentioned the fighting but told her some funny story about him and his mates finding a cave stocked with canned peaches, and how he'd gone off and eaten a whole can to himself, suffering badly for days with stomach ache. She knew he was trying to reassure her with humour but there wasn't much to laugh about these days.

Sitting across the breakfast table from her father, his head buried as usual in the Mail avidly following the progress of the battles, Dora said plaintively, 'Is there any good news Dada?'

'Dora– haven't you read the headlines today?'

'No,' she said sighing deeply, 'I don't want to read anything bad anymore.'

'But look,' Jack said pointing to the headline, *"Caen- The big Break-Through. The great battle of France has begun".* 'I've said lately that I was sure the end was in sight. Our boys are doing so well after Normandy. They're going to rout those Junkers and push them back to where they belong.'

He was jubilant about it and nothing could stop him running excitedly up the stairs shouting to his wife 'the end of the war is coming.' Sarah called back with her usual tone of wryness, 'It's hardly going to be today Jack. I've plenty of beds to change. You can come up and give me a hand if you've that much energy to spare.'

His booming voice carried on: 'But Sis, I really do think it won't be long now, presently we'll have the lads back and it'll all be a distant memory.'

Dora listening to the bits of conversation that floated down to her was indignant that Jack could write off the last five years of misery, anxiety and rationing just like that, let alone the horrors Arthur must be going through personally. And what about all the men who'd been killed or maimed and wouldn't be coming back. It was no use reminding him though, when he was in one of his jingoistic moods.

She turned to look at David, 'What do you think David – maybe Grandpa's right and we'll soon have Daddy home?'David just sat there grinning and nodding, far too involved in dipping soldiers into his boiled egg.

Ever since the war had started it seemed as if Jack had been rejuvenated. He only saw the deprivations as challenges to be overcome. Relishing being in the Home Guard, his uniform immaculate and reverting easily to his old RSM role, he marched the elderly men under his command about until they were nearly dropping. Always preparing them for night sorties on the coastline, Dora thought he would relish a German invasion if it happened. She and Sarah used to wonder what got into men when the word 'war' was mentioned. Why did they always want to come out fighting?

The only thing about war that annoyed and hurt Jack was turning the Garden over completely to vegetables and no longer allowed to grow his beautiful flowers and plants. Looking sorrowfully at the rows of potatoes and lines of runner beans he would say, 'Dora it's going to take such a long time after the war to get the Garden back to what it was.'

Dora breaking out of her reverie and hearing him running back down the stairs and making for the hall called out to him,

'Dada if what you say is right, when is Arthur likely to come home?'

'I don't know, Dora. The 8th have got a long way to go and probably more fighting in front of them. It won't be easy, early next year maybe ---.' His voice fell away, sorry now that he'd become so involved in what he was saying that he'd given her false hope.

As it turned out the Germans didn't surrender till the following May and it was a bolt from the blue when it actually happened. After the Allied bombing raids and the capture of Berlin in the April events moved surprisingly quickly. Mussolini was captured and hanged and two days later Hitler and Eva Braun committed suicide.

Arthur had been writing to tell her it was practically all over, but Dora could hardly bring herself to believe it. After all the suffering it was such an abrupt end to such a long war, almost an anti-climax. Despite longing day after day for it to finish, in some strange way Dora had got accustomed to living like this and now there was to be yet another adjustment. Was she prepared? How would their existing close little family cope with welcoming Arthur back and including him? And what would he do? It was hard to take in.

Jack was beside himself as each day brought more and more news to celebrate. He was like a messenger from the gods rushing into the kitchen on winged feet saying, 'Look, you two, they're signing the surrender tomorrow at Reims. The 7th of May, a date we'll always remember.'

Sarah was more relieved than excited, 'I don't know about you Dora, but I don't think I could have gone on much longer. I feel so old, tired and worn out. It was bad enough after the Great War. I do hope there's never another war in my lifetime.'

People in the town had already decided that for them the war was definitely over although there still hadn't been any official announcements. There were all sorts of arrangements being made for celebrations and street parties, and it didn't seem as if the government was going to have any say in curbing the enthusiasm. In the end, the Home Office was forced into issuing a formal circular instructing the nation on how they could celebrate: *'Bonfires will be allowed, but the government trusts that only material with no salvage value will be used.'* The Board of Trade did the same, *'Until the end of May you may buy cotton bunting without coupons as long as it is red, white and blue and does not cost more than one shilling and three pence a square yard.'*

Seeing all these notices Sarah remarked ironically, 'Honestly Dora, no one's going to take any notice of all these silly government regulations after all we've been through?'

Jack always one to toe the party line said, 'Sis, it may be the end of the war but things are going to be tight for years to come. I daresay there'll still have to be rationing.'

Finally the official news came. At twenty to eight on the seventh of May the Ministry of Information announced:

'In accordance with arrangements between the three great powers, tomorrow, Tuesday, will be treated as Victory in Europe Day and will be regarded as a holiday.'

Before Sarah, Dora or even David could say anything, Jack was in the loft searching out bunting and the old Union Jack flag which had seen better days. He was up and down Baker Street knocking on doors and collecting all the food he could muster from the neighbours. For once they all wanted to be part of the day.

'Oh Mr Roberts, we'll make the lemonade,' offered the Miss

Lewises, 'and we've got some streamers somewhere from the Armistice celebration.' The Davies offered chairs and tablecloths and sooner or later everyone was out on their doorsteps discussing what they would contribute. Baker Street had never seemed such a friendly place.

Sarah remarked under her breath to Dora, 'Pity they never made this effort before. It takes a war or the end of one to bring out the best in people. Mind you, it's probably your father, when he's in one of his gung-ho moods, no one dare refuse him.'

On the 8th, Jack was up at the crack of dawn and with the Home Guard set up trestle tables all down the street. Dora and Sarah had been up early making jellies and pink blancmanges, and all sorts of pies and sandwiches. David was set to work pasting red white and blue trimmings together, but spent most of the time putting paste into his mouth.

At last everything was ready. The children were in their best clothes, and the minister had managed with help, to drag an old piano on to the street from the bottom chapel.

Jack said, 'Come on Dora – give us a few tunes while we're eating.'

Dora did her best to enter into the spirit of the day, sitting David next to her on the piano stool, but all she could think about was Arthur waiting for his demob date. She was not going to be able to relax until he was home safe, and at the moment she had no idea where he was or what danger he might be in It was quite common for soldiers to get killed in these last days of war, as pockets of maverick Germans all over Europe were refusing to surrender and prepared to fight to the last stand.

At three o'clock on the dot, all the adults disappeared into their houses in time to hear Mr Churchill on the wireless. He reminded them that Japan was still not defeated but that with Victory in Europe the people of Great Britain,

'may allow themselves a brief period of rejoicing. Advance Britannia. Long Live the Cause of Freedom. God save the King.'

32

Demob !

The waiting was the hardest especially after all the razzamatazz of V.E Day. Aberystwyth was rife with rumours – some saying that demob was going to take eighteen months, and others that release would depend on age, service number and date enlisted. Dora didn't know what to think as Arthur's few telephone calls were hardly informative but at least he was back in Blighty so he was out of harm's way. It was just a matter of being patient. Dora felt she had been waiting for something all her life and this particular wait was the longest.

May went by and then her 30th birthday and then most of June and well into July. And then it came, there it was, one of the dreaded yellow telegrams. Her mother could see Dora toying with the envelope with shaking hands and said matter of factly, 'It's probably just telling you when he's arriving.' Dora hurriedly ripped into the telegram and that's exactly what it said in black and white:

'Demobbed Stop Arriving Aber Stop Saturday Stop Five o'clock train Stop Love Arthur Stop.'

Dora felt herself let out a huge sigh almost as if she had been holding her breath for the last six years. If she'd been allowed she'd have had a good weep with the relief, but she didn't dare with Sarah practically standing over her. Dora could hardly get through the week. What plans she and Arthur would make. They might even pack up and leave Aber altogether. In the next days she indulged herself in pipedreams, of her husband, a house, more children perhaps even four, and a different life in a new town.

Her father was thrilled too, looking forward to all the war stories and to hearing about all the battle action directly from his son-in-law.

A few days before the weekend he said, 'Dora, Sis, I'll finish at lunchtime on Saturday and we'll all go to meet Arthur off the train.'

'Oh no, you don't,' his wife interjected, 'it's only Dora and David who should be there. It's their special day. You'll have to wait your turn.'

On the Saturday Dora dressed David and herself up ready to leave for the station, the little boy was skipping beside her energetically seeming to soak up all Dora's suppressed emotions and helping ease the definite rumblings of apprehension in her stomach. Since their wartime marriage in 1940, she and Arthur had spent no more than a few snatched weeks or days together, and she wondered what it would be like living together day to day. Putting her fears aside Dora admonished herself, hadn't they been through so much already, weren't they entitled to a bit of happiness. Everything was going to be alright. They would have a good life together.

She and David ran up and down the carriages looking for Arthur. From the end of the platform, a slim figure in a smart navy blue stripped suit came towards her. For a fleeting moment he looked alien and unfamiliar, then David finally recognising his father out of uniform ran towards him and the moment was gone. Dora kissed her Arthur with tears in her eyes, 'We expected you in uniform.'

'I couldn't stand another moment of that khaki,' he replied, 'Burtons kindly fixed us up with our demob suits early and I thought I'd surprise you, fancy David knowing me out of uniform!'

Dora took a step back and looked at him hard, 'I can't believe it's all over and you're back for good.'

Arthur appeared much the same though a great deal thinner and browner. His light brown hair now had silver waves in the front, the parts not shielded from the North African sun by his forage cap.

Dora was full of questions, 'How do you feel? Are you tired? What was your journey like?'

He smiled, and nodded – but was too full of emotion to talk. She held out her arms and he held her close. Time stood still, and then a little voice piped up, 'Me, me, and me.' Arthur laughed, 'I forgot he's talking now.' She picked up their son and they held him together, then linking hands David swinging between them, and Arthur's kitbag on his shoulder they made their way back to Baker St.

Her mother had gone to enormous trouble, saving enough coupons to give them a decent tea, and had sorted out a couple of rooms at the top of the house, so they could have their own bedroom next to David's. At tea Jack couldn't wait to ask, 'What will you do now Arthur. I expect old Putt has kept your job at the Star open for you?'

'He said he would but it's been such a long time, I suppose I'll have to see him tomorrow and find out,' Arthur replied reluctantly.

'Oh no you don't,' Dora was adamant, 'after all you've have been through you need rest and decent food.'

Jack agreed. As an ex military man he could see the signs of battle fatigue etched deeply into Arthur's face. 'When you feel less tired why don't you have a few days in Llani and see some of your family?' he suggested kindly.

Dora looked at him gratefully. Maybe Arthur had not come back injured or wounded but war had certainly left its mark on him. That time in the hospital in Palestine must have affected him more than he let on. Now Dora had him back for keeps, she was going to make sure he was well looked after.

Dora tried to put herself in Arthur's shoes. Settling back into daily life again was going to be hard for him. Life was nothing like it was before the war. Six years of war had certainly left the country suffering. There was still rationing to cope with. Soldiers were returning and trying to get back their old jobs, many now taken by youngsters or women. Other Servicemen were emigrating or taking advantage of war grants, to put themselves through University. Often men were coming back to broken homes, wives who'd left, been killed, or who'd gone off with GIs.

Arthur would ask about people he remembered, 'What happened to Ivor Davies? – you know the tobacconists?' Dora said, 'It was very sad. His eldest son was killed at Dunkirk and his youngest in the Battle of Britain, his wife had contracted TB earlier in the war and was sent to a nursing home in North Wales and never recovered. All of it sucked the life out of him, and once he got the news about his youngest son he went out to the garage and hanged himself. It was as if there was nothing more for him to live for.'

There were so many distressing stories like this that Arthur stopped asking, but he was unsettled and restless with a tendency to wander round the house aimlessly. Regularly, he would say, 'I know I'm lucky Dora, to be alive and to have come back to you and David. It's just that I don't know where I fit in any more. Constantly obeying orders, going where I was told and being surrounded by men in uniform, I feel as if I've lost sight of the person I really am. I was so young and green in '39, and here I am nearing thirty with nothing much to show for all those wasted years. I feel like an old man.'

Dora did her best to reassure him, 'You're certainly not that Arthur,' and trying to joke him out of it added 'as if I'd be married to an old man! Things will get better Arthur you'll see. You just need time. Try and feel blessed for what you have and let everything else take care of itself. We'll have a few days in Llani and it'll give you a chance to catch up with the family.'

In the August, leaving David with Sarah, they made the trip back to Llanidloes. These days they had to stay at a hotel opposite the Market Hall as the old home had long since gone.

Visiting Arthur's old aunts was a tonic. Dora could hardly stop laughing. They fussed over Arthur and nagged him as if he was a little boy: 'Now Arthur, tell us all your news- but do stop wriggling. You'll upset my antimacassars. They're clean on today. No, don't lean your greasy head on that wall either as I'll never get the Brylcream out of it.' It didn't matter how much he protested they still shook their heads reprovingly as if he was a mere eight years old.

Dora could see the years fall away from Arthur. It was wonderful to think about the boy he'd been. This was when she could see David's resemblance to him the most and it helped set her mind at rest about her son's inherited looks.

Auntie Maggie Ted was the loveliest of the aunts and the one Dora liked the most, probably because she had married into the family and was always regarded as an outsider, like Dora herself. Before they attended the '*Thanksgiving Service for the End of the War*' at China Street Church, she gave them tea with homemade cake and jam and brought Arthur up to date with all the family news,'Arthur, Gwen's very good and writes regularly. She's out of the W.R.N.S. She and Bill got married, not long after you two, and they're settled in London. She sees Eric now and then–but he's not very well-he had some sort of fall before he left the Navy.

222

Eddie's coming home soon and will probably go back to his old job in the Foundry. Gertie and her family are in Rhayader as you know, and I don't know about Bobbie.'

Dora was pleased that she and Arthur had decided to make the visit. Even if his family were scattered to the four winds, at least he could feel that they had all got back safely. Returning home to Baker St she felt there was more of an air of optimism about him and said, 'Things will work out Arthur–you'll see. I've even managed to save some of your Army pay, so between us we have £50 in the Post Office. We've got a roof over our heads, a lovely little boy and our health and strength, what more do we need?'

But things weren't the same and one area hadn't improved at all. Dora was at her wits end as to how she could help her husband and son make any sort of connection. Arthur tried his hardest to play with David but had no idea how to handle a toddler, and David would run to his mother first. Were they ever going to form the close family she wanted? Desperately, Dora appealed for advice from her mother, 'I don't know how to bring Arthur and David closer together? What can I do?'

Sarah's only response was, 'It was the same when your father came home from the Great War. You were already running about and talking a bit. He tended to treat you like one of his soldiers and you responded to that but I think it's different for Arthur. You'll just have to be patient my girl. There's nothing for it.'

Meantime Arthur was unduly preoccupied about their future. He went round to the Star to see his old manager who was delighted to see him, 'Arthur you were such a good worker in the old days, but things have changed and these days we have a full staff,' adding regretfully, 'you see, we couldn't wait for you lads to come home. We've taken on female assistants who are not willing to give up their jobs, now they're used to a pay packet.

The war went on for so long we were forced to take them on.' Arthur could see how many more young women now worked behind the counter and supposed they were cheaper for the management to employ.

However Putt was beside himself with embarrassment, apologising profusely, 'All you've done for us Arthur. Sacrificing the last six years for our safety and all you've been through to come back to this. I'm so sorry. Don't worry, my boy, I'm going to do my level best to find something for you – maybe not here but somewhere. Just leave it with me.'

A few days later he rang Baker St, 'Arthur, come round and see me. I think I might have come up with something.' Arthur went round immediately. Putt said, 'I contacted the Regional Manager and he's the very thing for you, an Assistant Manager's job for you to step right into in Porthcawl. What do you think?'

'I don't know Mr Putt. I'll have to go home and talk it over with Dora first and let you know,' Arthur said uncertainly.

On his return to Baker St, Dora was ecstatic and all for uprooting and moving to Porthcawl immediately, 'Arthur, this would be perfect. It's a job you know well with responsibility, and it's still by the sea which you love. We could make a good life for ourselves in South Wales. There wouldn't be the problems with the Welsh either. I've always wanted to move from Aber.'

But however hard she tried there was no budging him. Possibly, after all Arthur had been through, another upheaval was just too much.

He would argue, 'Dora, you've got your family here and I can get over to Llani easily to see mine.'

'But Arthur they're not really my family. You and David are my family.'

It was no use, no matter what arguments Dora put forward he would not be moved, and to her bitter disappointment, he went round a few days later to turn the job down. Arthur was set on staying in Aberystwyth, and all Dora could think of was what sort of future could they expect to have now.

33

Late1945 - Finding Work

Arthur never wanted to discuss his wartime experiences. He would either change the subject or say, 'Dora, all I want is to do is the same thing every day, come home to you and David every evening and eat some decent food.' The latter was easier said than done.

Post-war Aberystwyth was as grey as the rest of Britain in the late 40s. Rationing continued. Dora did her best with meat and two veg, suet puddings and homemade cakes if she could get the eggs. In no time at all though Arthur began to put back the weight he'd lost. His face was less tense and he began to enjoy a peace time existence with his wife and son. However things were not as straightforward as they seemed. Dora found there were a lot of things about her reticent husband she had yet to learn.

On one occasion when they were taking David for an outing down the prom, Dora thought she heard someone shout, 'Hamer, Hamer – it is you, isn't it?' Prodding Arthur in the arm she said, 'Arthur, I think there's some men over there trying to get your attention.'

Before either of them could say anything her bemused husband was lifted off his feet and swung round and round. 'Put me down, put me down,' he gasped trying hard on to hold on to his dignity .

'Remember your old mate Danny and the gang. You haven't forgotten us already?' The man, who'd swung her husband round touched his cap, 'Sorry Missus, I was so excited to see Arthur, I forgot my manners. See, we were all in the Gunners together. We haven't seen him since demob.'

They all fell to reminiscing and laughing about all they had got up to on the quiet.

'Do'ya remember Arthur – all that time in Palestine. We thought you'd gone AWOL and there you were hospitalised. Would you believe it Missus, when your hubby was discharged from the hospital, he wandered about for weeks in the desert frantically trying to get back to his platoon, if it'd been me I'd have skived off somewhere permanently and sat it out till the end of the war.' They carried on joking making cracks about their officers, and the muddles they got up to with Signals, making it sound as if they'd been at some sort of party. After a while they all went their separate ways but not before getting Arthur to promise he'd come to the next reunion.

Dora could see the difference in her quiet, serious husband, and turned to him remarking, 'What an amazing group, it seemed like a lot of fun at times though I'm sure it wasn't anything of the kind.'

'No,' Arthur said, 'it was hardly a picnic. I don't want to be reminded of it. It's far better forgotten.'

'But you will go to the reunion, won't you? They'll be so disappointed if you don't. They seemed to think so much of you.'

'I suppose I'll show my face once, but that's it. It's in the past now. You and I have a different life.'

And that's all Dora could get out of him. Danny had been his best friend for years long before the war. They'd even joined the Territorials together, but it looked as if Arthur wanted to not only forget but blot out the past, not even sentimental enough to want to maintain an old friendship.

It was hard to understand. Being used to her father's extrovert personality, his love of all things military, and his strong involvement in the British Legion, it never occurred to Dora that Arthur wouldn't be the same.

But Jack of course was a man's man – enjoying a drink at the Conservative Club or a game of billiards, going to secret meetings of the Buffs or gossiping with his old cronies at the Legion. Dora was still uncertain enough of their relationship not to pressure Arthur. No doubt she would find out more of what made him tick in the fullness of time.

In the next few weeks, Arthur started taking himself off for solitary walks. He never offered to take her along or even David but amazingly enough often ended up at the Garden. Once there he would talk to Jack by the hour. It mystified Dora. These two men in her life were so very different and she was quite put out that he wasn't confiding in her, his wife.

Sarah would ask, 'Where's Arthur, I don't seem to have seen him for days?' 'He's gone down to the Garden again I expect,'

Dora replied sharply, 'I don't know what he and Dada find to talk about, I really don't?'

'It's hard Dora, coming back from war and trying to put down roots again. That's one thing your father does know about. It wasn't easy for him either in 1918.We had a lot of ups and downs before he took on the Garden. He was full of energy one minute, depressed and apathetic the next. Always trying too hard to hang on to old friendships with army mates and then disappointed when they let him down. You'll just have to be understanding Dora. He'll come round.'

'I'm sure you're right Mom. I hadn't thought it would be this complicated. I thought I could help him but perhaps he needs to find things out for himself.'

Later that afternoon Arthur came home buzzing with excitement, 'Guess what Dora- your father's asked me to go and work for him what do you think?'

Dora was aghast, 'But Arthur, you know nothing about gardening. I thought you were waiting for that job at the Post Office. They said they'd shortlist you after all your experience in Signals.'

'I know but I think I'd like to work outdoors. Your father's prepared to teach me. Look he's lent me this book of plants so that I can learn all the Latin names. I thought you'd be pleased.'

'Arthur, you don't know what he's like to work for. He's a generous big hearted man, but he finds it difficult to deal with customers. He can lose his temper easily, and end up cursing them if they're not proper gardeners, or if they treat his plants badly. I know his bark's worse than his bite but I don't think you'd find it easy working for him.'

'But I've been getting on so well with him lately,' Arthur replied, 'anyway if I could cope with the Army Sergeant Majors and all their shouting, I'm sure I can cope with your father's tempers. You used to help him out a lot and you two never fell out.'

'But that's because I wasn't working with him all the time and I was the one who had to apologise and calm the customers down when he'd frightened them away.'

'Still, Dora, I'd like to give a try. I've been talking to him a lot, and he's made me feel a lot better about myself. We seem to have come to some sort of understanding. You've always said how much you thought he wanted a son. Perhaps that's why.'

Dora could see arguing with him wasn't going to change his mind. Arthur was so keen to become part of a family and now he seemed to think hers was ideal, and was willing to do anything to join it. Amazingly he also seemed to be getting on better with her mother.

It was ironic that whilst Dora though loving her parents and owing them a lot, was trying her hardest to escape them and Aberystwyth, her beloved husband was running towards them. Dora knew when she was beaten. Everyone was conspiring against her. Overnight her mother and father had put their heads together and worked out how they could convert the upstairs rooms into a more self contained flat for her, Arthur and David. All the lodgers had long gone, so the rooms at the top of the house were standing empty and gathering dust.

Her mother said, 'We'll put in a sink and running water, and a gas stove into the middle room and that'll do for your kitchen. You and Arthur can have the room behind for a bedroom and David can sleep in the box room - then there's the front room you can have for a living room. We've plenty of bedroom furniture. You'll only need a table and chairs and perhaps a sideboard. You might find something in that new Utility furniture they're advertising.'

She and Arthur were to pay her mother rent and Arthur would work in the Garden for her father for a set wage. Dora knew she should be grateful that they had a roof over their heads and Arthur had a job – but at what cost? Dora had always thought after the war her life would change drastically. When David was born, she'd looked into renting a cottage in her beloved Llanbadarn, but Arthur's army pay wouldn't stretch to it unless she had a job and that was impossible with a new baby to care for. Staying on at Baker St reluctantly, Dora had nurtured the faint hope that one day she would move from there straight into her own house.

For the moment Dora had no choice but to resign herself to all the decisions that had been made for her. But nothing, absolutely nothing now, would deter her from looking for other options for her, Arthur and David. She must find them a way out, an escape route.

FAMILY LIFE

34

1946 - The Family

At the Garden there were plenty of customers as life got back to normal. There were many more funerals as peoples' health had suffered during these last six years. VJ Day had marked the final end of the War, with local men who'd been Japanese prisoners of war returning home, suffering from the effects of malnutrition, emaciated, and in poor health.

Arthur came home one night and said, 'John Lloyd- Jones died yesterday. He'd waited and waited for news of his son and when it came, he found he'd died of scurvy in a prisoner of war camp in Japan, and that was that. John's heart gave out and he went suddenly.'

'Oh that's terrible, the poor man,' Dora said, 'He was his only son, that Red Cross postcard he'd received signed by his son was all that kept him going.'

'Your father's very cut up. He was such a good Legion member that Jack's offered to do the flowers for nothing. You know he'll never make a business out of that Garden the way he's going.' Dora bit her lip. It was just like her father, his heart always overrode his head. But with two families dependant on the Garden's income it was far more critical nowadays to make it pay. She wanted to sympathise with her husband but her loyalties were divided. She'd warned Arthur all along as to how things would be, but he'd completely ignored her advice and been so sure that everything would work out.

A few weeks later out shopping with David, she spotted her husband wearily cycling up North Parade and waved across asking, 'Are you on your way home Arthur? It's too early for dinner; I haven't got anything ready yet.'

'No, I'm on my way to deliver and plant some bushes in Mrs Olwen Davies' garden. I still don't know that much but your father's sent me out anyway. The trouble is, you know your father, he's taken a deep dislike to her and says between her and her cat digging up the last lot of petunias, he can't be bothered anymore and refuses to deal with her. I've got to do something to sort her out. She's a good customer, spends a fortune on bedding plants with us even if her garden is a terrible mess.'

Every night Arthur would swot his way through 'The Dictionary of Plant Names for Gardeners' getting his wife to test him as he progressed, 'Give me the English names for this list of flowers Dora, and I'll see if I can remember the Latin names or remind me about geraniums – which family do they belong to?'

There was no doubt that Arthur was doing his best to become a gardener, but Dora often wondered whether he was he doing it to please her, her father or because he was really interested? Sometimes Dora felt quite deflated. All through the war she'd kept herself going worrying about her husband, not knowing whether he'd been wounded or even killed. All she'd wanted was for Arthur to come home in one piece. Of course she'd thought about 'after the war', and imagined what their life would be but in no great detail. It'd been more of a pink cloud 'happy ever after' kind of bliss surrounded by lots of children in a country cottage with roses round the door.

Learning to live with this comparative stranger on a day to day basis was not easy either. Over the years Dora had become attuned to Sarah's various moods and silences and Jack's flare ups, but to live with such a quiet man who rarely showed his emotions was something else again. He never seemed to lose his temper or even get that angry, Dora wished there was some way she could find out what was going on in his head.

Deciding to try a different approach, one day after Arthur had had his tea (it was always wise to ask him something on a full stomach) Dora suggested, 'What about meeting David and I tomorrow after work. We could go for a picnic in Cwm Woods. You could do with a change. You've been working so hard lately. What do you think?' She was always waiting for the 'I would but-------' or 'I'll be too tired perhaps another time' however Arthur as usual was more than willing to fit in with her plans, and rarely disagreed with her. Dora just wished that for once he would take the initiative. Why did it always have to be her? Was she being contrary in wanting Arthur to take the lead on occasion?

Arthur's responses to any proposals were generally, 'Yes, why not,' or 'Whatever you like Dora,' or 'That's a good idea.' He seemed to have no strong preferences. Whereas Jack and Sarah discussed everything and came to mutual agreements, Arthur left everything to her. It was pleasant to be with someone so easy going but Dora would have liked him to share more of the decision making.

But the day came when there was one very important decision to be made, and this time it didn't turn out quite how Dora expected. It was a Sunday afternoon after Arthur had been down to do the watering at the Garden, and they were both feeling at ease reading the Sunday papers, with David playing with his cars on the floor when Dora murmured, 'Arthur, have you thought about us having more children? You come from such a big family. I've always wanted brothers or sisters. We should think about it soon, David's nearly four now.'

Arthur very carefully and purposefully put down his paper and looking her straight in the eye said, 'Families are not all they're cracked up to be, Dora. You know my family.
All of us split into pairs when we were young – after Gertie was taken by my grandparents, Eric and Gwen stuck together and so did Peggy and I, and Eddie and Bob.

Peggy was the one who took care of me but once she had that accident in the schoolyard I was on my own. Money was tight with the seven of us. There was always a fight for the food and that meant only the strongest ate well and that certainly didn't include me. That's probably why I went down with rickets and Eddie at eleven ended up with T.B.'

'But what about your mother – she was such a loving woman?'

'Yes, but her leg limited her in what she could do.'

'But Arthur, it needn't be like that for us. I've enough love for a whole pile of children, it doesn't matter how many. I'm healthy, fit and strong and can take on any amount of physical work.'
'Dora, a large family costs money and we all had to leave home at sixteen and keep ourselves. Look at us now. None of us are close and we're spread across England and Wales with barely any contact.'

Dora could hear the underlying hurt and bitterness in his tone but she and Arthur were quite different type of people to his family. She was convinced they could do better in bringing up their own children. But Arthur sounded even more inflexible as he finished, 'Dora, I'm sorry but realistically we can only afford two children on my wage. I think we must be satisfied with that. At least we can make sure they have a proper upbringing and plenty to eat.' With that he buried his head back in his paper giving her no chance for further discussion.

Dora felt stunned and painfully disappointed, having no idea that he felt like this about children. They must have discussed children at one time but perhaps she'd only heard what she'd wanted to. In the back of her mind, there'd been this picture of the four children they'd have together but of course there was every chance he'd change his mind.

It was just unfortunate that today, the purpose of her conversation had been to gently lead up to telling him that she was already expecting their second baby, but obviously this wasn't the right time to break the news.

A few weeks later, Dora decided she really couldn't delay the news any longer and slipping it nonchalantly into the conversation at teatime announced, 'I think I'm pregnant.'

Arthur face went white, stuttering as if he'd misheard, 'What – what's that Dora?'

'We're having a baby you know 'the patter of little feet', she declared triumphantly. David sensing that something new was happening began banging his feet and chuckling loudly.

'That's right David,' said his mother, 'you're going to have a new little brother or sister.'

'Are you sure, have you been to the doctor—it can't be this soon,' Arthur stammered out, 'We were only discussing it the other week. It's not possible. I thought we'd be waiting a while.'

Arthur seemed so shaken that he never thought to ask Dora when she'd first known, or how long she'd known, or even if she'd known when they were discussing the subject. Dora was relieved some things were best kept quiet. Realising that for him this would be like having a first baby, she could understand his shock and panic, after all Arthur had been abroad during her pregnancy with David, not even being around for the birth. Nevertheless Dora was beside herself with joy.

David had been born on October 6th in time for Arthur's birthday on the 8th so Dora said to her husband, 'Looking at the dates, this baby may be born in time for my birthday on the 7th of June, wouldn't that be grand, one for your birthday and one for mine.'

By now having come to terms with the expected event, Arthur remarked drily, 'It's almost as if you'd planned it.' Assuming an air of artlessness Dora just shrugged her shoulders and floated off into the kitchen. Life continued much as before. Sarah and Jack were delighted about the forthcoming addition and Arthur was at last showing some signs of enthusiasm, with Dora secretly hoped for a girl again. When she'd been expecting David, she'd thought it would be a girl and when David arrived she'd wondered initially how she'd cope with a baby boy. This time for sure it must be a girl.

Just before Christmas, Dora went to collect David from school as usual. It was raining hard, and when she reached the school gates he was nowhere to be seen. Panicking she rushed home to Baker St. But no, there was no sign of him there. Racing back to the school again and this time going inside, there was David tucked up in the cloakroom, sheltering from the rain. Dora was furious with herself for not checking, and furious with the teacher for not looking out for her. Rushing back up Chalybeate Street, David kept tugging on her hand as she tried to move him along quickly. It was then that Dora caught her foot slipping on the wet grating and twisting as she went down, trying hard to protect both David and her unborn child. Passers-by helped her to her feet, asking her if she was alright, before she limped painfully home to Baker St.

Sarah was appalled when she saw the state of Dora's foot and her condition and sent immediately for Dr Thomas. Thankfully he had replaced her old arch enemy Dr Evans, and was a much older kindlier man.

He took one look at her foot and said, 'It's a bad sprain. You'll need to keep you foot elevated for a few days, but I don't know about the baby I can't hear a clear heartbeat. You may have ruptured the cord, Dora. We'll have to wait and see. Nature will take its course no doubt.'

He bustled out of the room indicating to her mother to follow, 'Mrs Roberts, a word. I expect Dora to lose the baby in the next few days. But you'll need to keep the foetus for me to examine.'

Sarah always a tower of strength in an emergency took on the household from looking after Dora, taking David back and fore to school, to cooking meals for their men folk.

Dora kept hoping against hope that her baby would be alright. But it was not to be. On Boxing Night when she, Arthur and David were due to go to 'Aladdin' at The Little Theatre, the terrible labour pains began. It was agreed that Arthur would take David, whilst her mother helped her through the worst. Even though Sarah had never had her own children she always seemed to know what to do.

It was too late for this baby. It never had a chance. Dr Thomas pronounced that it had been a boy. Dora felt sad but at the same time she so much wanted a girl she was prepared to accept what had happened. The old doctor warned her, 'No more babies for at least twelve months, young Dora. Your body needs to recuperate and get back to a healthy state.'

There were times when Dora found it heartbreaking to dwell on what they had lost and wondered how Arthur was feeling. Maybe he was relieved. But he never said anything at all about the miscarriage or even the baby, though he seemed far more solicitous than usual, and everything soon fell back into its customary routine. At the time so many people had such big families, that losing a baby was regarded as commonplace. Most people considered it Nature's way of getting rid of things that were not meant to be, and women were not expected to make any undue fuss about it.

35

1948 - An Addition

The winter of '47 was unbelievable. It seemed to go on forever. In all the years that Dora had lived in Aberystwyth she had never seen the sea frozen. It was a phenomenon. She, David and her mother were stuck in doors, coping with power cuts, and trying to make the coal last with just one lit fire in the house. Food was still rationed and now there was even a shortage of bread and potatoes. The Plynlimon Pass was closed and there was little in the way of fresh food being sent over the mountains.

Arthur and Jack were constantly plodding down to the Garden trying to keep the boilers lit for the greenhouses. The ground, covered in a few feet of snow was frozen solid with no business to be had. Seven weeks of this and there was no letup. Jack bemoaned 'his beloved plants' and Arthur worried where the next wage was coming from.

Finally in late March the thaw began. Arthur and Jack spent hours replanting for the year and trying to save and salvage as much of the dying plants and bushes as they could.

At the beginning of May, Dora felt unwell and had a strong feeling she might be pregnant again. Dreading seeing old Dr Thomas, she took her courage in her hands and made an appointment. As soon as he saw her the old doctor reprimanded her saying, 'Now Dora I hope you haven't come to tell me you're pregnant again. You didn't listen to my advice did you? It's much too soon for you to be having another baby.' But it was already too late another baby was on the way.

This time Arthur was elated. He seemed to be looking forward to the birth even more than Dora and kept saying, 'Dora it's going to be a girl this time you'll see.'

Dora herself felt a lot less thrilled. Instead of morning sickness she was plagued with evening sickness, and even her beloved cups of tea made her nauseous. Once the sickness had disappeared the cravings took over. This time it was apples and she found she was consuming a pound a day. Sarah said, 'Well at least we can cope with this craving though with that bad winter it's not a good crop this year.'

Eating for two and feeling a lot more relaxed in this pregnancy, meant that Dora was getting bigger and bigger, so the only exercise she could have was going out at night with Sarah or Arthur to walk round the block to Eastgate and down Great Darkgate St. This time Dora wasn't so positive it was going to be a girl, but whatever it was she wanted to see the end of this pregnancy. Perhaps Arthur had the right idea limiting their family to two children. Dora's enthusiasm for pregnancy had waned considerably over the last months, and she was not at all sure she was prepared to go through all this again and again.

David now five was beside himself with excitement. However much Dora explained that the new baby would only sleep and eat for some time and not be a readymade brother or sister to play with, David could not or would not understand. Arthur as usual was concerned about their future, and trying his best to save as much of his small wage as possible.

Since the summer business had picked up at the Garden and they were soon preparing the ground for the autumn. Arthur had learnt a lot more about gardening and he and Jack were hitting it off better. Dora felt at last they were all settling peacefully into their roles in the family, and hoped it would stay that way.

Sarah was crocheting piles of coats and caps – and with Dora's knitting and the sewing of napkins and baby nighties, they had all they needed for the new baby.

On her due date in January Dora said, 'It should be any day now. I'm certainly ready. I've got my case packed so all we've got to do Arthur is to get to the maternity home.' However, the date came and went and then three more weeks came and went.

Doctor Thomas said, 'There's nothing for it Dora, you'll have to go in and be induced. You can't have a ten month baby.'

Dora winced and thought not again, this seemed a rerun of the first time. At that time she didn't know quite what they'd meant by 'being induced' but this time unfortunately she was fully aware it meant large doses of castor oil and various other methods of torture. This wasn't at all how it was meant to be.

Arthur delivered her to the Maternity Home and left her to it. Hours later Sarah arrived with all the prepared baby clothes, 'No sign of it yet then,' she said.

'No, I'm to have a boiling hot bath soon. They think that relaxes your muscles and makes for an easier delivery.'

The bath which was much too hot came right up to Dora's neck, hardly allowing her to breathe through the steam, but it did its work. At long last with the threat of castor oil hanging over her head, labour started. Hours and hours passed punctuated by whiffs of pethadin with Dora giving up all hope of seeing a baby, until with one last monumental effort her ten pound baby erupted into the world.

Arthur, who had been pacing the corridor, was summoned by the midwife to meet his new daughter. He looked down at the baby in the cot and said, 'Good Grief Dora – she's enormous, she's got hair and it looks like teeth.'

'Don't be silly, Mr Hamer,' scolded the nurse, 'it's just a buildup of calcium on the gums. I believe your wife was eating a lot of apples through her pregnancy.'

Turning to his wife, Arthur bent over an exhausted Dora and kissed her, suddenly jumping back and saying, 'Ooh, I can't stand that hospital smell, I'll have to get some fresh air,' and with that he unceremoniously thrust a bunch of flowers on to her chest and rushed out the door, leaving Dora and the midwife open mouthed in shock.

'Well,' Dora said to the nurse, 'So much for a caring and romantic husband.' They both chuckled and shook their heads, women united, despairing at the frailty of men.

Dora didn't mind his behaviour at all, as all she could think about, was that at last she had the daughter she'd always wanted. Later after Arthur had recovered, he brought David along to see his new sister. Dora said to her son, 'What do you think of her David?' as he stared despondently down at the new addition. 'Is that her?' he asked, pulling at his lip, 'Spose she's alright for a baby but she's going to be no good to play with.'

A week later bringing home this enormous healthy bouncing daughter, Dora realised how much the birth had taken out of her. Delivering a ten pound baby was no joke. Once they reached Baker Street, Arthur had to carry the baby to the upstairs flat, whilst Dora barely able to stand up, laboriously crawled up the three flights of stairs on her hands and knees.

Sarah, stalwart as ever, rose to the occasion helping out as much as possible. Regrettably this also meant giving Dora the benefit of her advice. Still not able to walk properly, Dora would put the baby's cot by the open window to give her some fresh air. 'You should be taking that baby out in the pram,' her mother would remark, 'She needs some good sea air in her lungs. I could take her out if you can't manage it,' she offered.
But Dora was determined that she was going to be taking her own baby out for the first time, not Sarah.

Then there was the question of the name. Weeks had gone by with Dora still recovering and not able to go out. She said to Arthur, 'We really must register the baby but what shall we call her. What do you think?'

'What about Marjorie?' Arthur suggested.

'No, no, no, definitely not. I know who you're thinking of – that old flame of yours, Marjorie Hamer.'

'She wasn't an old flame, she was just a young girl I knew in the town,' Arthur added sheepishly.

'But didn't she used to give you extra sweets from her shop?'

'Just a few gobstoppers once in a while, there was no harm in that.' They looked at one another and burst out laughing at the thought of it.

'This isn't getting us anywhere,' Dora said, 'Didn't we both agreed on Jane after your mother, and after my original birth middle name? At least that could be one of her names.'

A few more days went by, and Dora said to her mother, 'We're stuck on a first name for the baby, what about 'Sarah'?'

Her mother grimaced, 'Please, no, I've always hated my name – don't saddle the baby with that.'

Arthur, who by now had been taking on baby duty, nappies and all, had nicknamed his daughter 'sweet smelling herb' – as he dangled one of the not very sweet smelling nappies at arm's length, holding his nose at the same time, came home from the Garden one day and said, 'I've had a brainwave Dora. I've been thinking all day about a name for the baby, and considering the names of flowers and herbs. What about 'Rosemary' as a first name?'

He laughed, 'After all it's supposed to be a sweet smelling herb and perhaps she'll become one later.'

Dora was thrilled that Arthur was so taken and involved with this new baby, as she always felt guilty that he'd missed so much of David's early childhood, and was quick to agree, 'That sounds fine, Arthur.' And so it was decided – the new baby was to become 'Rosemary Jane.'

36

1950 - Moving Out

Dora could hardly believe it when she read the letter. If only she dared ring Arthur – but it had been made clear to her on several occasions, that the telephone could only be used for Garden business, so there was no chance of contacting Arthur until he came home. Dora didn't know how on earth she was going to contain her excitement all day. When 6 o'clock came, Dora could hear Arthur tramping up the three flights his laboured footsteps echoing his fatigue; perhaps this wasn't a good time to spring something new on him. After his favourite tea of lamb chops, mash, and two veg. Dora asked, 'What sort of day have you had?'

'Just the usual,' was the tired response, 'What about you?'

Dora was still bubbling over with joy and couldn't keep it to herself any longer, 'As it happens, we had a bit of good news this morning.'

'What's that then?' Arthur didn't seem unduly interested as he concentrated on his syrup pudding and custard.

'You know some time ago we put our name down on the Council Housing list.'

'But that was ages ago Dora. I don't think anything will come of it. We seem to be quite settled here don't we?'

'Yes, but something has come of it. We've reached the top of the housing list as we're four in family now. They've offered us one of those newly built houses in Penparcau. Isn't that wonderful so what do you think?' Dora burbled on happily, 'We'd have a garden for the children and they could have their own bedrooms. We'd have privacy and be free to do what we wanted.'

'It's a bit of a stretch to the Garden isn't it. What about the rent? Could we afford it?' Arthur frowned as he reached for his cup of tea.

Dora not to be deterred and determined to meet all his objections forged ahead, 'You could cut across the Flats to the Garden and be there the same time as from here. I rang the Council offices and the rent's a tiny bit more then we pay my mother now. I can economise on food, and make more of the children's clothes----' her words tailed off, studying his expression.

Arthur could see how much this meant to her. Living day to day with two small children in a tiny flat, and always on call to her mother or father was not easy.

He smiled at her reassuringly, 'Let's sit down and look at all the money we have and the bills we have to pay, and make a budget.'

Dora, never one for planning, agreed meekly and almost too submissively. Whilst this budgeting was in hand and with David at school and her mother babysitting, the very next day Dora took a bus to Penparcau armed with the key from the Council Offices.

The house they were being offered was on Fifth Avenue. It was brand new, gleaming white, with three bedrooms and a spacious kitchen. At the back it overlooked green fields that led down to the river Rheidol. Dora started imagining all the curtains she would make, even bringing a tape with her to measure up. Of course, they would need mats for the cold lino floors, but her parents were big rag rug makers and no doubt would have some to spare. Her mother might let her bring the furniture from the Baker St flat, though this was probably debatable, as Dora hadn't yet got round to telling Sarah about any of this.

On the way back to the bus stop, she heard someone shouting, 'Dora, Dora,' and turning round she spotted a familiar face. It was Phyllis of all people, an old school friend she'd not seen for years.

'What are you doing up here, Dora?'

'Arthur and I've been offered a house on Fifth Avenue, and I just came to take a quick look.'

'Well we live a little further down that same road. It would be lovely to be neighbours,' Phyllis said.

Dora recalled that Phyllis had married someone called Hancock. She was Auntie Annie's niece, and it would be so good at last to have a woman friend close by, someone to drop in for a chat and a cup of tea. Sarah had always frowned on visitors to Baker St. A lot of Dora's friends were married or had moved away and since her own marriage she'd had little company outside the immediate family.

'I've got two sons now, Dora, my eldest Colin is six going on seven and my other's eighteen months. How old are your children?'

'My oldest is about the same as your Colin, and Rosemary's just a baby.'

They gossiped for a while about old friends, and then Dora caught the bus home, a warm glow in her heart, thinking how this could be just what they needed.

Arthur by now had sorted out all their finances and was becoming quite enthused, though taken aback that she'd already viewed the house without him 'You're right, Dora it is a good prospect for our family and we'll make it work.'

After worrying how her mother would take it, Dora was pleasantly relieved with Sarah's unconcern. It was always difficult and even dangerous to try and out think Sarah. In fact this time her mother didn't appear to mind one way or the other, but was helpful sewing curtains, sorting out extra saucepans, china and various household materials.

Though Arthur was positive about the move, he was uneasy about their limited finances but Dora herself was full of drive and couldn't wait to move. Her father was the only one with the glooms and dooms, warning, 'Dora, you might not like it on those council estates. They're moving all sorts of people from the slums there and you won't know who or what your neighbours will be. They could be rougher and tougher than you're used to.'

Dora thought he was probably exaggerating. After all she'd mixed with all types of lodgers and visitors at Baker St, and they weren't all nice, pleasant people.'

The day of the move David was bounding up and down with excitement. When Pickford's Removals arrived he proudly sat in the front seat with his father, whilst Dora leaving the baby with her mother until they'd moved in, caught a bus to Penparcau.

Dora soon had the place looking immaculate. It was blissful to only have her family to think about. No one calling up the stairs wanting her to help out at the Garden, or sell flags for the Legion or spring clean twelve rooms.

A few months went by and Dora could hardly believe that she had this spanking new kitchen to herself. True to her word, she spent all the first winter bottling blackberries gathered from the hedges, plums from the Garden, and apples gathered from the tree in their garden, to help the budget.

Even when some of the bottling jars exploded in the early hours of the morning she and Arthur only giggled at the mess and the cleanup. Nothing seemed to prick their bubble of contentment.

David had settled well into the local Primary School. He was a slight, delicate boy, shy and quiet, loving to help her with anything in the house and even with the baby. Rosemary, thank goodness, was a sound sleeper and spent most of that first year eating and sleeping.

By the summer all of them had got into a routine. When the river was running low, Arthur would roll up his trousers, paddle across and meet them in the lower fields for picnics. He and Jack still had their ups and downs but being away from Baker Street helped them lead a peaceful family life. Dora felt at last she had everything she had ever wanted. But it was definitely the calm before the storm.

One afternoon David came home with a bloody nose. Dora was furious. She settled him down with an ice pack, and waited for Arthur to come home for lunch. David now nearly seven was always being picked on and bullied. Arthur had tried to give him lessons on how to protect himself but to no avail. The little boy was too gentle to learn to fight.

That afternoon Dora in warring mode went up to the school and demanded to see the headmaster. 'He's not available,' was the curt response she got. By now Dora was seeing red, 'Then I'll wait until he is.' She was not going to have her lovely son injured again like this.

After some prevarication the school secretary went and collected the head from his office. 'I can't do anything about your son, Mrs Hamer. It must have happened outside the school gates. We don't allow such behaviour in this school.' Dora not willing to accept the platitudes he handed out decided to find out herself what had happened.

David usually went to school with Colin, Phyllis' son. Unfortunately Colin was often in trouble being a somewhat mischievous and aggressive boy, and could easily lead David into situations he couldn't handle.

Opposite their house lived the large sprawling family of the Lewises. The kids were dirty, ill kept and often unfed they were all the products of different fathers and ran round the area like a pack of feral animals. It was one of these children Colin or David had upset.

Explaining the situation to Arthur, Dora hoped that he would step in and take over and sort things out for her and his son. But all he said was, 'Kids get bullied now and then. David will just have to get used to it,' and made it clear there was nothing further he was going to do about it.

Dora decided to take it upon herself to confront the mother of the Lewises. Waiting till she was in the right frame of mind, Dora knocked on their door. Surely they could come to some sensible understanding. She was faced with the vision of Mrs Lewis, a fag hanging out of the side of her mouth and a head full of curlers saying, 'Wha' d'ya want?' As soon as Dora mentioned the fight between her son and the Lewis' youngest, she received a barrage of abuse and curses. It was hopeless.

Dora, feeling the fury rising in her, lost her temper, 'Look at the state of your kids, no wonder they run wild, they've got no proper home life.' And then losing it completely she went too far, ' You might as well have a red light outside your door the number of men who come and go. No wonder the kids are out of control not knowing who their fathers are!'

At this, the woman leapt for Dora's throat, but Dora had had the sense to back away aware that she might have said too much, and beat a hasty retreat to her own house.

Later that afternoon when she had put the baby down there was a knock at the door. A policeman, helmet in hand, stood there. 'We've had a complaint about you, ma'm. Can I come in?' 'The woman opposite has put in a formal complaint about you. Saying you slandered her, practically calling her a *'prostitute.'*

Dora couldn't believe how events had escalated from the morning, so shoulders back and standing up straight, she explained the conversation and the reason for her visit in rational tones. The policeman was a fatherly sort of man, and accepting a cup of tea from her said, 'You seem a well spoken decent person, ma'm but I have to warn you at least unofficially. That family will cause you no end of trouble you'll need to keep your distance from them in the future.'
After he'd gone Dora wondered how she was going to tell Arthur. But if she was hoping for sympathy and support, she was mistaken.

All he said was, 'I told you to leave things alone and it would die down. You've just made things a whole lot worse and David won't be the only one who'll suffer as we live opposite the family. What possessed you, Dora?'

Dora could have cried. Was she to be completely on her own running this family? This was so depressing. One thing she could always count on with Jack was that he would stand up for himself, her or Sarah, and would have no truck with anyone he came up against who showed him a lack of respect.

When she married, Dora thought she would always have someone at her back. Well clearly this wasn't to be the case in hers and Arthur's marriage, so at that instant Dora made up her mind to take a resolute stand on her own and her children's' behalf. Arthur would just have to go along with anything she decided. Her main priority would be to protect her children when they needed it.

Dora now had to both take and collect David from school, as relations with the Lewises had deteriorated even more. The whole family were now ganging up and calling her and her son names and constantly trying their hardest to provoke her. Dora began to wish she'd listened to her father. It was a pity she'd taken no notice.

There was nothing for it but she'd have to return to Baker Street, cap in hand. Taking Rosemary in her pushchair, she called on her parents at teatime when both Jack and Sarah were there.

Her mother said immediately, 'You must come back to the flat that's the only thing you can do,' and her father agreed, 'These people never give up. You can't be there for David all the time. And what about Rosemary?–in a few years she'll at the same school, and what will happen then?' The three of them decided on a date for the return move.

Dora now had to go home and break the news to her husband, who by now wasn't at all ready to return to Baker St, instead enjoying being in his own house. He'd begun meeting up again with some mates from the Battery, and they would go out for the occasional drink, so his reaction was as expected, 'It's just a storm in a teacup, Dora. It'll blow over. Can't you stick it out?' Dora thought resentfully, he wasn't the one who had to face the daily hullabaloo from that family as he was in the Garden from early in the morning till six at night.

'No Arthur,' she said uncompromisingly, 'I can't. I have to put the children first and that's that,' and softening slightly at his disappointed expression, 'there'll be other possibilities, you'll see.'

By the Spring of '52, the Hamer family was back in residence at 8, Baker Street and life seemed to be repeating itself, with Dora thinking here we are again, are we never going to escape Baker St?

37

Back to the Start

Dora had only just given David and Rosemary their tea, when she heard footsteps running up the stairs. She looked at the clock, it was only half past four, much too early to expect Arthur. But there he was bursting through the door. She could tell by his face that things weren't right. She hurried the children down to David's bedroom, leaving them to play. When she came back Arthur was sitting with his head in his hands.

'What's the matter? Don't you feel well again?'

Arthur hadn't been right for months, despite seeing doctor after doctor and a short hospital stay they couldn't find anything wrong with him.

'No, it's not my stomach it's the old man. Twice today, he upset customers, and turned them away. He spotted Mrs Lloyd coming down the road as he was digging the front patch by the gate and before I knew it he'd disappeared into the potting shed. Of course it was him she was looking for. Some of the bedding plants she'd bought for the spring had died and she wanted replacements or at least to talk to him and I did my best, Dora I really did.'

'I know you did love,' she patted his arm reassuringly.

'She insisted on seeing your father face to face. I went round the back and made him come out to talk to her.

But he was absolutely furious and went off in Welsh telling her very pointedly that she'd killed everything herself and he refused to sell her another thing. Once she'd stalked off he turned on me then and gave me what for.'

'You know Dada – he's all bark with a short fuse. He calms down as quickly.'

'But I can't stand it Dora, his tempers and his moods. I don't know from day to day where I stand. In fact after lunch he got worse because Major Edwards- Jones called in. You know how your father hates men who hang on to their service title after the war is over, and not only that but call themselves by double barrelled surnames just because their name is Jones.

Your father considers him a time waster, and insists on calling him Mr Jones to his face, which doesn't go down well but the Major's pleasant enough, and at least he's willing to take gardening advice. He'd seen something in a gardening magazine he wanted your father's help with. It was about building some sort of conservatory or summer house that he could grow grapes and various hothouse plants in. Your father thought it all a lot of new fangled nonsense and was quick to say that, sending the Major away with a flea in his ear.

I tried to reason with Jack but he huffed and puffed and said he was late for a Legion meeting and would I lock up. I'd had enough and came home early. This isn't good, Dora, we'll never make ends meet the way he's carrying on.'

Ever since the Penparcau debacle and their return to Baker St Dora knew it was urgent that they find a place of their own.

At this moment, it looked like Arthur needed a different job as well. With his continuous stomach problems one doctor had said that the condition could be caused by Arthur standing on damp soil every day, making a change even more urgent.

Dora was at her wits end. Things were not plain sailing at Baker St either. However hard she tried with Sarah and Jack, they seemed to want to have little to do with her children. They had once taken David on holiday with them to Liverpool but though he'd behaved himself, they never asked him again.

Every Saturday teatime, she would say to the children, 'Do your hair and wash your faces and hands it's time to go downstairs to see Granny for your Stamps.'

'Do we have to?' was the inevitable moan.

Her mother would have laid out a tea of wafer thin cucumber sandwiches and a Battenberg or a Victoria sponge together with the big silver teapot. Her father and Arthur were rarely home at this time.

'Sit there David you're a big boy now so you can have one of my bone china cups today,' Sarah would say.

Dora would be beside herself as David tried to manage his cup with one hand and wolf down two or three tiny sandwiches at a go. Rosemary being younger was allowed a mug and forgiven any spillages.

The Saving Stamps pretty with pictures of Prince Charles and Princess Anne would be produced with a flourish.

'I hope you've both been good children this week – this is your pocket money,' Sarah would say. She would cross question David about his school work and they would be allowed to stick their stamps in their books, and hopefully return upstairs for a proper tea.

David would have preferred to have been given a Dinky toy, and Rosemary was perplexed with the Savings book. It was supposed to start them on the right road to saving, but both children had no comprehension that these stamps represented money they could cash in.

Sarah would often say, 'Now you've had your tea, children, go upstairs. I want to talk to your mother.'

Dora's heart would sink – trying to think of what she had done or not done that week. If it wasn't about any misdemeanours they'd committed, it was usually about the British Legion. Both Sarah and Jack were dedicated to their work for the Legion, both having been presidents of their local branch the previous year.

'Dora we're holding a fete at the Parish Hall next Saturday. I've put you down for a stall and said you'll help.' Dora tried her best to interrupt saying, 'I'd have to bring the children with me as Arthur will be working.'

But her mother taking not the least bit of notice continued in full flow, 'I'd like you to dress Rosemary in that pretty organdie dress you made – you know the one with the frills and the big bow. I want her looking her best. She's to give the bouquet to the Lady Mayoress on the day.'

'I'll have to ask her,' Dora said diffidently.

'Ask her!' Sarah was indignant, 'That's ridiculous. What is she – seven now? She'll do as she's told, didn't she present a bouquet last year to the Minister's wife at your chapel and she was younger then?'

Dora kept silent as she knew Rosemary particularly liked Mrs Davies, the minister's wife, who having no children always made a great fuss of her, and would say to her little daughter, 'We nearly have the same name, Rosemary. My name's Rosamund so we 'Roses' must stick together,' and Rosemary would be thrilled to bits.

Whilst Sarah huffed and puffed about the matter
Dora finally managed to get out through gritted teeth, 'I'll still have to ask her.'

Sarah's face went into rigid mode stiffly saying, 'Very well, if that's the way you insist on bringing up your children, allowing them to do what they like------'and practically waving Dora away, dismissed her as if she was in the presence of royalty.

Dora nimbly ran up the three flights. It was always something. For Sarah and Jack the Legion was everything, and no allowances were made for family.

Her parents had also got into the habit lately of taking lengthy summer holidays and though Dora certainly didn't begrudge them their breaks as they'd worked hard all their lives, it meant that she and Arthur had such a lot to do that they hardly spent any time together.

On top of this was the matter of their privacy. No sooner would they sit down to tea, than Dora would hear Jack stomping up the stairs to bring his newspaper to exchange with theirs, or shouting to her about something he wanted her to do or just walking in on whatever might be happening and treating their flat as his own. It got so bad that Dora had persuaded Arthur to put a bolt on their living room door so that she could have a bit of peace, especially if she wanted an afternoon rest.

The day of the fete came round soon enough. Dora dressed Rosemary in the organdie, but was far too wary of the little girl's reaction to tell her what was to happen, as it was quite likely that Rosemary would dig her heels and refuse to go. The three of them set off for the Parish Hall, with David looking smart and grownup in his first long trousers and white shirt.

All went well for an hour or two and then Sarah came over and said under her breath to Dora, 'I've got the flowers ready – do you want to send Rosemary over?'

Dora put it to her daughter tactfully and calmly, whereupon Rosemary point blank refused to have anything to do with it. Dora was forced to go to her mother and break the bad news, and see if she could find someone else.

Sarah however, determined not to be bested by a mere child, started sending over a procession of people to try and change the youngster's mind. The more they tried the more determined Rosemary became.

Eventually a rather sweet old gentleman offered his services thinking some sort of charm offensive might work and said, 'You look so beautiful in your dress Rosemary, why don't you take my hand and I'll escort you up to the platform and help you hand over the bouquet to the Mayoress. She'd be so pleased to meet you and you'll like her, I know you will.'

But Rosemary was not to be swayed. She folded her arms and pointedly turned her back on the old gentleman. There was nothing for it, but Dora had to take the bouquet up herself feeling rather embarrassed about her daughter, but on the other hand quietly proud of the fact that Rosemary, even at such a young age, could make her mind up and stick to it. She herself had always done exactly what she was told by her parents and was still towing the line at nearly forty.

When she got home, she and Arthur laughed and laughed. Even though they knew Rosemary was no blood relation to the Roberts' – they both said in unison – 'she gets more like Sarah every day. She's a real chip off the old block. What a battle of wills they would have had, if she'd been brought up downstairs.'

38

1955 – 6. The Lease

At the beginning of the school holidays Dora was down in the front hall with Rosemary. They were on their way out to buy shrimps at the fishmongers. This was a treat for them both as they would bring the shrimps home wrapped in newspaper, top and tail them and eat them with a splash of vinegar straight out of the paper. Just as Dora was putting herself straight in the hall mirror, Sarah put her head round the door, 'Have you a minute Dora? It's urgent.'

Dora sent Rosemary to sit in the sun on Bethel's wall opposite and followed her mother back to her sitting room.

Sarah seemed unusually upset, 'You know, Mrs Hughes, our old landlady well she died a few months ago.'

Dora hadn't been aware of it but remembered the old lady well. The landlady had been a sweet soul and would often drop in to Baker St for a cup of tea and a chat and was on friendly terms with them all. Over the years they had been at Baker St., there had never been any problems with her as she'd always kept the rent at a peppercorn level. Under their lease, Sarah and Jack had carried out all the repairs to the upkeep of the building, and got used to treating Baker St. as if they owned it.

'Well, it seems,' Sarah continued, 'now the will's been sorted out, her daughters will inherit. With our lease coming up for renewal, they want to talk to us about renegotiating or they'll put the house up for sale. Honestly I don't know what to do or what your father will say. I think we'd be in a better position if your family wasn't living here. They might then consider your father and I extending the lease.'

Dora was shaken. Certainly she'd been toying for some time with the thought of them finding somewhere else to live, but it was so difficult on Arthur's small wage and with two growing children.

What on earth could they do? She and her mother didn't know what to say to one another, bemused at the turn of events and it was agreed between them, to think it over and talk it through with Arthur and Jack respectively.

No longer in the mood for shrimps, Dora took Rosemary down to the promenade. Sitting on a seat on the prom whilst her daughter built sandcastles on the beach, Dora kept turning things over in her mind. Life had not been going well at the Garden. Her father's tempers and his turning away business had become more and more of a problem for Arthur. To cap it all, Jack was of the opinion that David would also join them in the Garden when he left school. Dora had thought, 'Over my dead body!' David was a practical and artistic boy but not good at his lessons however Dora was confident that he would find his niche in time. It certainly wouldn't be the Garden though, as it could never provide an income for two men and a boy.

Dora wanted everything clear in her mind before she spoke to her husband. Rosemary was nearly eight now, so perhaps Dora herself could get a job though she wasn't trained for anything except keeping house, cooking and cleaning. True, she was good at it all after all these years. Maybe that was the answer then-follow in Sarah's footsteps, rent a house and take lodgers and boarders.

After Arthur had had his tea and the children had gone to bed, Dora broached the subject of the lease. At first he was in shock, 'I can't believe your mother and father let things go like this – surely they thought things would alter when Mrs Hughes died.'

Dora tried to explain, 'they had such an informal arrangement with Mrs Hughes for so many years that I think they look on Baker St. as theirs. Remember Mom took the house on back in 1917 with the Red Cross, nearly forty years ago.'

'But Dora, why didn't they think about buying no 8 themselves, wouldn't they have got first refusal from the Red Cross before it was sold after the war?'

'I think they did, but by then Dada was back and had started renting the ground for the Garden. He was dead against any sort of bank loans or mortgages, saying they were a millstone round your neck.'

Arthur was distraught, 'I don't know what we can do, Dora. We'll just have to find somewhere else to rent–perhaps a flat or maybe go back to the Council. I just don't know how we're going to manage.'

Dora quietly mulling over her idea of running a boarding house, deliberated as to whether she should mention it, but on second thoughts the enormity of it might frighten Arthur. There was no point in upsetting him unnecessarily, especially as his health was shaky. It would be wiser to do some investigation first.

Disturbing though all this was, Dora felt more alive than she had for a while, as if this was the challenge she had been waiting for. Perhaps it was fortuitous after all, forcing them to make a move.

Full of energy and optimism, Dora was up and out early next morning. Leaving David and Rosemary to play with the neighbours next door, she began her travels round the renting agencies and estate agents, but it was dispiriting. By mid morning her sunny mood had faded. It looked like her schemes might come to nothing.

Hard as it was, she had to face facts as the only savings they had was £50 in the Post Office, and a few pounds put by for the children.

Most of the estate agents looked down their nose at her, when they heard the amount Arthur earned. 'I'm sorry Mrs Hamer, we can't do anything for you in terms of a mortgage, and I think you'll find rents will be beyond your pocket as well.'

Dora felt that she was just reluctantly going through the motions in the afternoon, when her luck changed. Studying yet another estate agent's window, she spotted a house called 'Tan–y-Fron' in Llanbadarn with four to five bedrooms, quoting a weekly rental they might be able to afford. This could be the one and with no hesitation, Dora went straight in and asked for the key.

Astounding herself with her own audacity, Dora decided to enlist Sarah's help to go and view the house. Sarah's hard headed, practical streak was exactly what Dora needed, and she might as well make good use of it whilst her mother was making encouraging noises. It was also in Sarah's own interests, as this house could make all the difference as to whether Sarah and Jack kept Baker St or not. When she and Sarah arrived at 'Tan-y-Fron', other prospective buyers were already being shown round by their solicitor.

Dora hung back, letting the group go first, and it was then she heard a quiet voice murmur into her ear, 'I didn't realise you were interested in this house too, Dora.'

Of all people, it was her old friend, Henry, from the Wesleyan Chapel drama days. She knew he'd gone off to train as a solicitor, but hadn't set eyes on him in years. She and Arthur no longer attended the Wesleyan, since the children had started going to Sunday school at the Congregational with the children next door.

As he was leaving, Henry came close and said quietly and urgently to her, 'Come and see me in the next few days, Dora. I'm working for Davies Jenkins in Baker St, just two doors away from you at no 8,' and hurriedly moved off with his party.

Dora and Sarah continued their viewing, but the house needed a lot of work and the back garden sloped steeply and dangerously towards a brook at the bottom. Later talking to her father about the property, Jack said, 'That ground is known to be swampy Dora, with flooding from the brook when it overflows.' He tried his best to put her off Llanbadarn altogether saying, 'you really don't want to live there Dora it's not the place for you.' For some unknown reason he'd always hated the village, though Dora had no idea why.

It would be so nice one day, Dora mused, to be allowed to make up one's own mind and not have to listen to other people's advice and prejudices. Dora had always had a soft spot for Llanbadarn from when she was young. Her favourite house 'Sunny Side', down a lane by the church, was still there in its idyllic setting. Though 'Tan-y-Fron' was disappointing, Dora was determined not be put off Llanbadarn or to give up finding a house there. This would be a perfect place for the children. It was such a peaceful, secluded and pretty village only a mile and a half from Aberystwyth and on a good bus route, and what a change to be in the country rather than in the middle of a town.

39

A Guardian Angel

Dora decided not to tell Arthur about her disappointments in trying to find a house. His health was so worrying that she didn't want to make matters worse for him as he'd been in hospital now for six weeks, with tubes in his stomach to cure a possible ulcer.

Dora began to wonder if he'd ever come home. It wasn't too bad for David, at fourteen, allowed to visit his father but Rosemary at eight didn't have a clue what was happening. It was as if her father had disappeared from the face of the earth. One night Dora was alarmed to hear the little girl crying violently and wondered if she was having a nightmare.

'No, No,' sobbed Rosemary, 'Where's Dad, he's dead isn't he and you're not telling me.'

'Of course he's not dead,' Dora reassured her, 'though he's not well. But he'll be home soon, I'm sure,' she said crossing her fingers behind her back.

Dora hearing this put so bluntly by her daughter, began to wonder if she was kidding herself, was Arthur going to recover and come home? Who knew, what effects had been left from that time in hospital in Palestine? She'd often heard of men dying later from wounds they'd suffered during combat, and the war had played havoc with peoples' general health. What would happen if Arthur died?

The thought of it was unbearable. Dora knew she had to put her doubts to one side, be strong, and concentrate on keeping their family together. To prove to Rosemary that Arthur was alive and kicking, Dora had to beg and plead with the hospital authorities. Once Rosemary could wave to her father through the glass panel in the ward door, all of them were relieved.

After it seemed like a lifetime in hospital, Arthur was sent to convalesce for another four weeks at Tan-y-Bwlch, a nursing home outside Aberystwyth. He was still no better but every Sunday afternoon, Dora could take the children and walk across the beach to meet him. Outwardly he looked hale and hearty, putting on weight from the intense milk diet but still complaining of stomach pains.

As they moved further and further into the autumn, their family situation at Baker St. became more and more desperate. By now Arthur was back at work, but he seemed more tired than before and was starting to look drawn and ill again. Dora, fit, healthy and full of beans, was determined to become the 'breadwinner', or at least find a way to contribute to their income. To make matters worse, every evening Arthur would ask, 'How did you get on today- have you managed to find anywhere to rent?'The pressure was certainly building. Dora had still not told Arthur about her proposed boarding house venture. Only Sarah knew and as she and Arthur hardly spoke these days, Dora's secret was safe for the moment.

After their fruitless visit to *'Tan-y- Fron'*, Sarah had started being peevish with Dora as if all this uncertainty about Baker St was her fault, so a few days after the visit, Dora decided to mention Henry to Arthur but didn't go into details as to where they'd met, merely saying, 'You'll never guess who Mom and I bumped into the other day?'

'No who?'

'Do you remember Henry from the Wesleyan? He was in the Drama group with us. In fact he played the organ at our wedding. Apparently he's qualified as a solicitor now and is working just two doors down from here. The funny thing is after Mom had gone on ahead, he made a point of coming up to me and very, very quietly asking me to call in and see him in the next few days.'

'What do you think he wants, Dora? Perhaps it's just about old times. He always had a bit of a soft spot for you. I'm sure he'd have snapped you up if I hadn't got there first,' Arthur said teasingly.

'Don't be silly. We were just kids anyway – it's a long time ago. No, I have a feeling there's something more to it as there seemed to be an urgency in his tone anyway I've made an appointment for tomorrow morning.'

'Do you want me to come with you? We've got a funeral in the morning and that might be difficult.'

'No, Arthur, I'll go on my own and see what it's about. It may be nothing at all.'

The last thing Dora wanted was to worry her husband with the guesthouse idea – well certainly not at this stage.

The next day, Henry was delighted to see her. To Dora's complete astonishment without any preamble or any reminiscing went straight to business, 'You should have come to me earlier, Dora, about a house. It's definitely time, you and your family moved out of Baker St. and away from the Roberts'. You, Arthur and your children deserve better than a cramped flat at no. 8,' he said frankly.

Dora was nonplussed for a minute and didn't know quite what to say. How did Henry know about her family, and why would she have thought of approaching him. She hadn't even known he was working in Baker Street. It was very strange they hadn't run into one another before this, as it was such a small town.

She mumbled something about her parents and what she owed them, idly speculating on what gossip Henry might have heard about her background.

Henry however was refreshingly honest and direct, coming straight out with, 'Listen Dora, living with the Roberts and working for them is a route to disaster, surely you and Arthur need a house of your own with your growing family? I was surprised to see you at *'Tan-y-fron'* and really thought you might be interested in the house. In fact, I even discouraged the people I was showing round from putting in an offer, thinking you might want it.'

Dora felt embarrassed and uncomfortable, that she hadn't thought to let him know her opinion of *'Tan–y-Fron'* earlier, but outlined what she was looking for a suitably sized house to rent where she could take lodgers and boarders, preferably in Llanbadarn.

'You weren't thinking of buying then,' Henry queried.

Dora decided to be completely truthful, there was no point in skirting round their finances, 'No, there's no chance of us buying a house. Arthur doesn't earn much and we don't have enough savings for any of the building societies. We could manage to rent but only if I can make the house pay.'

Dora felt momentarily guilty saying 'we', as Arthur was in complete ignorance about her plans. She supposed she would have to tell him sooner or later, and it might just have to be sooner.

Aware that Henry was still speaking, Dora heard him say, 'You should have come to me Dora, because I think I can help.'

Dora was mystified. Whatever did he mean? Maybe he had some sort of contacts with the building societies after all he was showing people round when she met him. Thinking about it though, surely solicitors didn't usually do that type of thing did they-wouldn't that have been an estate agent's job?

But Henry was continuing, and appearing to address all her unspoken questions. His boss, Davies Jenkins, a solicitor and a wealthy landowner, had set up a number of private mortgages to offset his tax, lending to about five people at any one time, with one of his mortgagees about to finish in a few months time.

Dora thought–whatever is this to do with us?

But Henry was carrying on, 'Dora, I think I can talk Mr Davies Jenkins into overlapping his loans and letting you and Arthur have one of his mortgages. Could you find the right house to buy in the next month? Time is of the essence. What do you think?'

Dora felt faint and breathless, hairs standing up all over her head and goose bumps popping up all down her arms. How was this happening? Just when they needed help desperately, it was being offered 'on a plate'. It was incredible, astonishing, amazing – there just weren't the words for it!

Not waiting for a reply, Henry went on, 'Leave it with me for a few days and then come in with Arthur at the end of the week. If all's gone as I expect, we'll be able to talk through the details.'

Showing her out, Henry took one look at her pale face and reassuringly patted her arm, 'Don't worry Dora, I'm confident I can sway Mr Davies Jenkins. You'll be moving into your own house in no time.'

Dora's legs felt like jelly. If she'd been able, she'd have danced a Highland jig right there in the middle of Baker St. Instead, she went home for a much needed cup of tea, and couldn't wait to tell Arthur. It was as if all their Christmases had come at once, and Henry was a Guardian Angel sent down to rescue them.

There'd been so little hope – with Arthur's illness, the troubles at the Garden, Sarah's moods, and having to get out of Baker St. It had been overwhelming. Now there was a future and they had to grab it with both hands and run off with it and Dora was going to make sure they did.

Telling Arthur good news was a wonderful change. Always the pessimist he said, 'I can't see how Henry will be able to persuade his boss. I don't earn anywhere near enough. We're hardly good prospects.'

Dora decided it was time to 'bite the bullet' and outline her boarding house scheme. Amazingly Arthur perked up. Usually he would have picked holes in it all, but being only too aware of their difficulties said, 'Dora, I think this mightn't be such a bad notion. Both the children are at school and you know all about running a boarding house. You've always said, despite everything, your mother's given you good training. Added to that, you're full of energy and initiative I think you could pull it off.'

'You mean we, don't you,' retorted Dora, 'Remember we're in this together.' For the first time in their marriage Dora felt as if they were standing side by side. She knew they could achieve anything, if they put their minds to it.

THE HOUSE

40

1956 - The Big Row

Over the next month, Dora and Sarah looked at even more houses. Getting her mother involved in house hunting guaranteed not only Sarah's endorsement but her temper. Finally they found 'the one', a large semi detached house with a long garden standing opposite the church in Llanbadarn Fawr village. It had 3 rooms on the first floor that could be let, with two large attics for the family to sleep in. But there was no electricity or even a bathroom. However Dora was overjoyed, 'Arthur, we've found a house. It was a shop. It's got a big front window but that doesn't matter, I can always curtain it. It needs a lot doing, but it's right for us and would you believe it's actually called 'Rosemary'. It must be a sign, don't you think or fate?'

Arthur was not big on signs or even coincidences, 'If you think it's alright Dora then I'm happy. We can always change the name.'
'Definitely not,' said Dora, 'I want our Rosemary to be brought up in 'Rosemary'. I think it's meant to be.'

Dora forged ahead in leaps and bounds though Arthur was back in hospital again. He had collapsed one day at the Garden and the hospital had at last diagnosed appendicitis. It was a relief after the operation to see him gradually regain his health.

In the meantime, Henry had negotiated buying the house. Dora and Arthur had scraped up the deposit from their savings, and everything was going ahead. Henry had done a wonderful job persuading his boss and vouching for their reliability.

The two of them were both so grateful to him and thanking him said, 'Henry, we owe you so much for what you've done for us. You've really put yourself on the line. I only hope we don't let you down.'

'Dora, I don't think you will. You and Arthur are such good hardworking people you deserve a break. I always thought that you'd both got yourselves too tightly linked in with Mr and Mrs Roberts. At 42, you need to make your own way.'

During their earlier conversations, Dora had confided in Henry about her background. She felt he needed to know the facts about her parentage or lack of it. Though he was only a few years older than she and Arthur, Henry always managed to give them wise advice, allowing them to see things from a different perspective. Talking about the Roberts' he said, 'Duty is one thing Dora, but being this obligated to them and allowing your family to suffer because of it, is another thing entirely.'

Dora had never thought about it like that before. Her parents always preferred to deal with her alone, rather than have much to do with Arthur or the children. They seemed to want to ignore the fact that she was married with a family, making Dora often feel as if she was their property, bought and paid for.

A few days later, Henry's perceptive words came back to haunt her. It was one evening after Arthur was back from hospital and resting, and the children were in bed – there was a loud knock on their kitchen door. Opening it, Dora was surprised to see both Sarah and Jack standing there, as Sarah rarely ventured to the top of the house.

'We need to have a word with you both,' they said, 'We've had another letter from the Hughes' solicitor.'

270

Calling Arthur, Dora thought this sounds distinctly ominous, as these days even Jack never came upstairs to see them. From hers and Arthur's point of view, everything was going smoothly – where was the next blow likely to fall?

They all sat facing one another at the kitchen table, the letter on the table between them.

Sarah kicked off, 'The Hughes' are no longer willing to rent this house out. What they are suggesting is we have first refusal to buy. Of course, that's no good for us as we couldn't raise that sort of money or get a mortgage at our age.' but addressing Arthur rather pointedly, she persisted, 'As you and Dora are being offered a mortgage, we thought rather than move to Llanbadarn, you could take one for Baker St. instead and we could all stay here.'

Dora didn't know whether this was a question or whether they were stating a fact, but one look at Arthur's face was enough.

'How would that work?' Dora asked trying to postpone the moment, when she'd have to turn them down, 'with all of us, there'd be no extra rooms for me to take any lodgers.'

Sarah carried on dogmatically, 'We thought we could live in the front of the house, and your family could have the back. We would pay you rent and perhaps if you put the two children in together, you could let out one room for a lodger or as Rosemary's older you could go out to work, Dora.'

Dora was too flabbergasted to say anything. Was she always to play the subservient role in their lives, the barefaced cheek of it, to expect them to live as poor relations paying the mortgage, yet living in what was once the servants' quarters at the back of the house! Imagine putting a boy of fourteen into a tiny box room with a girl of nearly nine!

Dora was so infuriated and hurt by the way they had dismissed her family, she could hardly contain herself. Arthur's eyes were boring into hers, pleading with her not to lose her temper. He could see the signs and was loath to have some sort of confrontation. But Dora couldn't control herself any longer, years and years of rage and resentment had been building inside her. Years of being told 'your mother was no better than she ought' and always fitting in with whatever Sarah and Jack wanted. There's been so many times that Dora had been snubbed, overlooked or treated like an extension of the Roberts', but she was not going to have her family exposed to this type of treatment anymore.

Once at the Legion May Dance, when she'd known how much Rosemary had wanted to be picked as an attendant, Jack had come to her and said, 'Obviously Dora, we can't pick my granddaughter for anything. I'm on the committee, and there can't be favouritism, how would it look?' Even then she'd had taken it on the chin, seeing her daughter hurt and wondering how to explain to a disappointed six year old in floods of tears.

At last, Dora found her voice and trying hard to keep it steady and on an even keel said, 'But, we've put the deposit down on 'Rosemary' and we'll lose it if we withdrew at this late stage.'

'Oh never mind about that,' said Sarah, 'We'll find the deposit for Baker St., if you're willing to take on the mortgage.'

Dora could hold herself back no longer, and exploded with, 'So, first of all we're an encumbrance and you were pushing us to move out, which we're doing. Now everything's changed for you both, you expect Arthur and I to work ourselves to death, take on the mortgage, be relegated to living in the back of the house, and allow my children to be treated as second class citizens. You take no interest whatsoever in the children, unless there's something you want them to do. It's different for me I've fitted in with you both all my life, and done exactly what you wanted of me.

272

But my children are not going to have to do that. They are entitled to lives of their own choosing, and I'm going to make damn sure they do. No, we are definitely not going to take on Baker St,' Dora heard herself saying angrily, 'I'm sorry, if this leaves you in a difficult position. I'll always appreciate you taking me in and what you've done for me over the years. Now I owe it to Arthur and the children to put them first, and give them a home of their own and a future. This is my family,' (and she nearly added 'and my blood' but bit it back at the last moment).

Dora could see by his face, Jack was thunderstruck. In her whole life Dora had never spoken to him like that or stood up to him before. He'd always been her hero, despite the fact he'd never oppose her mother. In trepidation she waited for his temper to blow.

But instead in dead silence with clenched fists, he collected up the letter, turned his back on her saying, 'Come on Sis – there's nothing for us here,' and marched off down the front stairs, banging the living room door behind him.

Sarah astonishingly, stayed seated. Always far more realistic about life and loath to show any emotion, she commented coolly, 'It was to be expected. Don't worry. Jack will get over it when he cools off. It was a lot to ask. You're right Dora. You've your own family to think about,' and pursing her lips, she left the room.

Dora stared at Arthur. His face was ashen and he looked aghast, 'We've really burnt our boats. I hope you know what you're doing, Dora.'

'Thanks a lot,' she replied sarcastically, 'You were a great help.'

'To be honest Dora, I was thrown for a curve. I hadn't a clue what to say, I thought you might have second thoughts about us going and agree with them.

Whatever they're like, you've lived with them practically all your life, and until us they've been the only family you've known. It must be hard the predicament they're in. I thought you'd feel sorry for them and back down. You know what a soft touch you are usually.'

'Not this time, Arthur. They were so arrogant in their expectations–it floored me. I know I shocked myself with what I said. I've never spoken to them like that before. I hadn't realised how much resentment and anger I was carrying, and how much I need to get away from them and Baker St. I'm sure we're doing the right thing. I won't change my mind about that. The only worry is how are you going to keep working with my father after this?'

'Don't worry Dora, I'll survive. It will be difficult, there's no doubt. But I believe in you and if you are convinced then so am I. I can cope with Jack after all I've put up with him for twelve years, and now we've a new home to look forward to.'

41

1957 - The Final Move

Prior to the move Dora's sense of conviction wavered at times, especially when a wall in their new home practically collapsed on Arthur. Throughout it all, Henry was a tower of strength, not only as their solicitor but as their mentor and friend. Dora felt she could talk to him about anything. Neither she nor Arthur had many friends and certainly no relatives to turn to, so it was good to have someone there, who'd known them both when they were young.

Arthur would joke and tease about her rekindled friendship with the solicitor saying, 'Have you asked him yet why he's never married?'

Dora would toss her head and say, 'He's told me already, he never felt the inclination.'

But Arthur would never leave it alone, trying hard to get under her skin, 'Maybe it's because he lost the love of his life early on,' he said, giving her a knowing look.

'I don't think so. He's very religious. Other than his work I think he's dedicated his life to God. Now Arthur, that's my last word on the subject so stop it, no more.'

It was well known in the town, that Henry spent his weekends standing on a soapbox in Terrace Road, proclaiming how he'd been 'saved'. Dora found this awkward and would skirt round the crowd to avoid him. She knew it took courage to do something like that but it was not easy to understand that side of him.

However Arthur wouldn't let up on the banter saying, 'Perhaps he'll convert you, with all that bible bashing.'

'Honestly Arthur, the way you're going on, you'd think you were jealous of the poor man. He's a kind, thoughtful and caring man who's helping us through a very hard time, and never mentions Christianity to me. We should be grateful for everything he's doing, and that's an end to it.'

Dora sensed that unintentionally she had got to the heart of the matter when she'd mentioned the ' jealous' word, as very like herself Arthur was often insecure and afraid of losing her. She wondered if they would ever get to a point in their marriage when they could feel confident enough to trust one another completely.

∞

Moving day was now in sight, and Dora began to allow herself to relax. There'd been so much to do that she'd had no chance to take any pleasure in what was to come. Her father was still not speaking to her, and barely speaking to Arthur which made life tough. But throughout it all, her mother continued to maintain a calm neutrality, approaching their forthcoming move in a completely matter of fact way.

Two or three days before they were to move, Dora was busy packing crates with the little they had, when there was a gentle knock on the kitchen door. Sarah stood there her arms piled high with curtains, covers, and blankets. 'I thought these could come in useful once you settled and needed bedding for the lodgers. There's more in the lumber room. Come and have a look. Pick out what would be useful.'
They sorted through everything in silence but at least it felt like an amicable silence. 'If you come down to the kitchen, Dora, I've sorted pans and cutlery that we won't need.'

Dora was afraid to raise the subject of what Jack and Sarah were going to do next, thinking it wiser not to enquire but gladly willing to accept everything her mother offered.

No 8 currently had a 'For Sale' board prominently displayed on the outer wall. There were rumours round the town that a builder was interested in buying the property to convert into flats, though Dora didn't know, whether this was true.

Arthur was coming home from the Garden each night looking more and more worn. Everything was taking its toll on him; the work with Jack and trying to get the house ready. He would fall asleep, straight after tea, his head buried in the Daily Express.

David and Rosemary took very little notice of the move, only interested in how it would affect their lives. David, still at Dinas Secondary Modern, could walk directly up the hill from their new house, but Rosemary would have to take a bus to her old school, unless she went to the village school. However they were both looking forward to a garden and the run of a whole house, with David intent on having a dog.

Dora often felt that she was shouldering the responsibility for everyone, constantly saying to herself consolingly, 'You've broad shoulders, Dora. You can take it.'

The person who helped most through these dark days was Henry. She would drop in to his office, and he would get his secretary to make her cup of tea and reassure her, 'There's no problems Dora, all the searches have been done. There was a small problem with the land free hold, but we've bought it now and it becomes part of your mortgage. Is there anything else worrying you?'

Dora admitted that she was concerned about her parents saying, 'Despite all the work they've put in over the years, I know they've little savings having had such expensive holidays in the last few years. The Garden hardly brings in a lot, and has to pay out a wage to Arthur and my father. Now Mom and Dada are both in their seventies what will they do?'

'Dora, I can tell you something in confidence to ease your mind, but you must on no account mention it to them. I have heard on the grapevine that they've bought a small cottage in Eastgate–in the middle of the town. The only problem is that it's very tiny with only an outside toilet.'

Dora didn't like the sound of this at all, but what could she do now they were all being forced to go their separate ways. She only wished Sarah and Jack had had the foresight to invest in property long ago, but Jack had always turned his face against such a proposition.

Henry tried to reassure her by reiterating again, 'I do think that you and Arthur are doing the right thing. In years to come, you'll be pleased that you own your own house. Your children can grow up in the country and they can decide on their own jobs or careers.' Dora would go away comforted momentarily but still carrying a burden of guilt. It was silly to feel so bad about her parents, as she knew in past years they'd been offered many chances to move from Baker St.

Once a builder friend of Jack's had offered him a house he was building next to the Garden and on reasonable terms, but Jack wouldn't consider moving or even buying. He could be very pigheaded when it came to anything in his own life, and in those circumstances Sarah could never talk him round.

There was nothing more to organise, the great 'Moving Day' arrived on a freezing February morning. Arthur and David travelled down to 'Rosemary' in the Pickford's' van, while Dora and Rosemary cleared up, brushed and dusted the rooms.

Dora sent Rosemary down to say a farewell to her grandmother, so that she could do one last walk through. Those vast empty echoing rooms held so many memories, a lifetime's worth in fact, her lifetime so far.

For a second she thought she could hear the voices, whispering to her down the years. All those injured servicemen lying on their truckle beds, the summer visitors from Brum, the lodgers, she and David during the war, and now the four of them – the two children teasing their father on a Saturday night when he was setting off for the Conservative Club, running up and down the front and back stairs with his favourite blue silk pocket handkerchief. It felt like a death. No 8 had always had a presence, a character of its own and it was hard to leave it languishing back to its empty rooms.

Paying one last call to what was now the bathroom for the house, Dora thought about Gran in this room in the winter months, sitting upright in bed reading her Bible. What would Gran think? Gran and Sarah of course, rarely seeing eye to eye, but what would she have thought of Dora deserting them? In her heart of hearts, Dora knew that Gran would have been right behind her. She was sure she could hear Gran saying, 'Go for it, Dora. Go on. Take your family, make your own way.'

Finally Dora went downstairs to the back kitchen, where Sarah and Rosemary were sitting opposite one another at the well scrubbed kitchen table, saying nothing. Sarah offered Dora a farewell cup of tea. This was a turn-up for the book, but Sarah seemed to have something on her mind.

She turned to Dora face on and said plainly with no frills, 'You can do this, Dora. You can make a go of *'Rosemary'* I'm sure,' Dora waited for the sting in the tail and then it came, 'I've trained you well, and made sure cooking and cleaning are second nature to you. Don't forget you'll have my standards to live up to.'

Dora metaphorically 'rolled her eyes'. Trust her mother to come up with these last statements. Sarah was bound to make it personal to herself whether Dora succeeded or not. Of course Dora would have no part to play in it according to her!

But Sarah wasn't finished. In much softer tones she said, 'Don't worry about your father. He'll be alright eventually. It may take a while, but he will. It's hard for him to let go. Now be off with you both. You've a lot to do and so have I.'

Before Dora had even reached the door, Sarah had turned to busy herself with something else. If there was a tear, it was never evident, and probably never would be.

Holding Rosemary's hand tightly, Dora walked slowly down Baker St as if for the last time, trying hard not look back and headed for the station to catch a bus to their new life.

42

Freedom

Once the move was over, the only worry Dora had was Arthur still working with her father. Although her relationship with Jack had improved, things were strained. Jack had gone as far as letting them have some of the furniture he and Sarah didn't want but not as a gift and Dora had settled a price with her mother. Arthur and her father had taken the old handcart from the Garden, piled it high, and between them pushed it to their new house but Jack never ventured over the doorstep, leaving it to Arthur to unload on the pavement. Neither Sarah nor Jack would come to visit, but they expected Dora to call in on them every week.

Together Dora and Arthur painted and papered as many rooms as they needed for letting. In those early days, before the start of the lodgers, the children would joke 'about living on porridge and chips', and that wasn't far from the truth.

Money was tight and every spare penny had to go into the house. Dora was busy dyeing sheets and making up curtains from all the spare material from Baker St., till at last enough rooms had been refurbished.

The first lodgers were not the easiest. They were tough Irish 'navvies' hired to build the Hydro Electric Dam on Plynlimon. Dora would get up at five – pack their sandwiches, make them a big breakfast before they left for the day, make Arthur's breakfast at seven and the children's' at eight. There was no time to lose during the day. To keep costs down there were pies, tarts and Bara Brith to bake, to cope with all the mammoth appetites.

One night after she and Arthur were in bed, Dora thought she heard a racket coming from downstairs.

She nudged her husband and said, 'I think there's some sort of trouble with the men. I'll have to go down and see. You better come with me.' Arthur never a physical man was not keen.

Dora, in a bad mood after having her sleep disturbed found all the men involved in a poker game downstairs, drinking and with a couple of questionable women in attendance, and was furious. She banged open the front door as far it would go and yelled at the top of her voice, 'Out, out all of you-out this minute. I won't have my house treated like this.' She was completely livid by this time, with enough authority in her voice to frighten an army, 'You've got no respect for me, my house or my children. This is absolutely sickening.'

Two of the men, looking sheepish, tried to grovel and apologise, 'Sorry missus we're bang out of order. Please let us stay. It's the middle of the night. We won't do this again. We've got families to think of.'

Dora pushed the women out and one of the more drunken of the men who by now was patting Arthur on the head, saying, 'this little man doesn't frighten me at all.'

'We'll see about that,' said Dora seething with rage, at her husband being treated like that, 'Find out what a night on the street will do for you,' and she gave the drunk an almighty push.
Catching him off balance, he fell on his backside in the road outside looking stunned. Dora immediately double locked the door. Turning to the other two men she said, 'You'd better start behaving yourselves or it's the police next time.'

When they got back to bed Arthur said, 'God, Dora, you frightened me as well. I've never seen you in such a temper and so physical. Do you think there'll be more trouble? Remember that time in Penparcau?'

Dora snapped back feeling more shaken than she was willing to admit, 'Well someone had to sort them out didn't they, and it didn't look as if it was going to be you.'

Remarkably the next morning, the two remaining men asked politely if they could stay on. They arrived home later and presented Dora with flowers and chocolates, remorsefully asking her not to think too badly of them. They packed up the drunk's luggage and dumped it on him at work, 'You'll have no trouble there missus. We've sorted him good and proper.'

∞

Everything in 'Rosemary' was still very basic. Dora had had to learn to cook on the open range until they could afford a stove. There was just a walk-in pantry for storage. Keeping food cool was not easy and neither was all the washing. Sarah had passed on her boiler and the old mangle, but it was still a lot of hard work for Dora on her own. The outside toilet caused its own problems – with buckets and chamber pots to be emptied and jugs of water to be delivered to all the rooms every day.

In the months they had been there, several women in the village had come to the door asking, 'Do you need a cleaner?'

Dora remarked to Arthur ironically, 'I think people round here have got the wrong idea about us completely. Being 'Rosemary' is such a big house they must think we've got money.'

'Unless of course they know Jack,' Arthur replied, 'and think as he's got his own business and gives so much to the Legion, he might have bought the house for us.'

Dora laughed, 'Little do they know.'

When she was out doing her shopping in the village, locals had commented, 'surely you won't be able to do all that work on your own Mrs Hamer, I don't expect you're used to it.'

'Used to it,' Dora would say to Arthur in the evening, 'when was I ever not? What did they think I'd been doing all those years in Baker Street?'

Dora was always glad that Sarah had dinned into her, 'you must never be seen out in your pinafore or overall. You must always look presentable as if you've never been working at all,' though of course this rule might be working against her currently. At any rate, this was something to make them both laugh after a hard day.

One Friday tea time, Arthur came home exhausted as usual. He dropped his pay packet on the table. Later when Dora sat down to open and count it – she saw there was a pound missing. This was a disaster. Every pound or penny they had went towards the annual payment of the mortgage and the bills.

'Arthur, did you take out a pound for anything?'

'No, I brought it just as the old man gave it me. You'd better check again.'

But no, the wages were a pound down. Arthur was frantic. He was the saver in the family and kept check of all the money they had.

The next morning he confronted her father, 'Jack, did you miscount last night and give me a pound short in my wages?'

'No, Arthur. As you know we're not doing well. I had to dock your wages.'

'But why didn't you tell me at the time.'

Jack shrugged, 'I didn't see any need to.'

This was the last straw for Arthur. At heart he was a peacemaker. All along he'd tried to keep the lines of communication open between Dora and her parents. That night however he said to Dora, 'That's it–I've had it,-I've got to find another job. We need money to keep going. If this goes on and Jack keeps docking me, we won't be able to keep the house.'

That hit Dora hard. There was absolutely no way she was going to lose 'Rosemary'. Spurred on by grit and refusing to be beaten, Dora pored over newspapers for the next few weeks, until she came up with a possible job for Arthur. It was a caretaking job at the University on Penglais Hill, with better money than he was earning. The only problem was that he needed two good referees.

Showing it to Arthur, his first reaction was, 'I don't want your father to know about this. He's not going to be best pleased. He knows far too many influential people in the town and that definitely won't work in my favour, but I don't know what I can do about finding referees on the quiet?'

But Dora did. Returning to her Guardian Angel, Henry, she asked him if he would consider giving Arthur a reference. He said, 'Of course, I'd be delighted to give Arthur one, no question at all. What about a second person? Had you thought about asking your minister? He's new to the area, and wouldn't be familiar with your father or anyone who knows him.' In the end the references were sorted out. Arthur was interviewed and offered the job. Dora couldn't believe that the very first job she'd found, and Arthur's very first interview had been so successful perhaps their luck was changing.

Months later, Dora found out accidentally that their minister was a great friend of the Principal of the University and without telling Arthur had personally recommended him and made a case for employing him.

Dora mused to herself that there was definitely someone up there looking after their interests, first the house, then Arthur's health, then the job. Once Arthur was sure of the University job, he started to unwind from the strain; the only difficulty was telling Jack.

Dora said, 'This time, Arthur it's your turn to break the bad news and better sooner than later, as you know how the town gossips. Someone will be bound to give him the glad tidings first if we don't.'

Jack took it badly as they thought he would and wasn't a happy man, with Arthur receiving the rough edge of his tongue, 'You're ungrateful Arthur, these last twelve years I've taught you everything I know. You hardly knew a daisy from a dandelion when you started, and now you're leaving me in the lurch like this.' Though Jack was 77–he was fighting fit, and expected to carry on working for many more years. The Garden was his life and he couldn't understand Arthur wanting to leave it.

Over the years, Jack had brought in various men to help them on a part time basis accordingly on the Monday, when Arthur arrived to finish his last week, he found JJ working in the greenhouse and Jack barely acknowledging him saying, 'You needn't work the week Arthur. I've found someone else to replace you.' And that was twelve dedicated years of Arthur's life in the Garden written off in an instant.

Arthur jumped back on his cycle to return home. On the way he passed several of his old customers. As he greeted them, each one turned their head and looked the other way. The gossips had obviously been busy. Many of Jack's old friends thought 'it was a poor show' after all Jack had done for him. They were no doubt murmuring, 'Fancy abandoning the old man like that.' Other customers were sorry to see Arthur go, particularly the ones who'd had to confront Jack's bad temper and abuse.

Now both Dora and Arthur were starting afresh. As the weeks went by, Dora could see the change in Arthur. He was working with the old caretaker showing him the ropes, and looking brighter, happier and less stressed every day. It was a hard physical job and he often went up on Sundays to stoke the boiler but the people in Rural Science were a friendly bunch just like a family, and they soon took Arthur under their wing. He'd arrive home every Hogmanay and say 'Look what Jock's brought us back from Scotland this year.'

Dora would take one look at the haggis and say, 'I've no idea what to do with that, Arthur, and I don't even know if I want to, isn't it a pig's stomach or something, couldn't you get him to give it to one of the office girls, and just bring home the whiskey.'

The four of them would sit round in the kitchen laughing and joking prodding the haggis, with David making attempts at the Highland Fling and Arthur sampling the malt.

43

1959 - Home at Last!

Time had passed so quickly with such a lot to do, that Dora hardly noticed they'd been living in '*Rosemary*' for well over a year. There'd been some strange incidents since moving in. Some of the village people had reacted oddly, perhaps because it was such a close community. Most of the families were related, and everyone knew one another. Llanbadarn was close to Aberystwyth but it was a different world. The village itself with the Co-op, grocers and paper shop was a quiet, pretty place where life seemed to stand still. Old men would sit on the benches around the War Memorial gossiping amongst themselves in deep Welsh.

No one locked their doors, and neighbours would walk in and out one another's houses without a by your leave. Early on this caused major problems in the house. Dora and Arthur's neighbour, a Mrs Jones, who'd worked with Arthur before the war in the Star would drop in at all times of the day. On one occasion David, now a gawky teenager was stripped off, doing his ablutions at the kitchen sink, 'Ma', he said in a panic, 'Where can I go? There's someone coming down the hall.' Dora quick as a flash pushed him and a towel into the walk-in larder, and went out to meet her visitor, gently pointing her back the way she'd come. After that the front door was securely locked and bolted.

The other thorn in the flesh was old Davies, Mrs Jones' father who lived with her. He was a deacon at the Welsh chapel and took his Bible and the Sabbath seriously. Dora always seemed to be hanging out her wet sheets on a Sunday, as he paraded chapel members through his garden with them all standing tut- tutting to see such blasphemy on the Sabbath day.

Dora would complain to Arthur and say, 'That old man does it on purpose. It's nothing to do with him what I do with my Sundays.'

Arthur always conciliating would say, 'Let's grow the hedge higher. Then he won't be able to see over it.' But he was an ornery old man and next time they went down the garden, they found him clipping away at the hedge.

'Don't worry about that Mr Davies;' said Arthur, 'we'll do the hedge when it needs doing.' 'Oh no, you won't,' he said, 'this is my hedge and I 'm keeping it cut,' and went off into the house mumbling in Welsh.

Dora tried hard to get on with him. One day she saw him stepping out of his house all done up his best black suit and tie, 'Are you off to a funeral Mr Davies?'

'That's right,' he said amicably for once, seeming to be in a good mood.

'I'm so sorry,' said Dora 'is it family or someone close?'

'No, not all,' he said 'in fact, I don't know them. But there's nothing like a good burial is there to set one up for the day?' and he went jauntily up the hill to the cemetery.

Later Dora said to Arthur, 'I'm telling you this, Arthur, if I peg out in the next few years, make sure I'm cremated. Don't let him near my funeral!'

On another occasion, Dora had been out the front on a step ladder cleaning the big shop window and taking down the nets, when she was hailed by a rather weathered, old lady wearing a range of multi coloured garments that had seen better days. Getting over her first shock at the old lady's appearance, Dora could see the woman was close to tears. Hating to see anyone cry, Dora said, 'Come in for a minute. I'll make you a cup of tea. Sorry about the place but we're in a bit of a state. Come through to the kitchen.'

While the old lady sat herself down on their one wooden chair in front of the range, Dora busied herself with the tea.

Eventually the old lady calmed herself, after blowing hard on the proffered handkerchief explaining, 'I'm Mrs Jenkins. I run the corner shop. There's been a rumour going round that you're going to open a shop and sell papers-----.' The old lady gulped, and could barely carry on '---that means you'll take my business and I won't be able to make a living ----it's my only income, you see.' More tears welled up.

Giving her the tea, Dora said quickly, 'Oh, good heavens no. We're definitely not opening a shop. I don't know where these stories come from. I'm going to run a boarding house when we get sorted out.'

'Thank goodness---thank goodness---,' Mrs Jenkins said breathing a sigh of relief. I can't tell you how worried I've been. I'm so sorry to be a bother. I'll go and leave you to your work. If there's anything I can do to help – anything at all – just let me know.'

'Please, don't rush off,' Dora said 'stay and tell me about this house and the village.'

Mrs Jenkins, now much happier began, 'You won't believe this Mrs Hamer, but I was actually born in the little attic at the top of this house. My family left to move to the country after that. When I met Jenkins we moved back to the village.'

Dora showed her round the house and talked about what she and Arthur planned to do, realising that under the strange exterior beat a heart of gold. Dora was pleased to think she'd made her first real friend in the village.

Mrs Jenkins' shop was the centre of the village. People congregated there to shelter from the rain, wait for buses, or chat with their neighbours.

Every week people would queue to buy her cream and iced cakes, kept under a glass cloche, and dispatched carefully by silver tongs held delicately in large hands stained with ink from the papers.

One evening Dora was busy cooking tea, when David came in through the backdoor. He seemed to be holding something under his coat. Two little bright blue eyes looked up at her enquiringly. 'Look what Mrs Jenkins gave me. She's the runt of the litter–an albino. Old Jenkins was going to drown her but Mrs Jenkins saved her. They don't know what breed she is-a sort of cross between a sheepdog and a smaller dog. Can I keep her?'

Dora looked at his expectant face. It was no good he was as much of a soft touch for a lame dog as she was. Trust him to bring home the runt. Dora remembered only to clearly that other runt that Jack had got rid of when she was young and her own devotion to her Judy, and weakened.

'It's a bit late to ask me now,' she said, 'but you'll have to look after her yourself. I'm far too busy. It's hard work with a pup they need an awful lot of attention. What size will she become? I'm not at all sure we've got room for a fully grown sheepdog.'

David was thrilled and didn't care about her potential size, 'I'm calling her 'Lassie' like the film. Don't worry I'll take care of her. She'll be my dog.'

When Arthur came home he took one look at the ball of fluff lying by the range and said, 'Not another mouth to feed, Dora. When will it ever stop?'

But he was just as bad, bringing home a kitten for Rosemary when she was ill in bed and Rosemary now eleven, adding a rabbit that grew into a giant hare.

∞

Dora longed for Sarah to see the house. Despite their tricky relationship, over the years Dora had come to value and respect Sarah's opinion but things with her father were more difficult since Arthur had left the Garden. It was not easy to build bridges with Jack this time, as he seemed hurt rather than angry.

One morning hearing someone at the door, Dora was pleasantly surprised to find her mother on the doorstep. 'I thought I'd come and see for myself how you're getting on,' Sarah declared, 'but I don't want your father to know as he hasn't come to terms with Arthur's leaving yet.'

They walked round the house together. Sarah was positive, giving tips and hints of things to do. Always efficient she'd a lot to offer. Though Dora was pleased that her mother had come, there was still no real warmth between them. Perhaps they'd have been better off being in business together. Things would never change. If only it'd been Gran, who'd come. She'd have been so delighted for Dora. They'd have had a good chuckle over all the incidents in the village, and she'd have made a great fuss of the children.

However Sarah seemed to be preoccupied and as they sat and drank tea, she said in an unusually reassuring manner, 'Don't worry, Dora, your father will come round. He's always thought the world of you. I never did tell you and perhaps it's time I did. When you were turning thirteen, a man came to the Garden saying he'd been sent by your real mother and she wanted you back. The man wasn't your father but someone she was living with. Jack, though he was shaken, reacted quickly replying, 'That's fine we'll pack up Dora's belongings, and have her ready for you by Friday. You can come and collect her then, and pay the bill at the same time.' The man had expostulated, 'What bill, bill for what?' Your father apparently looked him straight in the eye and said, 'For the last thirteen years of course; Dora's clothes, her food, and her private music lessons. I daresay it will be a tidy sum.'

The man turned away hurriedly mumbling, 'Forget it. She can stay with you. I won't come back for her.' Sarah added, 'Your father certainly took a risk but it didn't look as if the man had that type of money. You see we had no legal hold on you, so your father had to come up with something.'

Dora didn't know what to say she was flabbergasted. Neither of her parents had ever mentioned this before. Unsure of her feelings and of her words, Dora just stared at Sarah for some minutes.

Sarah saw that this hadn't gone quite the way she expected, 'I only told you this, Dora, to make you understand how much your father loves you. He would never have let you go. He thinks too much of you. I probably shouldn't have told you. I thought, as you're an adult, it would be alright but I think it was a mistake on my part.' Sarah stood up and quickly pulled on her coat saying, 'I'll make my way home now.'

Dora could hardly wait to usher her mother out. Obviously Sarah hadn't intended to be malicious, rather that she'd wanted Dora to see Jack in a better light. However Sarah's confidence had only helped to reinforce Dora's feelings about being some sort of commodity to be bargained for, not a human being at all, or even someone's daughter. She hadn't felt like this since she was young, and it wasn't a pleasant experience.

Dora reran everything in her mind, going over and over what had happened. There was her real mother who'd left her with strangers and then wanted her back when she was old enough to work. Then there were the strangers who'd taken her in and brought her up, but treated her as if she was their property.
There was no doubt in Dora's mind that she loved Jack and he always seemed to love her. In her way, Sarah had done the best she could for her, but the only one who'd loved her unconditionally as a daughter should be loved was Gran.

None of it sounded right but it was pointless dwelling on it, after all Dora had other priorities in her life now. What was that saying 'the past is another country'? Probably it was best to leave the past where it was and concentrate on her present and future. Deciding not to tell Arthur anything about her mother's visit, Dora applied herself to her chores, and started preparing the dinner ready for the family to come home.

∞

Thinking about the children, Dora was pleased at how quickly they'd settled into the village.

Rosemary had point blank refused to take the bus to her old school and went to the village school with most of the lessons in Welsh, and had even joined one of the local Welsh chapels behind Dora's back. The first Dora had known about it was one Sunday morning when there was a knock at the door. Dora was confronted with an old farmer, dressed in his Sunday best, who said, 'I've come to take Marie Rhosyn to chapel. She's giving the lesson today.' Dora was taken aback and couldn't think who he meant but Rosemary was already running down the stairs in her coat and hat, 'Mr Williams has come for me, Mum, I'll see you later.' She banged the door behind her, leaving her mother open mouthed.

Rosemary always seemed to be running in and out peoples' houses and coming in with all sorts of tittle tattle. Dora could just imagine what Sarah would have thought. She would never have approved of such goings-on, believing 'you should keep yourself to yourself'. But Dora was delighted to see her daughter enjoying her freedom and independence at an early age. How she herself had longed to do that.

David at fifteen was due to leave secondary school. Dora had no idea what he would do – but he was 'good with his hands' and had turned into a sweet, generous boy with a kind heart.

Dora had started to establish routines for herself in the house and once the Irish lodgers had gone, she'd said to Arthur, 'Enough is enough, no more rough necks. We'll find a better calibre of lodger.'

Through Arthur's job they heard the University was looking for student lodgings, so Dora began the autumn, with two student boarders who stayed their full three years, becoming part of the Hamer family. '*Rosemary*' was soon full of life, noise and young people.

In the summer, like her mother before her, Dora depended on the visitors who came to Aberystwyth. People no longer stayed for a fortnight when the factories closed. Everything had changed with the arrival of more cars. It was now 'Bed and Breakfast' only, with visitors staying just a few nights.

On any lovely sunny spring morning, Dora would pinch herself to think that all this was hers – her domain, her business, her house and her family. Casting a desultory look at the piles of washing up in the sink, the loads of dirty sheets spilling out of the wash basket, the unmade beds and the cleaning crying out to be done, Dora would shrug her shoulders and head for the door. Putting the over excited Lassie on a lead and without a backward glance, Dora would savour the freedom of being her own boss at last, deciding to do everything in her own time and in her own way, and head out for an early morning stroll up Primrose Hill.

By now all memories of that long ago Christmas House had been lost in the mists of time, but occasionally Dora glimpsed a faint reminder of that childhood dream – particularly when they all gathered round the piano singing and dancing as she played, giving her an odd twinge of déjà vu, of something once seen but forgotten.

But these days Dora loved her life in all its realities. From the top of the hill she would look back down at the village and at *'Rosemary'*, its windows reflecting in the early morning light. They could definitely do with a clean she thought but reassured herself, I can clean my windows whenever I like – after all it's my house.

It had been a long time coming but it had been worth the wait. The hard years fell away and Dora knew she was home at last.

POST SCRIPT

So what happened to everyone in the book?

The Hamer Family spent nineteen happy and busy years in 'Rosemary' during which their son married, moved away, and set up his own business. Their daughter travelled the world, eventually returning to retrain as a Careers Officer and setting up her own business in the eighties. Arthur enjoyed twenty five years working at the University until he retired, returning part-time as a Guide.

In their sixties Dora and Arthur moved into a smaller house in Llanbadarn, always with Henry in the background doing their legal work and giving advice. This was Dora's dream house 'Sunnyside', the very house Dora had delivered insurance cards to in her teens and where she had sat outside romanticising about her future.

Did Dora ever find her real mother? Unfortunately not - though in her forties she did make enquiries but ended up with a blank. In the nineties, her daughter Rosemary tracked down Dora's real parents' marriage certificate and was able to reassure her mother that she definitely was not illegitimate as she had been led to believe by Sarah, and that in fact she had had a brother three years older than her but that was as far as it went. There were to be no emotional reconciliations.

What about the Roberts'? Jack worked in the Garden right through his mid eighties still riding his bike and wearing his beloved breeches. In time he succumbed to Parkinson's – no longer able to remember the names of his 'beloved flowers' and dying of a heart attack at the ripe old age of 89. On his death Aberystwyth town offered Sarah a civic funeral for all the work Jack had done for the British Legion, but she refused saying that Jack was hers at last and she was not going to share him any longer.

Sarah eventually moved in with Dora and Arthur living to 93, never settling or mellowing, still difficult and unbending in her old age. Dora never gave up hope that they would one day develop some sort of relationship. But it was not to be. Every day of her remaining years Sarah would demand 'to be with Jack', as it seemed he was the only person in her life she'd ever really loved besides her father.

Over the years after it was sold, 8 Baker Street became first of all a restaurant, and later three flats.

As they got older, Dora and Arthur moved back to the centre of Aberystwyth, enjoying sitting on the promenade looking at the sea that Arthur loved so much, until his death at 81.

In 1998 Dora, spirited and game as ever, packed up her belongings and all her memories of Aberystwyth and at the age of 83 moved to Gloucester to share a home with her daughter. They spent the next ten years developing the loving closeness they had found in one another and the psychic link they shared. Rosemary once asked, 'Are you disappointed that I didn't marry and have the grandchildren you so badly wanted?'

Dora replied honestly, 'Yes, I would have loved grandchildren, but I was proud of your adventurous spirit – all the places you went to, the people you met and the things you achieved. I loved your father but I would have loved to have had the freedom you've had, and done what you've done, and seen something of the world.'

Later in her early nineties before her death Dora would occasionally reflect back and comment on her own life and say to her daughter, 'I've been very, very lucky, maybe I didn't have a great start in life but the Roberts' took me in and were kind to me in their way, and I owe them a lot. Imagine where I could have ended up. I've had a good life and everything I've ever dreamed of - a husband - a family and a home of my very own.'

Author

Rosemary Hamer is retired and lives on the Wirral.
'The Christmas House' is her first novel.

Printed in Great Britain
by Amazon

80489696R00174